Families' Values

FAMILIES' VALUES

How Parents, Siblings, and Children
Affect Political Attitudes

R. Urbatsch

OXFORD
UNIVERSITY PRESS

Oxford University Press is a department of the University of Oxford.
It furthers the University's objective of excellence in research, scholarship,
and education by publishing worldwide.

Oxford   New York
Auckland   Cape Town   Dar es Salaam   Hong Kong   Karachi
Kuala Lumpur   Madrid   Melbourne   Mexico City   Nairobi
New Delhi   Shanghai   Taipei   Toronto

With offices in
Argentina   Austria   Brazil   Chile   Czech Republic   France   Greece
Guatemala   Hungary   Italy   Japan   Poland   Portugal   Singapore
South Korea   Switzerland   Thailand   Turkey   Ukraine   Vietnam

Oxford is a registered trademark of Oxford University Press
in the UK and certain other countries.

Published in the United States of America by
Oxford University Press
198 Madison Avenue, New York, NY 10016

© Oxford University Press 2014

Library of Congress Cataloging-in-Publication Data
Urbatsch, Robert.
Families' values : how parents, siblings, and children affect
political attitudes / Robert Urbatsch.
pages cm
Includes bibliographical references and index.
ISBN 978–0–19–937360–4 (hardcover : alk. paper)   1. Political socialization.
2. Political psychology.   3. Families—Political aspects.   4. Political
participation—Social aspects   I. Title.
JA76.U73 2014
306.2—dc23
2014004359

9 8 7 6 5 4 3 2 1
Printed in the United States of America
on acid-free paper

For my grandmother,
who knows a thing or two about family

CONTENTS

ACKNOWLEDGMENTS

As the classic formula goes, this book would never have been written with-out Bill Mishler and Jan Leighley. I come from the article-writing, not book-writing, side of the social sciences and so instinctively conceived of ideas about politics and the family as articles. But Drs. Leighley and Mishler disagreed heartily; when I submitted one such idea, the core of chapter 2, to the journal they edited, they summarily rejected it. This is the academic equivalent of being shot down without even a first date and similarly leaves everyone involved feeling vaguely embarrassed (and the petitionee poten-tially offended at being surmised to possibly have such low standards). So, in addition to my gratitude for inspiring the transmogrification of these explorations into a book, I also extend my apologies. Sorry!

Then again, I have collected a fearsome number of rejections-without-review on grounds of eccentricity of topic. This makes all the more valuable the support of Jeffry Frieden and Beth Simmons, two exceptional scholars and delightful people with the extraordinary patience to put up with me and whatever ideas followed me into their offices. Their encouragement in the early stages of both this project and in my career more generally, and the ideas they generously shared, helped lay the foundations for this book. Jonathan Rodden was equally accommodating, willing to discuss thoughts on anything from the importance of geography to the vast trove of data in Norwegian parish records, without batting an eye except for that one time I started talking about the constitution of Papua New Guinea. His input, too, informs this book in ways great and small.

More specific reflections on parts of this enterprise came from Sonal Pandya. Indeed, she coauthored my first project considering the role of family in political preferences, an examination of how the industry of one's spouse's employment changes one's economic policy preferences. I am very grateful for her taking time out of her burgeoning career to have these discussions.

Subsequent support came from several sources. Dirk Deam, a colleague with whom I speak too infrequently, shared some thoughts on chapter 5 as it developed, while Neil Malhotra graciously provided his characteristic far-above-my-pay-grade insight to some of the material in chapter 7 and stimulatingly sparred with me a bit about chapter 3; I only wish I knew him better so that I could exploit him even more ruthlessly. Mariana Medina, Christina Gish Hill, and Nell Gabiam provided useful comments and support about the project as it took shape, and Valerie M. Hennings directed me toward Oxford University Press. My thanks as well to *International Studies Quarterly* and the *British Journal of Political Science* for allowing the republication of some material that originally appeared in their pages—early versions of what became chapters 5 and 3, respectively.

More broadly, Matt Potoski proved an unfailing trove of mentorship on the strategy of authorship, David Pervin went beyond any call of duty in providing publication advice and good humor to a guy he has never met, and all the dedicated staff of Oxford University Press helpfully guided me through the process. Among the staff at Oxford, I owe particular debts of gratitude to Angela Chnapko for taking this project on and to Peter Worger for his assistance. To all of these friends and comrades, I extend my sincerest thanks. I also gratefully acknowledge the meticulous effort put into commenting by the various anonymous reviewers of the manuscript, into copyediting by the redoubtable Kari Lucke, and into the production side of things by Jayanthi Bhaskar and her associates.

I have also had unexpected thought-fodder from several students over the years—particularly unexpected, given that my teaching could charitably be described as "shambolic." (My lectures involve all the confusion and irritation you'd expect to be provoked by someone who unthinkingly drops words such as "shambolic.") I especially tip my hat to, in no particular order, Brendan Corcoran, Peter Ross, Basil Mahayni, Adrian Florea, Mark Nieman, In Han Yeo, Cord Overton, Bo Won Chang, Jeong Ju Moon, Hyun Ju Lee, Rachael Voas, Justin Knight (whom I owe a lunch), Michael Kostboth, David Kearney, David Cox, Elizabeth Leuthauser, and Chris Wertzberger (who owes me $100). Dana Schumacher and Jason Chrystal deserve shout-outs for directing some of these students toward me and many lesser lights away from me, as well as for their general moral support.

Acknowledgements traditionally close with thanks to the author's family. For obvious reasons, that convention seems particularly apt here. Thanks, then, to my family, for relentlessly defying all the predictions I make throughout the book. If we hadn't been so eccentric, I might never have started thinking about all this. But next time, try to cooperate at least a little, will you?

Families' Values

CHAPTER 1

What We Know About Families and Why We Should Know More

How do you decide what you believe in? If you think back over your life, you may sometimes be able to point to particular incidents or experiences that led you to have particular opinions about war, or abortion, or income redistribution. Just as likely, though, the origins of many of your attitudes will be an ineffable blur: things you believe are just things you have always believed, with little obvious starting point. Yet *something* must have led you to those positions.

Some of the forces that produce particular political attitudes are fairly straightforward: Wealthier people must pay more in income taxes even as they rely less on public services, so it makes sense that, more often than their poorer compatriots, they prefer a smaller government. Similarly, growing up in an area where everyone espouses a particular viewpoint creates psychological pressures to conform to that local norm; people from Sweden will think of different policies and perspectives as more "natural" than will Australians, just as those from rural Mississippi are likely to prefer different policies than people from urban Massachusetts. But these broad tendencies contain many exceptions. Some rich people are quite acceptant of higher tax burdens to support government services, and even in deeply traditional parts of the world, some people are willing to push against local mores. While some of this variation may be random, the sheer extent of deviations from simple models' predictions about preferences suggests that other systematic influences may lurk in the background.

That one potential source for this variation might be the family is not a new conceit. Analysts have identified several pathways by which family members can influence one another politically: Family members' discussions lead their beliefs to converge, and having a spouse or children could promote traditional moral attitudes. Nevertheless, the family is a central, protean force in social and psychological life, which suggests that it may have broader and more varied effects on political beliefs. Marriage and childbirth affect basic personal characteristics like life satisfaction,[1] which could in turn alter political attitudes: Being happier associates with more support for incumbent elected officials,[2] as well as with different positions on specific policy issues.[3] Moreover, family experiences—raising a child, say—seem to influence core elements of personality, such as conscientiousness and agreeableness,[4] which influence political ideology in turn.[5] As such, familial influences likely extend well beyond the direct transmission of beliefs. Consciously or not, relatives filter and change how people think about the world.

This book aims to investigate some of the varied effects that families have on political belief. The central argument is that relatives are relevant to public opinion and attitudes in ways extending well beyond commonplaces of family resemblance: Close relatives can influence beliefs in a much more complicated and interesting variety of respects. This broader perspective on family influences on attitudes creates a role for relations such as sisters or brothers, who tend to disappear from most accounts of family political socialization. It also leads to new predictions regarding issues like foreign policy or trust in government, where family gets relatively less attention, and points to mechanisms like concern for the future and attitudes toward risk that can get lost beneath the more direct and obvious influence of family political discussions. Though the particular hypotheses explored here are, with luck, of interest for their own sake, the goal is not only to show that they apply but also to demonstrate that much scope remains for broadening the way in which we think families can exert political influence.

Much of the research presented in this book is new, but this introductory chapter provides a backdrop by showing the more traditional literatures on political socialization and family values, where analysts have established several mechanisms of family influence that we can apply to new questions. It additionally hopes to bring more attention to underappreciated past findings suggesting unexpected, innovative links between families and political beliefs. The next few sections set up this prior lay of the land concerning the interconnections between the world of family and the world of politics.

THE RELATIONSHIP BETWEEN FAMILY AND POLITICS

People have linked family to the political realm throughout history: Plato and Aristotle, for instance, discussed at length the ways that households trained the young for political thought and participation.[6] Part of this training occurred because households were seen as miniature states—or, conversely, government of a polity was just household management writ large—an analogy that still has purchase millennia later.[7] This general sense that families and nations were similar entities on different scales complemented more specific, testable ways in which governments were thought to affect families or vice versa.

One primary strand in the literature linking family and politics has concerned how government policies influence the structure of families. Do income tax rates change how likely couples are to divorce?[8] Does having a larger public sector associate with more grandparents living in the same household as their grandchildren?[9] Does allowing no-fault divorce affect how many children people have?[10] Although government policies are rarely the primary determinant of most family-related choices—even aridly doctrinaire economists acknowledge that their own decisions concerning marriage and children do not reflect a textbook cost-benefit calculus[11]—the policy environment does seem to make a difference for detectable numbers of people, as do other outcomes, such as macroeconomic performance, that governments may indirectly be able to affect. In one striking example, fertility rates decreased during the Great Depression alongside the desire to have children,[12] but government-relief spending alleviated this tendency.[13] Governments, then, have at least some effect on how their citizens form and dissolve families, even if direct subsidies of fertility have not always had their intended effect.[14]

The reasons why governments have attempted to shape family structures have fluctuated, but recently one consideration has been particularly important politically. The feeling that family-related behaviors reflect and produce broader moral philosophies has been important enough to enter the lexicon as "family values," an explicit linkage of kinship and politically relevant attitudes.[15] Particular family formations, in these debates, demonstrate that society has successfully instilled norms of social conduct, especially in caring for children, perhaps even sacrificing personal ambition or enjoyment to do so. A sociological approach to modern American politics confirms that family structures correlate with political cultures, with more conservative areas perhaps unsurprisingly having more traditional family organizations.[16]

The nature of this relationship, though, is an open question. It could be that particular family structures lead to the associated political viewpoint, so that, for example, people who grow up in more traditionally organized households are likely to become conservative *because* of that household organization. This notion that family causes politics matches most of the analysis in political science as such, but it is not necessarily the whole story.[17] Causation could go in the opposite direction: Conservative ideology may be what drives people to more highly prize traditional household organizations and, say, bear more costs to avoid divorce. Or there might be no causal relationship at all—both political outlook and family structure could both be produced by some other characteristic (such as income or religion) but have no direct connection to one another. This ambiguity haunts many studies of public attitudes, including those looking for potential familial effects; it raises methodological issues that studies of family influences must confront. Most commonly, the central problem is one of selection: The cliché that one cannot choose one's family rings disappointingly hollow here, as one can choose one's mate and whether to have children. Or someone else got to choose one's family, as when one's parents decided to have a certain number of children and thereby produced a certain number of siblings. This is problematic, because the group of people who decide to have more children (or who beget a large family accidentally) may differ from the types of people who end up having smaller families: The former group could be richer or more religious than the latter, for example. In this case, it is difficult to tell the difference between the effect of having richer—or more religious—parents and that of coming from a large family, because the two potential influences correlate. A simple comparison between the average child with many siblings and the average only child may then not reveal anything about the actual effect of family size but only about the effects of having grown up in a wealthier or more devout household.

While some element of selection is common to virtually all family relationships, it plays out in different ways when discussing parents, spouses, and children. This highlights that the discussion to this point has painted with a very broad brush, discussing the causes or consequences of all sorts of kith and kin. Thinking more precisely about how family has its influences quickly tends to resolve into different effects for different relatives: People are not influenced by their parents in the same way as they are influenced by their children. They deal with the two different relationships at different phases in their own lives, for one thing, and in the opposite hierarchical situation. As with parents and children, so with other relatives: Each relationship tends to have a quite different context. As a result, most familial effects on political attitudes are more finely detailed, speaking about the effects of parents instead of some general family value imposed equally by any relation. When reviewing what is known about family influences, then, it makes sense to split the discussion by different classes of relative. The next three sections do just this, looking separately at the effects of the three most frequently studied familial influences on political views: parents, spouses, and children.

FAMILY AND POLITICAL ATTITUDES: THE INFLUENCE OF PARENTS

The most studied of all family relationships in politics, with formal empirical testing going back decades, is the way that parents' views influence their children's.[18] Parents who are conservative, or Democratic, or opposed to budget deficits will likely express those views to their children, both in active attempts to inculcate their own values and, less consciously, as those beliefs lead them to perform day-to-day actions observed by their children. To the extent that children listen to their parents, then—admittedly, sometimes a vanishingly small extent—children's beliefs converge to the parents'. Moreover, besides direct communications with their children, parents can try to control other factors in the children's environment (friends, extracurricular activities, attendance at religious services), and these other experiences may further mold political attitudes. At the very least, parents provide political information that children can use as a starting point when they formulate their own political identities.[19]

A great deal of evidence has been put forth supporting the idea that children readily absorb these sorts of parental influences, over and above the basic empirical truism that parents and children often share political outlooks. The individual steps of the argument hold up. Children do seem to be more malleable in their political beliefs, so that they are relatively likely to react to environmental influences such as parental teachings.[20] Meanwhile, parents do actively attempt to instill particular beliefs, even controversial ones, in their children.[21] Some of the evidence supporting parental socialization theories is more circumstantial: Parental transmission seems to be strongest when parents are consistent in their political positions and interested in politics.[22] This makes sense, as these are precisely the parents one might expect to seek to convey messages to their children. Similarly, mothers typically spend more time with their offspring, giving them more opportunity to socialize the children—and when the parents disagree politically, mothers' political views are substantially more likely than are fathers' to transfer to the next generation.[23]

Naturally, there is no straight-line, automatic determination of children's political ideologies.[24] Children can, and often do, rebel against their parents' attitudes, forging new positions not just in response to the changing standards of the times they grew up in but also from personal inclinations and experiences that work against parental beliefs.[25] The circumstances under which parents' opinions fail to stick are somewhat unclear and merit further exploration (chapter 2 pursues one relevant path). Even acknowledging the cases when children oppose their parents, however, in the vast majority of cases there are limits in how far this opposition goes. One of the most thorough analyses of family influences in politics, in fact, focuses on the idea of "bounded partisanship": Family members may not always share each other's views, but they are unlikely to be diametrically opposed.[26] When children move away from their parents' positions or partisan affiliations, that is, they are more apt to end up with a neutral position than with an outright endorsement of what their parents rejected.

Even allowing for these more limited claims on the ability of parents to determine their children's views, the logic of parental socialization has faced recent challenges. Several plausible factors completely unrelated to parental teaching could produce the shared beliefs of parents and children. For example, parents and children are usually socioeconomically similar—rich parents tend to raise rich children—and both groups could simply be reacting to their shared circumstances instead of to each other. But the most assertive assault on the relevance of socialization points out that parents' influence on their children does not start at their first political conversations: Long before, at the moment of conception, parents passed on genes. The new social genetics asserts that this biological inheritance could determine political preferences, at least in part. It could also produce many of the effects originally proposed as proof of socialization theories. Parents who feel strongly about politics being more likely to have children that agree with them politically, for example, could merely show that those parents had strongly encoded genetic preferences across several genes, at least some of which transmitted to the children.

The workhorse model used to explore these potential biological bases of politics, as in many studies of genetic influences, is the twin study. Comparing identical twins (who share essentially the same genetic material) with fraternal twins (who share only some genetic material) allows some estimation of how much of political personality comes from genetic influences instead of environmental factors. Most such studies find a substantial role for genetics in determining political attitudes, while household variables such as parental attempts at socialization are far less influential, perhaps even irrelevant.[27] That is, identical twins turn out to be much more politically similar than are fraternal twins, which suggests that genetic factors drive ideological preferences.[28] Other research designs also lend support to the idea that genetics matters for political preferences.[29]

This rise of biological explanations reflects a broader sense throughout psychology and the social sciences that most parental influence comes from the genes that they pass on rather than from the upbringing they provide: from nature, not nurture.[30] Those who downplay the role of nurture typically do set some limits: Outright physical abuse of a child, or failure to provide adequate nutrition, does appreciably affect child outcomes. Within these bounds, though, attempts to promote self-confidence with frequent expressions of love and support, or to instill particular political values through demonstration or indoctrination, seem to have relatively little purchase. Such efforts may change the way children behave in front of the parents, but outside the home, their effect appears far more limited than does the effect of genetics. Hence, according to these arguments, parents' attempts to promote particular personality traits such as self-confidence and leadership are largely futile; the seeming effects of upbringing on relevant political behaviors or beliefs may instead be genetic.[31]

With the troubled history of genetic arguments in politics, these claims were bound to cause controversy. Besides implying limits on free will, a philosophically problematic notion to many, genetic arguments raise the specter of bygone theories of biological determinism; social Darwinism and eugenics moved in very unhappy directions. The geneticists' claims are much less absolute. They point to propensities, not to deterministic imperatives. Nevertheless, methodological and theoretical questions mean that while genetic factors are a promising focus for study, their precise impact is as yet unclear.[32]

FAMILY AND POLITICAL ATTITUDES: THE INFLUENCE OF SPOUSES

Even if parents have been the most studied of family influences, other relatives have also broken through to the attention of political science. Most frequently, these have been spouses.[33] Wives and husbands are obvious candidates for sources of political influence for several reasons. Courtship, marriage, and household management generally require a fair amount of communication, often about politically relevant issues, providing a great deal of opportunity for the expression of attitudes. Unlike with parents and children, the bulk of interaction between spouses occurs as adults, so both halves of the couple can meaningfully discuss politics throughout the course of their relationship. Some have even spoken of spousal discussions as "resocialization," as the spouses echo the parents' effect of instilling political preferences, if in a more reciprocal form in most spousal relationships.[34]

Despite these points, some features do make spouses relatively hard to evaluate when identifying sources of political influence. Most notably, spouses generally involve a conscious process of selection (typically by the partners themselves, though potentially also in arranged marriages). Those who can choose their own mates can select spouses who already agree politically. This alternative possibility means that wives and husbands who share political views may not have had any socializing effect on each other: They came into the marriage with similar political perspectives.

Indeed, mate selection and politics seem to be intertwined. What sociologists and biologists call "assortative mating" (the tendency for individuals to choose mates who resemble them) happens along many dimensions—income, attractiveness, ethnicity—but political ideology seems to be among the most important.[35] Conservatives most often pair off with conservatives, liberals with liberals. Not only does this reduce one potential source of spousal frictions; it also reflects the processes by which people find mates. A regular church attender, to take one example, will spend a good deal of time at church functions with others likely to share her beliefs. If she marries a fellow congregant, or if acquaintances from church introduce her to others in their social networks, she may have a similar political worldview to her new mate whether or not she intentionally sought out someone with whom she agreed politically.

Assortative mating provides more than a political resemblance. It also often means, because of all the other dimensions along which spouses resemble each other, that they share an economic and cultural milieu just as parents and children do. This is not just about churchgoers. Many people meet their future spouses at college and so are unlikely to marry someone of considerably lower education—which could make them seem to be socializing or selecting one another politically when in fact they simply both hew to the patterns of their shared class.[36] When both halves of a couple like the same policies, then, when is it because one influenced the other? Not only must we worry about the possibility of selecting spouses on political ideology, but those common background and demographic factors must be taken into account.[37]

Notwithstanding these alternative possibilities, some evidence remains to suggest that spouses affect each other in ways that tend to lead their political positions to converge. Most individuals discuss politics more frequently with their spouses than with anyone else, and personal discussions in general seem to sway political beliefs.[38] Consistent with this idea (albeit also with other possible stories), conformity between wife's and husband's beliefs tends to increase over the course of a marriage.[39] The process can involve more than gentle suasion. At the extreme, there may not be convergence but outright adoption of the spouse's political views. Particularly among more traditional cultural groups, it can be that spouses do not really converge in belief but that wives profess attitudes and vote as their husbands prescribe regardless of their own opinions.[40] Whether as a matter of conscious submission or unconscious adoption of social norms, wives do seem to be more likely to conform to their husbands' previously expressed view than the other way around—even when the wife expresses greater interest in politics than the husband does.[41] Typically, though, the movement toward shared preferences is less dramatic: The same bounded partisanship process seen with parents seems to work within married couples as well.[42] Spouses do not always support the same party or ideology, but they tend not to actively support opposing views. One partner's advocacy will, by this argument, tend to constrain the other partner to being, at most, neutral.

While increased discussion may, as so often in marriage, fail to bring agreement,[43] spouses may shade political views in other ways. Some have argued that simply being married may in and of itself affect attitudes, regardless of the views of the spouse.[44] Marriage does change circumstances in several ways that might have political implications.[45] Having a legal bond to a partner puts another potential income-earner—whether through wages, government benefits, or other source of earnings—in the household, for instance, providing some insurance against economic downturns and so potentially shaping policy preferences. Proving these arguments presents many of the same difficulties as does showing the effect of the spouse's political preferences: Married people are the ones who choose to get married, which could reflect underlying ideological predispositions (e.g., valuing that insurance more) that marriage did not change. Hence, observing differences between the married and the unmarried may not demonstrate any causal effect of marriage. But the balance of the evidence suggests that marriage, like other major life transitions,[46] can influence political beliefs.

FAMILY AND POLITICAL ATTITUDES: THE INFLUENCE OF CHILDREN

While the conventional wisdom has long acknowledged parents' and spouses' roles in forming political preferences, children historically have attracted less attention. Infants and young children clearly have little capacity or inclination to socialize their parents into particular ideological views, bar the occasional precocious Marxist. While even quite young children can exhibit some political knowledge,[47] parents' ability to curate this knowledge means this is unlikely to be an independently reasoned perspective. By the time children are old enough to exert more conscious sway, their parents are old enough to have political beliefs entrenched by decades of adult experience.[48] Theories that parents have different preferences from nonparents most often involve the alleviation of childcare costs rather than any actual political influence on the part of the child. For example, parents might be supposed to be especially likely to support public education funding. Even these theories see, at best, only mixed empirical confirmation.[49]

More recently, though, parents have been conjectured to have wholly different ways of looking at the world and thinking about issues: Children cause their guardians' views to shift about a variety of issues.[50] This idea concords with popular discussions of politics, which often define voters by their parental status, with breathless media stories about parents as an identifiable political class of swing voters.[51] The usual expectation is that parents will be more conservative and right-leaning, for several reasons.[52] The inherently gendered nature of childbirth and lactation, followed by societal pressures that tend to assign more responsibility for childrearing to women, may emphasize traditional social roles both within the household and in dealing with society. At the same time, having charge of a child's welfare creates feelings of responsibility and protectiveness that may prefer traditional policies rather than potentially risky changes— "conservatism" in the most literal sense. It may even be that parents, in their Sisyphean attempts to keep children under control, simply identify with authority figures; parenthood seems to inspire at least some people to become more punitive in their attitudes toward criminals.[53] Most of these potential rightward shifts have greatest force in social issues: "family values," as the phrase appropriately has it. In economic terms, though, children are most associated with hardship—the costs of childcare, potential disruption to a parent's income—which tends to pull to the political left.[54] This may contribute to the inconsistent evidence for parental conservatism in actual real-world studies.[55]

Other approaches have sought differences not between parents and nonparents but between parents of different types of children. One of the most striking indications of child influence comes from studies showing that specific child characteristics can influence parents. These are most intriguing when they involve "horizontal identities" that are not necessarily shared by parent and child: deafness, for example, or homosexuality.[56]

The characteristic that has garnered the most attention, with its universal implications, is the child's gender.[57] Daughters associate with parents having more liberal and feminist positions, corresponding to the usual gender gap of women being more liberal and feminist.[58] This is true whether looking at very broad factors of partisanship, voting, and ideology,[59] or at more specific and explicitly gender-rights-related survey responses.[60] It even appears when the stakes are quite high, opinions were likely already formulated, and the commitment to positions could be costly: National legislators seem to vote and make policy based on their children's sex composition.[61]

Child gender is particularly useful when trying to identify whether children have effects because it is the unusual thing that parents rarely control directly[62] even as it can vary in easily detectable ways within families. Showing that this essentially random variation has observable effects on political preferences therefore provides credible evidence that the effect of children is actually causal. Otherwise, children—like spouses before them—involve a selection process: People who decide to have one or more children may have always differed in their political philosophy from those who were never to have children. It is plausible for them to have always liked children more and so put more value on public expenditures relating to the young. Because on average those who have daughters are (before their children are born) like those who have sons, however, observed differences between people-with-daughters and people-with-sons show evidence that the child's sex was what caused the two groups to diverge.

Even with its power to reveal real effects with great clarity, gender is not the only potential source of variation among children. When the children reach adolescence and adulthood, they can adopt all kinds of political perspectives (even if genetics or childhood socialization predisposes them more to particular beliefs). Parents can then pick these new views up from their progeny, producing convergence from the other direction as the parent shifts toward the child's views. While few studies have looked at this issue, those that do have tended to find some supportive evidence.[63] It is certainly true that parents usually remain in regular contact with their children after the latter have left the house, even if the communication is not as frequent as it was during the children's first years. Children can then rub some of their views on their parents, just as other conversation partners do.

WHAT'S MISSING?

As this brief review suggests, scholars have established several solid hypotheses about how families relate to individuals' political preferences. People tend to share their parents' ideologies, whether because of socialization or genetics, and they choose their spouses, in part, on the basis of political compatibility. Parents tack more toward typically female preferences when they have daughters than when they sons. All of these factors suggest that those within the family will most often have predictably similar political views for a variety of reasons. In addition, there is the consistent suggestion that those with more family ties—a spouse, more children—will tend to be more conservative.

This is all reassuringly intuitive, and very much worth studying: It is crucial to confirm the seemingly obvious, lest we retain the obvious belief that the sun goes around the earth. Obvious forces are also likely to have the largest impact—that is part of what makes them obvious—and so are apt to be major contributors to any model of social outcomes that aspires to completeness. Nevertheless, social science is at its best and most thought-provoking when it finds the middle ground between the obvious and the implausible: surprising yet persuasive claims that can tell us something novel, casting additional light on social and political relationships rather than reinforcing previously held ideas. It is worth pushing beyond the most-studied influences to seek out new insights.

Another motivation for pushing beyond the points laid out above is that those points pass over many of the central experiences of family life. Sisters and brothers, for example, made only the briefest and most incidental of cameos in the discussion—and even that was purely methodological, when twins served as a handy means of studying genetic influences on individuals' politics.[64] This belies the huge social, logistical, and emotional effect that siblings often have on one another's lives. Of course, one could reasonably suspect that the author of a study arguing that familial influences on politics are understudied would leave out the literature on siblings to make the need for further research look more urgent, but research on sisters and brothers is surprisingly scanty. Occasional, tantalizing scraps pop up here and there: Reserving a large proportion of the Rwandan legislature for women may have caused sisters and brothers to get along less well,[65] and several studies have suggested that those without elder siblings—firstborn children—are more likely to obtain political leadership roles.[66] Outside of these sorts of occasional reports, though, little systematic effort has considered that siblings might affect the political world. Not all of the personal needs to be political, but surely it is worth considering that people as important as siblings could have an effect on beliefs or behavior if coworkers (of all people) can be alleged to, as they often are.[67] Siblings are not alone in their neglect. It is even harder to find any analysis over the role of, say, grandparents, even though any living grandparents would probably be the most common source for profound formative experiences involving the elderly, so that having been able to know one's grandparents might be expected to influence opinions over public pensions, health care, and other age-related policies.

This leaves ample room to apply the same, widely accepted ideas about family political socialization to new relationships. We can also take a fresh look at previously studied relationships, moving beyond any tendency to family convergence. This is especially important because social changes may have eroded some of the traditional bases for family influence. It has, for example, been argued that as filial piety has decreased in recent decades, so has the tendency of children to share their parents' political orientations.[68] Some scholars have already taken steps to pursue questions other than family political resemblance, showing the potential for finding interesting consequences of other dimensions of family life. One study[69] looked at how parents' mixed messages affect political engagement: If mother and father defy the tendency to pair off with a political cohort and instead disagree about ideology, does the lack of certainty turn the children off politics? It seems not; instead, the family debate inspires children to think more about political matters, spurring interest. But only a few moves have yet been made along these lines. Many areas at the intersection of family and political attitudes still remain *terra incognita*. This next few chapters attempt forays into that uncharted territory.

How, though, can we most effectively generalize from the established family effects on political beliefs to other relatives as causes of attitude shift and other issue areas in which those attitudes are shifting? Fortunately, disparate as they are, most of the theories discussed in the past three sections pass through a limited set of paths connecting cause to effect. These same causal mechanisms reappear throughout this book as the central theoretical mechanisms by which families have their effects:

- *Direct influence*. Much of the traditionally discussed effect of relatives comes from observing those relatives' political views and following suit. Whether the cause is the compelling information that people provide in support of their opinions, a simple desire to conform, a more complex desire to extend a shared identity into shared norms, or other processes, hearing or seeing a liked person express attitudes often translates into sharing that person's attitudes.[70] This was most evident in the discussion of parents, but other family members, such as siblings, could have analogous effects.
- *Social network effects*. Relatives are—one hopes—not the only interlocutors in the world. People also speak to a wide range of other individuals

outside the family: friends, coworkers, neighbors. However, family can influence which of these nonfamily people one talks to. Parents can choose the school, church, and extracurricular activities that their children attend and thereby those children's peers; having children influences where and with whom one spends one's time (e.g., by inducing more sitting at the playground with other parents). These nonfamily parties that one meets because of relatives offer another way for family members to exert political influence. Relatives can also affect the dynamics of the network within the family: One tends to spend more time with cousins when one shares a living grandparent, for example, and the presence of siblings changes how children and their parents interact.[71]

- *Self-interest.* Family members change the sorts of government policies from which one benefits. Most obviously, having children increases the benefit one receives from publicly sponsored childcare or education, from tax deductions for dependants, and from child health services. A parallel logic appears for many other relatives and policies. Having aged parents to care for implies an immediate payoff from old-age pensions and generous public health care, for example. To the extent people take the self-interest of those around them into account, family also provides an obvious source for costs and benefits one might experience secondhand. For example, having a daughter who could face discrimination and hence unhappiness because of her gender may inspire a father to feel a personal interest in measures that protect women's rights, even if the daughter is too young to induce those effects by articulating such possibilities.

- *Personal experience.* People often extrapolate, and learn most intensely, from their own life experiences,[72] and family is typically a rich source of early experience. Having to have the self-reliance to care for younger siblings or the diplomacy to finesse relationships with older siblings, for example, provides perspectives and skills about human relationships that can color attitudes toward society and the state.

Naturally, these general mechanisms play out in various specific ways when applied to individual questions and circumstances, and later chapters expand on these capsule descriptions. These basic mechanisms, however, serve as the foundation for future chapters' discussion.

PLAN OF THE BOOK

Even when focusing on these channels of family influence, many relatives could have relevant effects, and an unlimited range of political attitudes could be affected. With so much potential ground to cover, this book chooses to focus on breadth, exploring a variety of hypotheses relating to different political issues, family relationships, and aspects of those relationships that matter. This sort of sweeping approach, while not apt to produce detailed conclusions about any one question, has many advantages. It completes a preliminary survey to determine which hypotheses have enough support to merit further, more detailed scrutiny. The more exploratory strategy, venturing across many research questions, demonstrates that there is ample scope for finding new research questions: When so many different combinations of family and political issue produce potential theories, the likelihood is that other, as yet unconsidered possibilities also reap interesting conclusions. With this in mind, each of the following chapters has at its core a different hypothesis to investigate.

The diversified approach also has the advantage of allowing efficient use of the data available. Many surveys provide rich troves of data about respondents' political attitudes, but unfortunately few of these surveys have any information about the respondents' families. Typically, these surveys report only whether the respondents are married; with luck, they may also note whether the respondents have children. Conversely, sociologists have generated a wealth of datasets with fantastically detailed representation of family interactions—showing how often people see their uncles, how far away from their grandparents they live, and so on. Alas, these studies tend to have very little information, if any, about political attitudes; a statement of political party affiliations (such as a response to "Are you a Democrat or Republican?") is frequently the limit of relevant content. The overlap between studies discussing politics and those examining political relationships is much more limited, and any one of those studies might exclude a key question about family or about politics.[73] Studying the relationship between family and political preferences, then, often requires jumping from one survey or topic to another: Just when a hypothesis seems to be in reach, a vital corollary question proves not to appear in the survey. Roving across issues and family members reduces this problem by allowing concentration on the issues and situations where relevant data is available.[74] The advantages of breadth, then, while real, also make a virtue of necessity.

Even with these magpie tactics, certain thematic through-lines recur to maintain the coherence and structure of the investigations. Family is inextricably linked with gender roles, which provides one natural thread tying the various chapters together. This is explicit when talking about siblings and children, where the gender of the party involved is one of the key variables of interest. It comes up as well, albeit less directly, when looking at parents; parental conformity to the traditional family roles of one breadwinner and one homemaker—usually, of course, with a marked gender association between being female and being the homemaker—also receives some attention. Risk acceptance (or aversion) also ties to many aspects of the family and resurfaces as a theme in several chapters: with how parents' behavior exposes children to the world, with what behaviors older siblings might model, and with what hazards children might face. Exploiting these sorts of connections aims to let the chapters and their ideas speak to each even as the discussion moves across a variety of political issues.

Each chapter internally mirrors the structure of trying to maximize breadth of coverage within thematic unities. As each chapter reviews a particular topic or hypothesis, it has a certain level of coherence built in; to apply the hypotheses most broadly, however, most chapters use a range of measures that get at the underlying concept in question but from different perspectives. For example, when chapter 6 looks at demands for more social insurance (such as welfare benefits), it considers together two precursors of those demands: sympathy for poor people and trust in the government. These two attitudes are not customarily interchangeable—yet both are pertinent to the discussion at issue, and looking at these two variables emphasizes the breadth of potential outcomes implicated by the theory. This empirical strategy sometimes forgoes more obvious variants of the measures concerned[75] in order to touch on a larger array of specific public opinions or policy preferences.

Few points in the chapters that follow speak directly to the most common theme of the works discussed above, namely political socialization by spouses or parents leading to ideological convergence. This process undoubtedly still holds new insights that could reward further study, but it has already had its basic ideas explored and so is less central to the aims of this project. Still, as a first starting point, it behooves the discussion to stick to research questions that relate to relatively well-established ideas and hypotheses. Nothing in this book is intended as a radical departure from what we know about family; it instead aims to build on the previous insights to show that much room remains to push research in all sorts of new and potentially fruitful directions. As such, it attempts to build directly on previous studies: It extends many forces already seen to influence political attitudes within the family to new substantive issues or takes things known about family and applies those familial characteristics to political issues. Through the accumulation of several extensions of this nature, though, it hopes to produce a larger picture that is qualitatively different from that which came before.[76]

Within these considerations, the book follows some of the family members that matter most—parents, siblings, and children—in a roughly chronological approach as to how they appear in the lifespan. It starts with parents (broadly construed throughout the book as "the guardian figures in the respondents' childhood households"), who are the focus of chapter 2. Given that parents' beliefs have received so much attention as influences on their children's political outlooks, the chapter looks at another characteristic of parents: not their attitudes but their behaviors. In particular, it considers a much-discussed but not explicitly political choice that parents make: whether one of the parents is a full-time homemaker.[77] Having a parent at home is likely to expose the child to a different set of influences and to send different signals about what constitute normal roles for people in society. This divergent socialization process has a number of potential consequences, most of which suggest that, on many issues, children with a stay-at-home parent should lean further to the political right. After laying out this possibility more fully, the chapter considers whether survey respondents actually follow these patterns, taking into account the probability that parents who stay at home may be more politically conservative or otherwise distinctive to begin with.

Chapter 3 is the first of two chapters concerning the role of siblings. As noted above, siblings are a rather unusual group to consider when considering the formation of political values. Because of this, it is worth showing that siblings really can have an influence—that the real effect is not noise produced by other family or childhood attributes for which siblings might falsely receive credit. To show this, I rely on a simple natural-experiment design, one that assigns respondents to different groups *randomly*, not based on any characteristics of those respondents. This randomness assures that any systematic difference between groups could not be driven by any preexisting features of its members but must instead derive from group membership, just as with having a daughter instead of a son. In this case, the random assignment is the sex of a sibling—in particular, the sex of the respondent's next-older sibling, the one most likely to be influential by being older (and therefore looked up to) and simultaneously in the same home (and therefore able to assert influence, consciously or not).

Given how much sex and gender matter for political beliefs and behaviors, sisters' influence is likely to differ somewhat from brothers', even within the same family. If they did not, gender gaps would not spring up as often as they do, since women and men grow up, on average, in similar households. In particular, the general tendency for females to be more left-leaning than are males suggests that those with an older sister may also tend to have more leftist positions. The chapter explores some of the ways that this dynamic plays out.

Having established that siblings can have a role in shaping political ideology, the book moves in chapter 4 to looking at a more frequently studied implication of siblings: birth order. While it may be frequently studied, being a firstborn child instead of someone with older siblings has mostly been applied to a few questions, such as leadership. I take a different approach, noting that psychologists studying child development have found relatively little reason to believe that birth order matters for the pertinent aspects of personality and belief. What siblings do seem to matter for, on the other hand, is how well-behaved one is as an adolescent. Notably, younger siblings have sex before marriage in greater numbers—and at earlier ages—than do their more upright firstborn siblings (similar patterns hold for alcohol and tobacco use). While this finding is quite widely known in the pediatrics literature, it has not made the jump to the possible political implication that younger siblings might even as adults be more relaxed in their attitudes toward sexual conduct. This could matter for attitudes about many passionate contemporary debates, as over abortion or gay rights. The chapter looks at whether and how younger siblings might differ in their opinions.

Chapter 5 moves on to the next generation: children. Following the model of chapter 3, the discussion of children's influence begins with a natural experiment to establish that the children are actually the animating cause of any effect. Sex is again the basis for the natural experiment, though here the relevant variable is the sex composition across all the respondent's children. This, once again, builds off a common research design in the literature, but the design is most typically used to ask about political issues that relate explicitly to gender (abortion rights, affirmative action preferences)—sensibly enough, since what is varying is the gender of the children. Chapter 5 looks to push the design further, looking at attitudes about war and foreign policy. Men, after all, are more likely to bear the direct costs of fighting in war, and being cued to think about the welfare of young men by having sons of one's own may make these sufferings more vivid and costly. At the same time, having children can inherently give more cause for concern about the future, so trading off the immediate costs that a war will definitely bring against possible longer-term benefits of military action may play out differently for parents.

Family size is a variable that crops up repeatedly throughout the discussions of why relatives matter, and chapter 6 gives it center stage. The primary question there looks at the effect of having different numbers of children. One likely consequence of having responsibility for more children is greater reason to fear economic problems, whether because the expense and commitment of raising a larger family makes one more susceptible to job loss and exhausting one's savings or because the psychological pressure to provide for one's greater number of dependants simply increases worry and anxiety.

This sense of insecurity could have potential consequences for several political attitudes, but perhaps the most immediate is preferences over government social insurance—in other words, the welfare state. Fearing that one might lose one's job or otherwise find income insufficient to cover needs makes insurance valuable as a possible source of revenue to tide over the loss even as it may enhance sympathy for those who suffer economic misfortune and poverty.

Chapter 7 sums up the theories and results of the previous chapters, further discussing the broader conclusions and potential implications for research connecting families and political preferences. It also takes up a question where causation goes from politics to family characteristics rather than the other way around: Does having stronger political associations, in particular identification with specific political parties, increase people's willingness to have children? Evidence suggests that it might.

A NOTE ON METHODOLOGY

Before proceeding to these substantive topics, it is worth pausing briefly to discuss how data is used and presented in the analyses in this book. The approach is generally standard to the point of tameness: The data sources are all prominent, widely used resources in public-opinion research. Indeed, chapters 2 through 6 rely on data that is freely available online, from the American National Election Studies and General Social Survey, to facilitate replication and extension of the conclusions found here.

The statistical methods here, too, aim to be as transparent as possible. The models are all regression models, the most common means in the social sciences of looking at relationships and testing hypotheses while taking other possible explanations into account (i.e., controlling for other factors). Indeed, in chapters featuring statistical tests with a natural-experiment design, some models are even bivariate (i.e., not involving control variables) in part to make them more accessible even for readers who do not have much background in quantitative methods. To further increase the accessibility of the results, all the statistical models in the book are linear ("ordinary least squares") models. This sometimes goes against recent conventions in the social sciences, so the appendix further explains this decision for those interested in statistical methods. Here, suffice it to say that linear models can be read as effect sizes: a value of 0.10 means that whatever is being predicted increases by 0.10 units (on whatever scale that variable may be measured on) for each unit by which the predictor variable increases (with interpretation again reflecting the size of the unit in the measurement used).

The models here are simplified in another, presentational way. The analytical chapters present their models' findings as graphs of effect sizes, not in tables of coefficients. This, although again not the most common approach in the social sciences, follows the practice recommended by most statisticians and visual-communication gurus.[78] The results presented all derive from regression models, and readers who are more familiar and comfortable with thinking in terms of the mathematical coefficients rather than their pictorial representation can reverse-engineer those numbers or consult the appendix for more details. If the dot by "one additional sibling" in a hypothetical figure sits at about 0.10 in the graph, then the model estimates each additional sibling to increase the variable being predicted by 0.10 points. Similarly, the length of the bar around that point estimate gives the 95% confidence interval, from which more statistically inclined readers can get a sense of standard errors, t statistics, p values, and other statistical quantities that might be of interest. Although these eyeball estimates necessarily lack some of the precision of tables of numeric values, they should provide a sense of the substantive impact and confidence level associated with each estimate.

Chapter 2, with the first presentation of model results, contains some further discussion of the graphical-regression presentation and how to read it. Some later chapters raise further methodological points, which are addressed as they arise. These, though, are the basic methodological tactics of all the models in the book. With those in place, we can turn to the first topic: how parents' work choices affect their children's conservatism.

CHAPTER 2
The Conservative Children of Stay-at-Home Mothers

In thinking about the ways that family can form people's political beliefs, the obvious place to start is with parents. Parents take central responsibility for socializing most people, especially during the childhood years, when important dimensions of personality and belief systems take root. Even in adolescence and adulthood, many people continue to count their parents, or the memory of their parents, among their most important role models and guides. This is partly why parental effects were so central to the previous studies discussed in chapter 1. Moreover, almost everyone experiences the influence of some sort of parental figure, when "parental figures" are construed broadly to include stepparents and other nonbiological guardians. (When referring to "parents," I generally mean this social, not biological, sort of parenthood.) While grandparents only sometimes live long enough to have a chance to directly shape their grandchildren's beliefs, and not everyone has siblings, spouses, children, aunts, or uncles, the overwhelming majority of people have at least one parent as an active presence in their lives.

For all the emotional and physical power that parents have over their children, though, some children defy their parents' political inclinations. Take, as a prominent example, the children of Ronald and Nancy Reagan. Icons of American conservatism the Reagans may be, but despite the genes they passed on and lessons they might have tried to impart, both of their biological children (Patti Davis and Ron Reagan) forcefully and publicly adopted quite left-leaning views.[1] Clearly, parts of political socialization remain outside parents' control. It is precisely this slippage that makes parents interesting: What causes their political messages to take or to meet curt rejection? Under what circumstances might other influences drown out the parental teachings?

Parents do present some difficulties that make their influence difficult to analyze. When asked about third parties like parents, survey respondents' perceptions may not accurately reflect the true answer. Surveys do not generally check respondents' remarks about other people against how those other people respond to the same question, even when this sort of cross-check is theoretically possible. In addition, parents' period of most intense involvement in their children's lives tend to be when those children are young, but most information about political opinions—including the polling on which this chapter relies—reflects surveys of adults. This pushes for retrospective, and hence ambiguous, responses. Given the many years of interaction that children typically have with their parents, it can be unclear when a reported parental characteristic was in effect: Was it during the survey respondent's childhood, when the child was most likely to have spent considerable time with the parent? Or during adolescence, which is the most common period for children to leave the parental home and so the most recent time when the survey respondent interacted with the parent with the deep exchanges of someone who shared a household? The survey respondent might also provide the current answer or, if the parent is no longer living, whatever was true during the last years of the parent's life. These different possible interpretations by the respondent may lead to the same answers for some questions, such as parental year of birth or even occupation, but for many others the answer probably changed over the course of the years. For opinion-related questions, the response could even be entirely anachronistic: If asked to identify a dead parent's preferred political party, for example, a respondent might project how the parent would vote at the time of the survey. This may be especially likely in the American South, given the region's thoroughgoing switch from solidly Democrat to solidly Republican during the second half of the twentieth century.

These types of problems may not be very daunting in practice. If people misperceive things about their parents, it may well be the perceived value, not the reality, that has the strongest influence on the child's political development. To use the central question of this chapter as an example, a survey respondent may believe that his mother worked outside the home because she found it professionally fulfilling to do so, when in fact she would really have preferred not to be in the paid labor force and was simply trying to earn money to make household ends meet. The mistaken belief about the family financial situation and the mother's attitudes toward work neverthe-less would be the raw material that the respondent used when formulating political attitudes: The perception, not the reality, is the direct cause of the child's opinions. The imprecision in establishing when particular parental circumstances were in place is also not fatal, as the instances that are easi-est to remember are likely to also be the moments that particularly shaped the survey respondent's outlook. The uncertainty about when exactly those moments were does preclude consideration of interesting, if ultimately secondary, questions such as when parents' influence is most keenly felt in the formation of their children's political preferences. There nevertheless remains room to consider the more central issue of what parental features or behaviors might affect children's politics. The hazards of relying on the child's memory and impressions are moreover less worrisome when study-ing matters readily observable to the child, as these questions eliminate the need for speculation or extrapolation.

One topic that fits this bill is whether a parent, traditionally but not always the mother, served as a full-time homemaker during the survey-tak-er's childhood. This holds interest for a variety of reasons. The shift in women's, including mothers', labor force participation was one of the great sociological changes of the twentieth century. In the year 1900 it was rare, especially among the middle and upper classes, for a mother to work when she had young children at home. By the year 2000, it was commonplace in most Western societies, though by no means universal. Exploring the consequences of this shift may speak to important trends over time. More pointedly still, the decision of whether or not to work outside the home is a dilemma that continues to face parents today, and responses to it vary. The consequences of parental workforce participation are accordingly of interest even when considering variations in outcome at one point in time, without reference to historical trends. Most important, psychologists and sociologists have noted several features of the parental workforce decision that can alter the way their children think about the world, suggesting that parents' work choices may alter outcomes throughout the child's life. The question posed here is: Do those outcomes include political attitudes? There is reason to believe the answer is "yes," in particular that having had a stay-at-home mother may predispose people to conservative ideologies.

STAYING HOME

Political and economic analyses have most often focused on the causes, not the consequences, of mothers' decisions—within social and economic constraints that sometimes virtually compel particular options—to stay at home rather than work. The mother's choice not to engage in paid labor is very worthy of the attention it has received, of course, but it need not completely overshadow the political consequences of that choice for her children. After all, copious, longstanding literatures in both sociology and developmental psychology have drawn out many implications for children of having a working mother. It stands to reason that a factor central to general child development may also affect individuals' political development and socialization. Yet political science has only rarely taken up the influence of working mothers.[2]

One particularly important potential consequence of mothers' working concerns general political ideology: the child's placement on a left–right scale. As a central feature in public opinion and determinant of many other political preferences and behaviors, individual ideology is of broad interest throughout political science and economics. More crucially yet, the psychology and sociology literatures noted above have spoken to a variety of effects on personality and prospects resulting from maternal employment outside the home. Personality and prospects, in turn, link to established determinants of conservatism, as some personality types seem more apt to embrace conservative or liberal ideas.[3] In the broadest terms, the two mechanisms that connect maternal working to children's eventual political orientation involve, on the one hand, policy evaluation and, on the other hand, personality. These two mechanisms complement each other and may intertwine in some regards, but they allow for some theoretical separation.

Before examining these pathways by which maternal working might influence children's political outlook, though, it is worth noting that many of the factors discussed below could also apply to stay-at-home fathers where mothers are in the workforce. Much of the theory surrounding parental behavior applies equally to both parents, and the story here may really be about whether all parents or guardians in the home have external employment. A stay-at-home father married to a working mother has, however, traditionally been rare and often reflective of unusual circumstances, such as paternal disability in the era before workplace compensation. This rarity makes it hard to observe stay-at-home fathers in significant numbers in available datasets, which rules out an empirical test establishing whether the same differentiation exists between fathers who are only homemakers and those in the paid labor force. Speculatively, though, the effects discussed here are probably more likely when the mother, rather than the father, stays at home, as the scenario of a stay-at-home mother, being more socially common, is more likely to be reinforced by broader society. That is, when the stay-at-home parent is typically the mother both within an individual's household and in society as large, the two effects reinforce each other more strongly.

With that preliminary established, we can turn to exploring the mechanisms by which parental work decisions influence the children. Even though young children do not often evaluate policy for themselves, childhood experience heavily influences many values and beliefs. One readily noticeable trait observed by children with full-time homemaker mothers is sex-role differentiation. Those whose mothers have no outside job are more likely to regard women and men as having quite distinct roles both within the household and in society at large.[4] If there is no expectation that men and women—and, by analogy, any particular individual or group within society—will have equal responsibilities, it may be less obvious that equal rights and opportunities are worth the social cost to provide. This may shape attitudes both toward feminism in particular and to a broader sentiment about the state's obligation to equalize disparities in general: Overall egalitarianism is closely bound up with attitudes toward sex roles.[5] The greater acceptance of distinct sex roles connects via this mechanism to more acceptance of inequality and a reduced impulse for redistribution. These outcomes align with traditional preferences of the right.

At the same time, the decision for an adult to commit full-time to household maintenance suggests a devotion to the family and a valuation of its preservation that, in households where the mother works outside the home, may be less manifest to children, even if equally felt by parents. Put another way: Households with a homemaker rely more on their own resources and less on the availability of other providers of social services. This has multiple potential consequences for politically relevant opinions. For one thing, it may enhance the perception that threats to the traditional nuclear family may be costly and disruptive; there would then be more impetus for social conservatism.

In addition, those whose childcare was primarily undertaken within the nuclear family have less evidence to suggest that it takes a village to raise a child. Childhood experience suggests greater familial self-reliance is possible than would the experience of someone whose childcare was outsourced from the household, suggesting in turn that public or social services are more expendable. Of course, a decision to exit the workforce and care for children may in fact reflect the unwanted *absence* of affordable childcare or other outside options: The parents may in fact have desired maternity leave, government-provided day care, or other social services to reduce the burden on themselves. This preference would still tend to be less observable than in households where the mother holds a paid job while raising her child(ren). Even if such preference is made clear to the child, there remains the fact that the family could, in the event, rely on its own resources to provide childcare, so that the publicly provided service is, on the face of it, more dispensable. Individuals frequently extrapolate from their own personal experience—assuming it is representative, even when in practice it is not—and in this case it could increase the child's likelihood of concluding that public services are wasteful or superfluous. The opposite process could operate if financial exigencies force some parents to work when they would prefer to stay home with the children: The child's interpretation of this behavior, too, may or may not reflect parental motives. Having observed parents' working may accordingly lead children to assume that it is natural for households to have to rely on outsiders for services such as childcare and so they are more open to public provision and intervention in matters of household economy.

As to the effect of maternal work on personality, having a mother employed outside the home connects with many aspects of personal development, whether that employment is during early childhood, adolescence, or in between. Having been taken care of by a larger number of caregivers, a factor that associates strongly with maternal work, is particularly important.[6] The reasons found in the literature for this are more suggestive than conclusive.[7] It may arise from the trauma of multiple attachments, or the greater potential for inconsistency in authority figures' behavior when there are more authority figures in play, or perhaps even because experiences curated by a single primary caregiver may be less stimulatingly varied, even if that caregiver strives for diversity. (If parents following the traditional male-breadwinner female-homemaker model are more conservative than those who do not, this striving for diversity by stay-at-home mothers may be unusual, but it still possible—especially as the outcome of working or not working may not reflect a mother's most-preferred option.) Regardless of the precise cause, those raised by homemaker mothers tend to demonstrate less curiosity about the world,[8] while conversely those whose mothers work are less anxious about interacting with others, perhaps because of childhood experience of having to deal with a wider range of interlocutors.[9] Personality, in turn, has a wide range of important links to political ideology. Most notably, comfort with and openness to new experiences tend to associate with liberalism in most studies.[10] This provides a further mechanism whereby maternal working may induce more left-leaning preferences: A working mother leads to a higher level of psychological openness, which then tends to induce more liberalism. It may even be that parents who work exhibit different parenting styles because of the different set of obligations they are balancing. If, in particular, they put less emphasis on the message that children should obey authority figures such as parents, they may instill attitudes that also lead to greater liberalism.[11]

Hence, there are multiple reasons why stay-at-home mothers might tend to have relatively conservative children even when those mothers are not themselves conservative. Indeed, maternal workforce participation implicates at least three and possibly all four of the categories of familial influence noted in chapter 1. Mothers' example and ability, especially if they stay at home, to convey messages to their children give them *direct influence*. The choice to work also changes children's *social networks*, with childcare workers and perhaps other children in a day-care setting more likely to form bonds with the children when the mother works. Childcare also means that the children of stay-at-home mothers also have different *personal experience* than do the progeny of working mothers, which may influence perceptions both of what is normal and what is optimal. It may even be that the mother who stayed out of the workforce for years would benefit most from different public services—for example, if that employment gap made it harder to get a job later on in life, therefore making her more dependent on pension income—which would create *self-interest* effects from having had a working mother.

Yet the links between mothers and ideology may not all argue that maternal working produces more conservatism. In fact, one of the most thoroughly theorized effects of maternal employment, on cognitive development and general intelligence, may suggest the opposite relationship. Both theory and empirical results connecting maternal work and child brain development are inconclusive, with effect sizes typically being small, inconsistent, and unstable.[12] Still, a persistent strain in the literature pushes the notion that more direct maternal care promotes child development. Intelligence has in turn been controversially tied to a reduced propensity for conservatism.[13] Together, these ideas produce the opposite hypothesis to that explored here: Children of stay-at-home mothers would be expected to be more *liberal*, not conservative. A similar possibility arises from the notion that children of working mothers may believe, however accurately, that economic conditions were the source of the mothers' decisions to work. They may accordingly support income redistribution to prevent others from having to suffer the same perceived deprivation. Of course, when theoretical mechanisms point in opposite directions, the question of which dominates becomes empirical, to be resolved by looking at what patterns emerge in real-world data.

CONSERVATISM AND MATERNAL WORK IN SURVEY RESPONSES

Testing the proposition that stay-at-home mothers tend to produce more conservative children requires a data set with information about both adult political preferences and childhood circumstances. Fortunately, one of the flagship datasets of political research, the American National Election Study (NES), did include the relevant questions for many years. In particular, information about maternal occupation was part of every (biennial) edition of the study from 1970 to 1992 except for that of 1990. Overall, this provides around 22,000 observations of potentially usable data.

The primary concept to be predicted is the degree of right-leaning ideology. The most immediate available measure of this asks the survey respondents to rate their own conservatism on a 7-point scale, where higher values indicate more conservative positions. This measure does have some disadvantages. Different respondents' perceptions of what it means to be conservative, liberal, or centrist might vary, so the subjective ratings might not be consistent across people. In addition, the direct measure of ideology is missing for large portions of the sample who were not asked the question or chose not to answer. In the extreme case, the conservatism question was not in the 1970 survey at all, and even in later years around one-third of the sample typically did not provide a conservatism rating for whatever reason.[14]

To ensure that none of the findings stem from these quirks of measurement, the models below also consider an alternative measure of conservatism, namely partisan identification. With the US two-party system, there is a marked tendency for those who strongly identify with the Democratic Party to be left-leaning, while those who identify strongly with the Republican Party tend to be more conservative. This correlation is by no means absolute: Especially in the early years of the surveys used here, Southern Democrats were often extremely conservative, and even in later years the "big tent" nature of American parties left room for considerable ideological diversity within each. Partisanship also explicitly captures nonideological factors, such as affinity for a particular charismatic politician. In addition, third parties count as "Independents" regardless of their political positions—members of the Green Party or the Libertarian Party will both end up in the middle of the partisanship spectrum even though their ideologies may be neither particularly centrist nor similar to one another's.

Despite this imperfect match with what the theory predicted stay-at-home mothers would influence, association with parties provides another rough guide to overall political perspective that can serve as a useful cross-check to the explicitly ideology-based measure. Partisanship has additional advantages as well. It is available for most survey participants, including those in 1970, and to the extent partisan sentiment reflects acceptance of the national party's platform, it provides (at any point in time) a more objective ideological meaning than does self-proclaimed position on a scale.[15] Partisanship also has the benefit of holding independent practical interest. With the central role of political parties in political activity, associations between maternal work and party choice have implications for many questions of voting, elections, and political behavior. Thus all models below were run twice, once to predict ideology itself and once to predict party position. Partisanship is, like ideology, measured here on a 7-point scale, with higher values suggesting greater conservatism by showing more association with Republicans and less with Democrats.

For the central predictor variable of interest—mother's workforce participation—the data set includes a simple binary indicator of whether the respondent's mother (or mother surrogate for those with dead or otherwise absent mothers) had no job other than that of homemaker when the respondent was growing up. This measure is not quite consistent across the surveys; the 1970 survey differs slightly from later years', in that no separate question explicitly asks whether the mother had a job outside the household. Instead, that survey featured a general question about the mother's job, one answer to which included mentioning that the mother was not in the civilian labor force. This does combine military personnel, students, and perhaps those whose occupation is unknown with pure homemakers. This conflation is unlikely to greatly alter the results, as mothers falling into these categories comprise less than 0.1% of the overall proportion of those not in the labor force for the years where the data set does clearly distinguish among the groups. In addition, running the models below without the 1970 survey also produces similar outcomes to those reported. Most[16] models below accordingly include the 1970 survey alongside the other years' data. In all years, the variable is coded as missing for those without any mother or mother surrogate in the childhood household. Since higher values of the variables of interest imply, respectively, at-home mothers and more conservative outlooks, the expected effect of having a mother with no job outside the home is positive: Those with stay-at-home mothers are hypothesized to score higher on the conservatism scale.

In addition to the variables of interest, several other concepts are relevant for the models. One of the central complications in studying the effect of working versus stay-at-home mothers is the potential for spurious causation. Households where the mother works are not selected randomly, and many factors plausibly influence both the tendency for the mother to work and the tendency to socialize children conservatively. This implies a potential need to incorporate a wide range of possible confounding factors into the models as control variables. However, the classical logic of control variables in hypothesis testing implies that they guard against spurious causation only when they—or the concepts they reflect—antedate and so could have caused the explanatory variable of interest. Since the independent variable here (maternal work behavior during respondents' childhoods) occurred early in respondents' lives, standard control variables also ought to be factors that either were established by the time of respondents' youth or reflect features of the survey rather than those of the individual respondent. The most important of the survey features is the year in which the survey occurred, especially given the trend in maternal workforce behavior noted above: As time has passed, women have been progressively more likely to work outside the home even as they helped raise children. The models below all include year-of-survey variables to capture other differences across the decades.

Some of the other factors that held since or before respondents' childhoods, and thus could have affected mothers' workplace decision, are fundamental demographic characteristics that, because they likely also affect political opinions, merit inclusion in any model of attitudes.[17] Among the most important of these is age. The fraction and demographics of women who are out of the workforce has shifted substantially over time, even as opinions vary over the life cycle. These two shifts may coincide to create the false appearance of an effect of mothers' work decisions. Similarly, surveys consistently find men to be more conservative than women, and women may be more likely to exit the workforce to care for male children—as put by one review of the literature, "mothers may be [more] focused on fulfilling the conventional maternal caregiving role when they have sons rather than daughters."[18] An observed correlation between having a stay-at-home mother and conservatism may therefore be spurious if it does not control for the sex of the survey respondent. Finally, different cultural groups may also vary both in their general political outlooks and in their beliefs about the proper role of the mother in the households. The models therefore control for ethnic and regional cultures, along with a measure of urbanization of the respondent's childhood location.

These demographic features comprise a basic model. Respondents' demographics, though, are not the only likely determinants of their preferences; fortunately, the NES at least sporadically contains measures of several other potentially pivotal childhood influences. One vital measure is the father's occupation, which heavily influences family incomes and social status. These are both likely to be important determinants of the political atmosphere in which respondents came of age, even as it is likely to affect mothers' options concerning work outside the home: In lower-income households, mothers are more likely to have to accept paid labor to be able to afford basic family needs. To take these circumstances into account, the models include indicator variables for every paternal career listed in the survey (including "not in labor force").

As important as paternal careers are the political sentiments of the parents themselves. As chapter 1 discussed, these have evident, clearly established correlations with children's political orientation. Political sentiments are moreover likely to strongly affect women's labor force decisions: Those ideologically inclined to traditional gender roles are obviously less likely to embrace mothers' working outside the home. The NES's measure of parental ideology is partisan identification; the above caveats about the imperfect correspondence between partisan affiliation and left–right ideology hold even more strongly here, as partisan positions shifted across the century of childhoods included in the data. Party positions nevertheless offer an explicit measure of parents' political views. The NES asked only about parental political views in seven of the survey years with data on mothers' workforce participation, so including this variable substantially reduces the number of survey-takers in the sample.

A final available variable of relevance is whether the respondent's parents were both born in the United States. If immigrants' traditionalism or lack of assimilation affected their workforce participation patterns, this could also influence the relationship under study here. Immigrants are moreover apt to be more conservative on several issue areas and subsequently to convey conservative messages to their children.[19]

DO OTHER ADULT CHARACTERISTICS ABSORB MATERNAL EMPLOYMENT EFFECTS?

While focusing on control variables that could have affected respondents' childhoods makes sense for the causal argument presented here, it does have several unfortunate consequences. It radically diminishes the number of observations available, because the NES did not consistently include questions concerning parents across the survey iterations. Most notably, the questions about parental partisanship are as mentioned above available for only seven of the eleven surveys; this one variable thereby singlehandedly reduces the sample size by over 40%. Focusing exclusively on factors known about respondents' formative years also imposes strict limits on the concepts that are measurable, since the NES asks only a few questions about respondents' parents and childhood characteristics. An approach looking only at childhood variables, for example, does not have direct measures of potentially interesting features like how educated the respondent eventually became. It may therefore be worth testing the robustness of the link between maternal working and conservatism using control variables for features that emerge only during adulthood.

Doing this does raise concerns for what inferences can be made and how precise estimates will be. After all, the whole course of the argument here is that childhood conditions may influence adult outcomes. Taking account of factors that arose later in life may mask the real effect of childhood circumstances by causing "endogeneity bias." To take an analogy, consider the link between childhood nutrition and adult income. A better diet during one's youth could possibly affect not only mental qualities that lead to higher income but also adult height. Height has other causes, too, of course: genetics, for example. Moreover, height may independently influence income if employers are biased about personal appearance; if companies pay people more for being tall (consciously or not), height will have an effect on income over and above the extent to which it indirectly captures the effects of childhood nutrition. It is in consequence tempting to use height as an independent predictor of income. But insofar as childhood nutrition affects height, treating height as though it had a separate, independent effect will misleadingly reduce the seeming impact of childhood nutrition. That is, the effects are *not* wholly independent, and so the predicted difference between those with good and bad diet will appear to shrink to smaller than what it in reality is.

Similarly, if maternal working partially determines respondents' adult income, for example, and that income pulls people to the conservative end of the political spectrum, then controlling for income will undercut the actually causal effect of mothers' behavior. Or, to take a concern that might afflict another control variable, if males' tendency to conservatism stems from socialization rather than intrinsic biology, causation could be reversed here. As mentioned earlier, there is some evidence that mothers are more apt to stay home after bearing sons than daughters. The greater exposure to stay-at-home mothers that boys then receive may be what produces the gender gap in conservatism. In this case, controlling for sex induces bias in the estimates— but once more, any such bias strictly reduces the likelihood that stay-at-home mothers will associate with more conservative children. An observed connection between left-wing orientation and maternal working is then less likely and hence more compelling in the presence of the potential bias.

While it would always be better to have a perfect estimate of the effect size, this sort of systematic bias may be acceptable. After all, its primary result is to stack the deck against the hypotheses considered here. The statistical models tend to underestimate the size (and statistical significance) of the effect of childhood variables, so that adding control variables from adulthood should reduce the probability of finding that maternal workforce behavior affects political ideology. This reduces the worries about including such temporally misplaced control variables, and what worries remain are outweighed by the adult-era variables' potential usefulness in indirectly capturing background and childhood characteristics that also shaped parental household work decisions.

Most of the demographic characteristics—year of birth, sex, ethnicity, and the like—do not typically change between childhood and the time of the survey, so those measures carry over comfortably to models using characteristics of adulthood. Translating some of the other childhood variables into contemporaneous equivalents is also relatively straightforward. Instead of using how rural was the location of where the survey respondent grew up, for example, it is simple to substitute in how rural the respondent's place of residence is at the time of the survey. The same holds for the state where the survey took place, which replaces the region where the respondent grew up.

These variables can be supplemented with new concepts unavailable among the childhood-era control variables. Education and household income levels, notably, are mainstays of models of individual beliefs and preferences. With respect to broad ideologies like conservatism, education potentially exposes people to more information and ways of thinking about the world, while income changes the incentives for supporting government intervention in the market, a position traditionally anathema to American conservatives. Yet the NES contains no direct measure of these for respondents' childhoods; parental occupation probably indirectly indicates education levels and incomes, but the connection between jobs and occupations can be loose—and the link between parental variables and child education is more tenuous still. When using measures from the time of the survey, however, explicit measures of income and education are available. NES models looking strictly at factors that are measured in childhood contain even less scope for measuring religiosity, which relates closely to social conservatism. Religion is especially interesting here, as it often reflects parental influences even as it affects political preferences. It is also a complex, multidimensional concept to measure, with sects (such as Catholicism or Buddhism), intensities of belief and social behaviors all varying across individuals. The reported results here focus on frequency of church attendance. Finally, rootedness in the community may produce conservatism, and various measures of how long respondents have lived in their current towns and houses are available to account for this.

DIFFERENCES IN CONSERVATISM

Figure 2.1 summarizes the statistical results that come from bringing together the above variables, with each of its six panels showing the

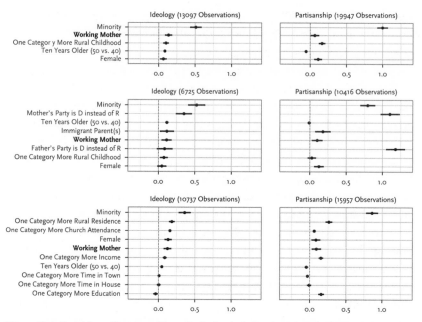

Figure 2.1 Variables affecting self-rated ideology (left column) and partisan identification (right column), on 7-point scales. Top-panel models are baseline; middle-panel models include control variables from childhood; bottom-panel models include control variables from adulthood. All models control for survey year, place of residence, and father's occupation. Bars show 95% confidence intervals. More positive numbers indicate more left-leaning beliefs.

estimates from a different model. The graphs on the left in Figure 2.1 show models looking at the ideology-based measure of liberalism, while those on the right look at party identification. For each of these measures, three different models are shown, with the topmost giving a reduced model with only demographic features, the second row adding additional variables available for the respondents' childhoods, and the bottom model adding instead information about respondents during their adulthoods. For each listed change in the variable, the circle shows the estimated effect on liberalism while the bar indicates the 95% confidence interval for that estimate. As an example, the top entry in the upper-left panel shows females to be—when everything else in the model is held constant—about 0.07 points more liberal than are males, or equivalently that males are 0.07 points more conservative than females. (Recall that both dependent variables are on a 7-point scale, so that a 1-point change represents the difference between, for example, "conservative" and "extremely conservative" or "weak Republican" and "strong Republican.") This 0.07-unit change is clearly small as applied to any individual, yet for an *average* effect across a population, it is relatively substantial: The gender gap in attitudes that it denotes is large enough to be noticed in all sorts of popular and scholarly analyses.[20] Note as well that the confidence interval for that gender gap effect stays entirely on the right side of the dotted vertical line indicating zero effect. This indicates that the effect is statistically distinguishable from zero: A positive association this large would not be expected from random noise if there were no underlying connection between one's sex and conservatism. In other words, we can be statistically confident that being female correlates with being more liberal rather than with being more conservative or equal in ideology.

As to the figure's substantive implications for the central question of how maternal work relates to conservatism, stay-at-home motherhood has the expected effect of increasing conservatism in all six models, when the effects of other variables in the models are accounted for. This estimated effect is not large in magnitude—only around one-eighth of a point—but it is comparable in size with that of several well-established effects. For example, the gap between children of stay-at-home and working mothers is about twice as large as the gap between men and women when using the ideological measure (and around the same size as the gender gap when using the partisanship measure). Similarly, the rightward-pushing effect of a stay-at-home mother is on average similar to that of a 1-point change on the rurality scale (e.g., having grown up in the suburbs rather than in the city). Moreover, this effect of mother's work status also attains high levels of statistical significance: The results suggest grounds for confidence that the observed relationship was not simply a fluke of random variation.

While the implication of all of Figure 2.1's models is the same with respect to the central finding that children of mothers who work outside the home grow up to be more liberal on average than do children of stay-at-home mothers, the slight differences among the model results can also be enlightening. It is for example notable that the predicted effects of maternal working are somewhat smaller in size for partisanship than for ideology—that is, the effect of maternal work is closer to the zero line in the rightmost column of Figure 2.1. This is consistent with the idea that the stay-at-home parent effect most directly influences ideology, perhaps because of the misalignment between partisanship and particular beliefs. Similarly, the models with childhood-era control variables tend to produce slightly smaller effects of maternal work than do the models with adulthood-era controls, which hints that the maternal work decision associates with other elements of the childhood environment that can influence people's politics. Even when looking at the model using childhood-era controls and measuring attitudes through partisanship, though, there is still an appreciable and statistically significant connection between people's conservatism and their mothers' work behavior.

Reinforcing confidence in these estimates, the control variables also have plausible predicted coefficients. Estimated levels of conservatism are highest in middle age, while women and (especially) racial or ethnic minorities generally lean further to the left than do men and whites. Paternal occupation has a less marked effect on model fit than does parental partisanship. When looking at children's partisanship,[21] as might be expected, the offspring of Independent parents tend to be more Republican-leaning than are the progeny of Democrats (the baseline category), while children of Republican parents generally turn out to be more Republican still. Also, following venerable findings in the literature,[22] mothers' political views appear to translate into child ideology more directly than do those of fathers: Mothers' affiliation with the Republican Party has a substantially stronger conservatizing effect than does fathers' affiliation in the models. More education associates with a more leftist outlook, all else equal, while higher incomes, residence in a rural area, and religiosity all connect with more right-leaning sentiments.

Finally, native-born parents' children are typically more conservative than are immigrants'.[23]

While these baseline results are a promising indication that maternal workforce participation may tend to incline children toward a more leftist perspective, they are by no means conclusive. Other variants of the models here also produce similar estimates. For example, mixing variables from childhood and adulthood does not change the tenor of the results. In the extreme case, which includes all of the variables in Figure 2.1 along with all the variables just mentioned from adulthood, the coefficient on stay-at-home mothers is 0.09, with a confidence interval ranging from 0.01 to 0.17. This is slightly smaller than the estimated effects seen in the other models but still compares to well-attested phenomena like the gender gap and attains standard levels of statistical significance. To extend the model in a different direction, we can include the interaction of mothers' party affiliation with their workforce behavior. In such a model, maternal Republicanness exhibits no observably stronger effect on child ideology when the mother stays at home (although the rightward-pulling effect of a stay-at-home mother remains). This hints, albeit not conclusively, that it is not simply greater exposure to the mother's principles that pulls the children of homemakers politically rightward. Hence, even when accounting for a variety of other potential influences, mothers' work choices do consistently associate with their children's ultimate political ideology.

ARE ALL DIMENSIONS OF CONSERVATISM AFFECTED?

Even upon considering both ideological and partisan measures of conservatism, conclusively establishing the causal effect of maternal workforce participation is difficult with the few measures of parental characteristics available. With only indirect proxies for the parents' conservatism, control variables cannot eliminate the possibility of spurious causation. Another approach that may help get around this difficulty is to consider the theoretical effects of general parental conservatism and consider where they might differ from the likely implications of working mothers—that is, to look for the distinctive fingerprints of maternal work effects. One likely place to look for such fingerprints is within specific issue positions. Some factors that are part of a right-leaning worldview are more likely than others to connect to maternal work choices. If children of stay-at-home mothers show equal tendency toward conservatism even across issues where mothers' working has no obvious implication, it would imply that mothers' working may be less important for political socialization than was the parental ideology that happened to lead mothers to work. On the other hand, if children of stay-at-home mothers are only more conservative regarding issues with tighter theoretical connection to maternal work, it suggests a more direct role for maternal workforce behavior in shaping beliefs. Examining which issues appeal differently to those with homemaker mothers has the additional advantage of casting a more precise light on the effects of parents' career choices.

As a broad, multidimensional ideology, conservatism has implications for a wide range of specific issue preferences. If this general conservatism transmits to children, then, several concomitants would be expected: a tendency to prefer a smaller role for the state and less redistribution; more traditional social mores; support for a more militaristic foreign policy.[24] Many of these, as discussed above, are precisely the conservative tenets that the presence of a stay-at-home mother may induce. However, the foreign policy preferences bear less obvious theoretical relation to maternal labor force participation. Certainly, the direct implications of family experience are much more remote for foreign policy, even if intrafamily relations sometimes feel like warfare, and a change in foreign policy is unlikely to bring particular benefits to families with working mothers. It is possible that stay-at-home mothers' effects on personality could translate to particular foreign policy preferences, but the potential mechanisms (say, because an authoritarian personality leads to more willingness to deploy unilateral force abroad) see little obvious support in the previous literature on either personality or foreign policy. This is not to say that family is irrelevant to preferences over foreign policy—chapter 5 further explores the connection. Nevertheless, the maternal work decision is not tightly connected to those mechanisms.

If a mother's status as homemaker is merely an irrelevant reflection of underlying parental conservatism rather than an active inducement pulling the children's preferences rightward, then, the expectation would be that homemaker mothers would beget children with more conservative positions across the board, including in foreign policy. If, by contrast, maternal careers have an independent effect on child attitudes, differences would tend to occur on domestic, but not international, issues. Even within the set of domestic issues, the theory suggests that maternal behavior more directly socializes some over others—in particular, one might expect the largest effects for attitudes toward women's role in society.

One way to explore these possibilities would be to repeat the models from Figure 2.1, replacing the broad measures of conservatism with a series of narrower dependent variables. That is what this section does, reporting results from analogues to the middle panel, that is models with childhood-era controls. (Using instead other models from Figure 2.1 produces similar results.) The first of these narrower measures concerns beliefs about women's proper place in society. For this variable, respondents place themselves on a 7-point scale where a value of 1 signals that the respondent believes that women's place is in the home, while an answer of 7 represents the belief that women and men should have the same roles in commerce, careers, and politics. This is perhaps the component of traditionally conservative ideas most directly relevant to having a stay-at-home mother and so would be expected to have a strong relationship: Those whose mothers worked have obvious reason to believe that women can assume useful positions outside the home as well as inside. Broadening this concept from women in particular to egalitarian attitudes in general, another model looks at general beliefs about equality in society. These are measured with an index encompassing six questions about the costs and benefits of greater equality, which together produce a 25-point scale running from -12 (most adamant that society should equalize opportunities) to 12 (most acceptant of inequality). The six questions are phrased without reference to any racial, gender, or other demographic group but are simply about whether all Americans should and do have equal chances in life. Note that for both the women's role variable and the egalitarianism variable, the more traditionally liberal position associates with higher values, as it did in Figure 2.1.

Another potential effect of exposure to a working mother concerns traditional values and social policy. Scholars have long since noted that feelings about abortion correlate with opinions about the equality of men and women,[25] so abortion is one place to expect policy implications of sex-role attitudes. Conveniently, abortion is also the moral issue most consistently asked about in the NES. Hence the measure of traditional values looks at the number of conditions under which the respondent thinks the law should allow abortion, on a scale from 1 to 4.[26] The coding is such that those who think abortion should be allowed under more conditions have higher values of the variable, so that the traditionally liberal preference once again represents higher values. To look at opinions about the size of government, because, as noted above, having a working mother may increase support for income redistribution and public service provision, the measure is a 7-point scale where higher values indicate less support for larger government.

Finally, as the placebo test—that is, one in which the theory presented here does not argue for a significant relationship—of foreign policy preferences, the table includes a model predicting support for defense spending, also on a 7-point scale. As all of the variables to this point have been measured so that higher values (that is, more rightward positions on the figure) associated with more liberalism, this variable is coded in the same way. Since defense spending is an anomalous issue where conservatives have traditionally favored greater government activity, this means that higher-valued codes on this variable imply support for the more typically liberal position of *lower* defense spending.

Figure 2.2 shows the results of modeling these five specific issue areas. Within each issue, those who had at-home mothers have more traditionally conservative positions, but the magnitude and statistical significance of the coefficients vary widely across the variables being predicted. As would be expected, one of the strongest effects is that those whose mothers worked are much more likely to feel that women's role should be equal to that of men. The effect of maternal working is about three times the size of the gender gap (which, however, is not in the expected direction, perhaps because the regression does not account for women's tendency toward greater religiosity—including measures of religiosity at the time of the survey reverses the effect) and substantially larger than the estimated difference between forty- and fifty-year-olds. This preference for relative equality between the sexes translates into general concern for equality as well, as shown in the second panel of the figure: Those whose mothers worked outside the home are more concerned that everyone in society has the same rights and opportunities. Again, the effect of mother's work is larger than the gender gap (though only about one-third larger, in this instance) and comparable in size to, though slightly less than, the effect of

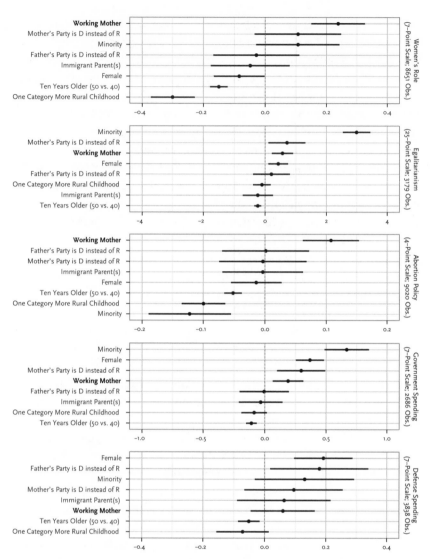

Figure 2.2 Issue-area preferences. All models control for survey year, place of residence, and father's occupation. Bars show 95% confidence intervals. More positive numbers indicate more left-leaning positions.

having a Democrat rather than Republican mother. Those with full-time homemaker mothers also are less enthusiastic about legalized abortion, as seen in Figure 2.2's third panel. Here, unusually, no gender gap appears in the coefficients, although this too probably stems from the absence of a direct control for greater female religiosity. Maternal work has essentially equivalent effect to having grown up in a one category more urban environment, or, as an alternative benchmark, to the estimated difference between the abortion attitudes of a thirty-year-old and those of a fifty-year-old. Concerning preferences for government spending, the effect of maternal work is, though statistically significant at standard levels, only about half the size of the gender gap.

For defense spending, however, the effect of a working mother is smaller than it is in most of the other issue realms. It also fails to attain statistical significance at anything approaching standard levels, despite there being more observations and so greater power for the model to identify effects with precision here than in some of the other issue areas. Nor is this unique to defense spending; other measures of foreign policy opinion that link to conservatism—attitudes toward war, isolationism, and the like—also see only small, insignificant effects from mothers' working. While this is not of itself conclusive proof that maternal job decisions have a causal impact on children's political outlooks, it further contributes to the pattern of evidence suggesting that maternal work behaviors, not merely the parents' own political attitudes, do affect the politics of those they raise.

CONCLUSION

The argument and results here suggest that children of full-time home-maker mothers tend to be more right-leaning both in their general ideology and across several domestic policy issue areas, such as abortion regulation, the size of government, and concern for equality in society. These are theoretically predictable consequences of childhood experiences that suggest the family has resources to take care of its own, that groups within society may have quite different roles just as mothers and fathers do in the respondent's experience, and that the family is a central unit of life and therefore worthy of protection. More broadly, these results tend to suggest that ideological attitudes will be self-reinforcing across generations: The children of mothers who worked will generally be more insistent on their own—and their spouses'—equal role within the home and society. This can lead not only to social stability but also to one potential source of change across generations: Even a population of conservative parents may be likely to produce relatively liberal children if the female part of the population had to work. Although it is impossible to conclusively establish causes for the political beliefs of any one specific individual, the story here may be part of the explanation of how Ronald and Nancy Reagan's children pulled left-ward. Nancy Reagan continued to work as an actress (and board member of the Screen Actors Guild) for some years after the birth of her children, exposing them to other role models and influences during a formative time.

As always, these results leave open many questions. This chapter considered the broadest levels of family ideological influence; the rich literatures on child development and socialization suggest that the effect of a working mother may interact with many other family dynamics. Daughters may see more influence than sons, for example, or firstborns more than their younger siblings, owing to greater interaction with the mother. (Related effects are the focus of chapters 4 and 5.) More fully considering the causes of mothers' decisions to work, a hard or impossible task with most extant surveys, may further enrich such lines of inquiry. Women with more stressful careers, for example, may be both more likely to give up their jobs upon the birth of a child—and to have daughters.[27] Those in stressful jobs that do continue working after the birth of their children, in addition, may transmit different impressions about jobs and society than do those whose careers are less psychologically taxing.

In suggesting these possibilities, as well as with the main question explored in this chapter, the central difficulty is to be certain that an observed relationship is causal. This is typical in social science, especially using nonexperimental data, and for few problems is this issue more fraught than in proving the effect of parental influence. In moving on to the next generation and considering potential effects of siblings, however, the potential for demonstrating that the influence of siblings is causal and not merely spurious can be expedited by a simple natural experiment: the essentially random variable of the sex of those siblings. The next chapter takes up this idea.

CHAPTER 3

The Ideological Pull of Siblings

Social interactions are particularly important for the formation of opinions; there is good reason the process of political preference formation is usually called "socialization." Parents, teachers, peers, fellow members of clubs and organizations—each provide cues about proper behavior and the workings of society. This chapter turns to a different group: sisters and brothers, whose conspicuous place in the lives and perceptions of young people suggests they might be a vital influence. However, they rarely take starring roles in political analyses, perhaps because any independent effects of individuals' siblings can be difficult to discern. The same parents and, often, community influences that affect individuals themselves also usually shape those individuals' siblings, which makes it hard to identify the effects that siblings, and not the surrounding community, might have. Moreover, in most households, all members share racial and socioeconomic characteristics, which means some of the more obvious sorts of influences are too unusual to easily generalize from.

Nor is this difficulty in singling out what effects siblings might have the only obstacle. As a practical matter, siblings' tendency in many societies to establish separate households makes it costly to gather information about them or interrogate them about their political beliefs: Very few studies collect data on both sibling composition and interesting political beliefs. More theoretically, the same psychology literature that emphasizes the importance of siblings also suggests that many factors potentially diffract the influences that the sibling relationship might have. The size of the age gap between siblings makes a difference in sibling effects,[1] as may family demographics such as socioeconomic status[2] and systematic differences in parents' behavior toward different siblings (if I fall into a life of crime because Mom always loved you best, is it you or Mom that influenced me?).[3] In large families, the multiple overlapping dyads of significant interaction—oldest sibling with second sibling, oldest sibling with third sibling, second sibling with third sibling, and so on—require considerable effort to disentangle. Even defining "sibling" can be a complicated business, with the possible influences of half-, step-, foster, and adopted siblings.

Despite these hurdles, examining the role of sisters and brothers may repay the effort. The lack of emphasis on siblings in political science sits uneasily with evidence from the other social sciences that siblings extensively affect each other's perceptions and behavior.[4] Scholars of social and developmental psychology are especially emphatic (though not unanimous[5]) about the persistent, influential effects that siblings have on one another; sociological and economic studies add some broader context to sisters' and brothers' likely impact.[6] Although these effects are larger and more studied during youth, when siblings are most apt to spend time together, many of the relevant psychological features show a high degree of persistence after adolescence.[7] The smaller number of studies that do look for sibling effects in adults, moreover, often find them.[8] For example, having siblings can alter basic, typically lifelong traits such as conscientiousness or extraversion.[9] In addition to these psychological effects, siblings affect behaviors—such as childbearing—that may themselves influence political views,[10] as will be further considered in chapter 6. When siblings have such a range of effects, it seems likely that they might also affect outcomes of direct political interest.

In addition, some of the difficulties of studying siblings are more surmountable than they may first appear. Consider the pernicious problem of being unable to pinpoint effects of siblings. While siblings are similar on many characteristics—to each other, to their parents—there are ways in which they do vary. Most important, they differ in sex, and these differences arise in partially randomized ways that expedite empirical analysis. Because the selection of a new child's gender is most commonly left to nature, we can expect people with sisters to be—aside from the influence of their siblings—very similar on average to people with brothers, so any differences between the two groups likely derived from the influence of the sibling's sex. Handily, too, sibling sex is also a highly visible, persistent feature: Even someone at great distance from, or out of contact with, siblings can reliably report those siblings' sexes, which allays some of the problems of hunting down and surveying both halves of a sibling pair.

In addition to these empirical advantages, sex is useful because it plays a major role in many processes that feed into political-preference formation.

Having someone as close as a sibling be male instead of female is therefore promising as a source for observable variation in political outcomes. Psychologists and sociologists have extensively considered variation in siblings' sex, finding widespread effects on behavioral and educational outcomes.[11] Even economists have got in on the act, finding that sibling sex can matter for earnings potential.[12] A possible role for sibling sex echoes other, known political effects of family gender composition, such as the tendency discussed in chapter 1 (and that arises again in chapter 5) for a parent's mix of sons and daughters to affect issue preferences and voting behavior. Given the relative malleability of beliefs during youth, when interaction with siblings typically peaks, the potential influence of sisters or brothers may be even larger than that of daughters and sons.

This leaves a great deal of room for potential effects. Much of this room, though, raises the old issue of being hard to associate conclusively with the effect of the sibling. Simply looking for people who have a sister, say, will disproportionately find people who came from large families, and while the sex of any individual child may be somewhat out of parents' conscious control, the number of children they have is much more likely to be explicitly chosen. And some parents seem to have more children until they get one of each sex. So simply looking at whether someone has a sister will tend to be comparing people from very different families—larger ones and those larger for a specific reason. That sort of a research set-up thus misses out on the potential randomization and hence the greater security of a quasi-experimental design; the size of the family holds great potential interest (it will be the subject of chapter 4), but it tends to require more complicated research designs encumbered with many control variables. Finding a more straightforwardly testable theory consequently requires looking not just at the existence of a sibling with a particular trait but instead identifying one particular sibling before considering the characteristic of that sibling.

The obvious sibling characteristic to consider, as just discussed, is sex, and the obvious sibling to choose is a person's next-older sibling. Siblings who are near each other in age (and, hence, rank within the family) typically interact more with one another than do more disparate pairs; siblings closer in age are more likely to serve as playmates and companions. This means that a sibling closer in age is a more promising source of effects than would be, say, a person's eldest sibling, who is more likely to have been a relatively distant presence during childhood—and, indeed, more proximate siblings usually overlap most in outlook.[13] At the same time, sibling socialization tends to flow from older siblings to younger, both through explicit attempts of older siblings to mold the younger and through younger siblings' efforts to imitate the older:[14] Throughout their youth, people tend to look up to and emulate their older siblings. Political beliefs are thus more likely to flow from older siblings than from younger ones. Taken together, these two processes (influence tied to proximity in age and flowing from older to younger siblings) mean that one's immediately older sibling should tend to be especially influential in shaping personality and behavior: The elder sibling closest in age has the greatest chance of impressing his or her views.[15] This naturally does not inform outcomes for only children or eldest siblings, but it still affects large proportions of most countries' populations: Most people have at least one elder sibling.[16]

What effects, then, might the next-older sibling's sex have on political preferences or beliefs? The most frequent finding is that siblings tend to conform. In the process of socialization, the younger sibling's tastes and ideas tend to converge toward those of the older. This holds across a range of outcomes, such as hobbies, educational experiences, or attitudes toward smoking and alcohol consumption.[17] It even holds when the outcomes in question are sex-typed; people with an older sibling of the opposite sex are less apt to restrict their interests only to matters traditionally associated with their own sex.[18] None of this may be conscious. The toys around the house for an older sibling may unintentionally provide cues for the younger siblings, or parents may find it more convenient to take their children to similar schools or extracurricular activities regardless of the younger siblings' personal inclination. Whatever the cause, all else equal, individuals whose immediately older sibling is female are more likely to act in typically female ways, while those whose immediately older sibling is male will be more likely to follow commonly male patterns.

If this process extends to more directly political outcomes, those preferences showing a gender gap will show a parallel sibling–gender gap. A wide variety of political questions do exhibit consistent sex differences, whether for sociological or biological reasons (or the interaction of the two).[19] In many contexts, for example, political participation differs between men and women.[20] Differences are even more striking on matters of public opinion. Men and women have especially divergent preferences over overtly gender-related issues such as sexual mores and family roles.[21] The different perspectives extend well beyond these realms, however, spanning policy issues from criminal justice to the environment.[22] Indeed, sex differences turn up even in very broad measures of partisanship and ideology.[23]

How would an older sibling transmit these sorts of preferences to younger siblings? It is unlikely, after all, that children spend much time sharing information about explicitly political questions or otherwise directly socializing attitudes toward government policy—though this objection is clearly not fatal, as demonstrated by the literature of sex-of-child influence on parents mentioned in chapter 1 (and further explored in chapter 5). Various means of influence are nevertheless possible. As a source of direct influence, siblings tend to shape attitudes toward risk, both by modeling behaviors that younger siblings adopt and by explicitly discussing likely consequences with their siblings.[24] Since risk aversion tends to influence preferences on a wide variety of political questions, sibling influences concerning risk may induce concomitant ideological shifts.[25] Other broad psychological factors besides risk—sociability, for example, or competitiveness—may similarly beget sibling influences, though sex differences in risk attitudes are particularly well established.[26]

In addition, siblings affect participation in organizations and extracurricular activities; when these involve groups with particular outlooks toward social relations, this may shape subsequent political beliefs. As a result, siblings can have the social network effects described in chapter 1 alongside their direct influence. For example, girls tend to be more engaged with religion and church groups, while boys have historically been more likely to prefer competitive sports teams.[27] But activities and social networks diffuse across siblings. That is, people are generally more likely to join groups that their older siblings belong to, so if these types of groups tend to involve or produce divergent social attitudes, sibling influence could also affect preferences.[28] Those brothers that consciously or unconsciously entice their younger siblings into sports-related activities, then, might simultaneously lead those siblings into a greater taste for competition that those who follow their older sisters to church would be less apt to receive.

Finally, if policy preferences stem from chapter 1's mechanism of self-interest, it may be that younger siblings are socialized to dislike policies that redound to the disadvantage of their elders. For example, if females suffer from discrimination, they may complain of it to their younger siblings and motivate opposition to policies that put women at a disadvantage.[29] This would echo similar phenomena where relatives of people with a particular condition ranging from disability to imprisonment go on to become advocates for policies regarding that condition.[30]

Alongside these direct socializing influences of siblings, indirect socialization by third parties could also reflect sibling sex. Younger siblings can observe the socialization by parents and others, including any sex-typed messages that they may transmit. Many parents attempt to avoid treating daughters differently from sons, but even they often subconsciously treat children of different sexes contrastingly from a very early age.[31] Moreover, even if they would be able to treat a set of all daughters or all sons neutrally, behavior tends to differ once both sexes of children enter the picture, with daughters getting more stereotypically female attention once they have a brother and sons getting more stereotypically male socializing once they have a sister. Traditionalist parents socialize their daughters still more differently from their sons.[32] While the parents tend to target these sex-specific messages at the older child, they may naturally spill over to the younger as well, either reinforcing or countermanding the messages presented directly to that child. Since socialization by sex typically involves instilling different attitudes toward politics and competition,[33] this could influence attitudes toward the matters considered here.

The most fundamental place to seek sibling influences in political belief would be in the most encompassing forms of ideology, the most typical expression of which is the left–right scale. Sympathy toward positions on the left or right frequently leads to a host of other issue positions. Furthermore, this dimension of belief also correlates markedly with sex: Women, on average, consistently fall to the left of men on the political spectrum, in the well-known political gender gap.[34] The multiple processes that lead women to greater sympathy for the left should then leave older sisters more left-leaning than are older brothers, on average. Following a sister in birth order is then more likely to expose an individual to left-leaning sentiments, while following a brother is relatively more likely to involve exposure to right-leaning attitudes. If these broad preferences transmit as hypothesized above, then, those whose next-older siblings are female would, all else equal, be further to the left than those whose next-older siblings are male.

As noted in chapter 2, abstract ideological identifications may translate only weakly into feelings about concrete issues, so it is useful to have a more specific question of policy preference to supplement the left–right dimension. Along these lines, one of the most far-reaching differences in attitude between men and women—and one extending several of the issues considered in chapter 2—relates to the sexes' relative keenness for state intervention. Women are typically more favorable than are men to an expanded role of the state.[35] This general preference shows up consistently across specific economic issues as well: Whether considering tax rates, government budgets, or state-owned enterprises, men are likelier to prefer the outcome with the smaller state and more expansive private sector[36]—particularly in the United States.[37] There are several well-established sources of these gender gaps, as a variety of factors produce similar outcomes. Women's skepticism about markets may result from observing sex-based pay discrimination, from socialization that is less sanguine about competition, or from their traditional role as consumers bearing disproportionate shares of household shopping responsibilities. Whatever the cause, women's relative reluctance to embrace the market recurs throughout the public opinion and political economy literatures—and such reluctance could spill over to younger siblings whom girls and women help socialize. An individual whose next-older sibling is female, after all, has a close, lifelong association with someone relatively likely to be acceptant of interventionist state activity. By contrast, if that next-older sibling is a brother, the association is instead more likely with someone relatively dubious about the state. With this example and influence, the younger sibling's preferences are likely to tack toward those of the older sibling. As a result, a person whose immediately older sibling is a sister is more likely to support state intervention than is an otherwise identical person whose immediately older sibling is a brother.

These effects on ideology and attitudes toward state intervention could manifest themselves in various ways in practice. One possibility is that for two siblings of the same sex, the mechanism discussed here would not alter the expected position of the younger sibling. That is, all children of a given sex in a family might have the same innate proclivities before sibling effects strike. In that case, two sisters—or two brothers—would start with the same predicted position, so that the younger's ideology could not converge any further to the elder's; someone following a sibling of the same sex would accordingly be predicted to have the same attitudes as an only child who had no sibling influence.[38] Alternatively, the older sibling could substitute for a more mixed set of influences on the younger sibling: Cues from the older sibling could replace or drown out some effects from parents or a diverse group of peers or media sources. In this conception of sibling socialization, the preferences of both sexes will systematically shift from the sex's average. Women with older sisters, having experienced a particularly female-dominated set of influences, would be expected to be more liberal, and more likely to support state intervention, than would a woman without older siblings—who would in turn prefer more interventionist than would women with older brothers. An analogous pattern would hold for men. In this case, though, those with older siblings of their own sex would be more ideologically extreme than are those without any older sibling.

The expected difference between someone with a same-sex sibling and someone with no elder sibling is thus not clear-cut; theory allows for multiple possibilities. However, there would still be definite predicted differences between those with an older sister and those with an older brother. The former would be further to the left and more sympathetic to state intervention than are the latter: women because they experienced the market-friendly rightward pull of a brother and men because they forewent the state-friendly leftward influence of a sister. This should hold whether or not those with a next-older sibling of the same sex would share their positions with only children.

Sibling socialization has its limits, especially when based on as blunt a distinction as sister versus brother. While sex has ties to a wide range of political cues, it typically works indirectly—it is more useful here because of its quasi-randomness than because it is likely to have a larger impact than would more detailed information about the siblings' political attitudes and personality. In any case, households with several children all of the same sex exhibit less consistent conformity to societal sex roles than do other family configurations.[39] That is, girls in a family with only daughters are less likely to follow typically female interests and outlooks than are girls in a family that also includes sons, perhaps because of the aforementioned differences in parental behavior when caring for children of both genders. This implies that a model with effects of all older siblings cascading down predictably through the younger siblings is unlikely. This is especially true because interaction with other children probably involves less explicit political content than does the influence of adults, and the remoteness of children's conversations from policy or partisanship may diffuse some of the effects they have on political attitudes. It would in any event be unsurprising if a mechanism based on sibling sex mattered less than sex differences themselves do in empirical studies: The effect of being female is probably typically greater than the effect of having an older sister, whether because of other sorts of socialization (e.g., peers) or because of intrinsic biological distinctions. Also, some people partly establish their own independent identity by explicitly moving away from or totally rejecting their siblings' beliefs and interests, just as parental socialization does not always stick. Still, the immediately older sibling may have a socializing effect pulling toward their own sex role on average, even if many families are, for one reason or another, less apt to reflect such a pattern.

DATA AND PREDICTOR VARIABLES

While chapters 1 and 2 both bemoaned the rarity of public opinion surveys including both substantive political questions and systematic information about family, their plaint goes double when looking for information about siblings. The major exception is the 1994 American General Social Survey (GSS). Most other polls and political questionnaires ignore siblings altogether, and even other iterations of the GSS do not contain the extensive data about brothers and sisters that the 1994 survey featured. Since gender gaps have probably not qualitatively changed since 1994 (though some evidence suggests they may have narrowed in several dimensions[40]), the data set probably still expresses the general relationship between gender gaps and sibling–gender gaps. The survey's inclusion of the crucial sibling data along with questions about ideology and attitude toward state intervention in the economy accordingly outweigh the drawback of somewhat older data. An additional benefit to the slightly older data set is that the births of most survey respondents—and their older siblings—antedate the ubiquitous availability of ultrasounds. This reduces the potential for selection effects in sibling gender, thereby enhancing the randomized, natural-experiment study design.[41] For these reasons, the models below employ the 1994 GSS data, despite its conceded age.

Within this data set, the first necessary task is to determine the sex of respondents' next-older siblings.[42] This is generally straightforward, as the GSS typically includes birth years and sexes for all siblings. There are, however, some complicated cases. As values are reported only for the nine eldest siblings, complete data may not be available for respondents from very large families. If all nine reported siblings are older than the respondent, as occurs in a small number of cases, it is impossible to tell whether the next-older sibling appears in the data. Additionally, multiple siblings born in the same year are ambiguous: They might be twins or separate births in the same year, especially if the siblings do not share a mother. These differing configurations produce differing expectations for the theory here, since twins tend to have much weaker influence on sex roles than do older siblings and so are not counted as older siblings here.[43] It is quite common for respondents to share a birth year with siblings; these are clearly twins in most cases, but in some instances, they may instead be older or younger siblings.[44] Likewise, sometimes there appears to be a tie for next-older sibling, with multiple older siblings born the same year.

Where these ambiguities exist, they are frequently immaterial to the hypothesis, since both potential next-older siblings are of the same sex. Results presented below hold up with the exclusion of the remaining uncertain cases, which number fifty-one in total (out of 1,904 respondents with older siblings). Other questions concern step-, half-, or adopted children, who may have been less available as a socializing factor, or deceased siblings, who might have died before they exerted a socializing influence. The data here does not provide usable information about the date of death of deceased siblings, but it does disclose which siblings are not full biological siblings. Using the data only for full siblings only slightly changes the reported results, as relatively few of the survey participants are coded differently when excluding step- and half-siblings.[45]

As noted above, sibling sex greatly facilitates empirical analysis, because it is effectively a natural experiment. An older sibling's sex is typically randomly determined without any role for explicit selection effects, especially for full, biological siblings. The essentially exogenous nature of this random assignment is thus independent of typical causal factors, which alleviates the need for control variables: The randomization leads the effects of confounding factors to be equal across groups in expectation. The baseline models below accordingly do not require or contain control variables.

Yet the randomization might not be perfect. Persistent patterns in the way that child sex interacts with decisions to have more children may make it prudent to control for a variety of demographic factors. In particular, many (but not all) Americans have a preference, alluded to above, for having a child of each sex, which often leads to families continuing to have children until there is at least one son and one daughter.[46] If, as some have suggested, this practice is more common among those holding out for sons rather than daughters, it could systematically affect the likelihood of one's older sibling being female among affected subpopulations. Some groups may additionally have different propensities to have male or female children[47] or to engage in sex-selective abortion, even in the United States;[48] if these populations also diverge in political preferences, any apparent effect of sibling sex may be spurious.

The 1994 GSS does not include many of the most directly relevant possible variables: It contains, for example, no information about parents' views that might hint at whether they were likely to have tried to have kept having children until they had one of each sex or about their politics. However, the survey does contain proxy measures that can indirectly capture some of the underlying concepts of interest. Just as in chapter 2, the most relevant variables involve the respondent's childhood home; factors such as income or education that the respondent acquired in later life are most likely to be consequences, not causes, of parental decisions about having children. The survey does nevertheless include information on several dimensions that might reflect the parents' propensities to have children with particular sex configurations. The models below include controls for the respondent's sex, age, and ethnic or racial minority status. In addition, as proxies for other parental characteristics that may be relevant, the models include measures for respondent religiosity (in the form of fundamentalism, the measure GSS includes) at age sixteen, along with information about the region and urbanness of residence at that age.[49] These characteristics of the respondents relate to elements of the childhood home or parents' attitudes that could influence both potential sibling socialization effects and respondents' underlying propensity to hold particular political beliefs.

For the first dependent variable, general political ideology, the GSS has several potential measures. The most direct measure asks respondents to place themselves on a 7-point scale whereby 1 represents "extremely conservative" and 7 "extremely liberal."[50] As with the similar variable used in the last chapter, this self-evaluation may be unreliable if respondents vary in their perception of what ideological positions these labels describe.[51] This problem may not be of great moment here, since the socialization mechanism under study contributes to perceived placement of ideological categories. Nevertheless, other measures of ideological position offer useful reassurance about the consistency of the measure.

One related variable in the two-party system of American politics is partisanship: closer association with the Democratic Party tends to indicate more leftism, while those Republicans tend to espouse a more rightist policy. This, as discussed in chapter 2, provides a more anchored perception of ideology, although it has its own drawbacks. For one thing, in 1994 the Republicans' transformation into the right-leaning party in the South was still quite recent, and partisan identifications might not yet have adapted to the change.[52] For another, partisan attachments often reflect factors unrelated to ideology—most relevantly for any family-related analysis, people often stick with their parents' partisan identifications even if they disagree on actual substantive issues. But partisan sex differences have generally mirrored the explicitly ideological gender gaps, so this may serve, if less precisely, as a measure of ideology.[53] As measured here, partisanship is also on a 7-point scale, with "strong Republican" at 1 and "strong Democrat" at 7.

A third measure of overall ideology, preferred candidate in the 1992 presidential election, amplifies both the strengths and weaknesses of the partisanship measure. Looking at specific candidates removes regional variation in partisan ideology that may afflict the other measures; at the same time, comparisons of Bill Clinton and George H. W. Bush may signal concerns about personality as well as ideology, and the two candidates were relative centrists, further attenuating the role of ideology in the election. Moreover, the 1992 election saw a large number of voters eschew both major parties in favor of an independent candidate, Ross Perot, whose ideological classification confuses the tidy left–right spectrum of the election. To convert these complex possibilities into a measure of attitudes, the models below look only at those who supported either Clinton or Bush, indicating with a value of 1 those who voted for Clinton and nonvoters who profess to have preferred Clinton in the election (and indicating with zero those who preferred Bush). Besides dropping observations from the data set—namely, those describing Perot supporters—and thereby reducing the reliability of the estimates, this also injects noise into the estimates: If, for instance, highly conservative respondents plumped for Perot because of their elder brothers' influence, then part of the actual effects of siblings was jettisoned from the analysis.[54]

Hence, the three measures move progressively further away from a direct measure of ideology, the concept implicated by the theory, even as they show different implications of ideological differences. Note that for all three measures of ideology, then, higher values associate with the more right-leaning position; since women are more likely to prefer the left-leaning position, the hypothesis predicts that those with a sister for a next-older sibling will have lower scores on these measures than do those whose next-older sibling is a brother.

Figure 3.1 shows the results of models predicting these various ideological variables. The top panel presents the model without control variables, while the bottom panel includes them (including the unreported variables indicating the region in which the respondent grew up). Note that the effect of being a minority is so strongly associated with partisanship—non-whites are far more likely to identify with the Democratic Party and its candidates—that, in its most natural coding, it overwhelms all other effects to the point where they are difficult to make out in the figure. To improve readability, the minority variable is accordingly rescaled in Figure 3.1 by having its decimal point shifted one digit to the left. Similarly, to improve comparability across the three predicted variables, the 1992 variable is rescaled to be on the same 7-point scale as the other two measures, even though it is a binary measure. Thus the effect of 0.12 displayed for having

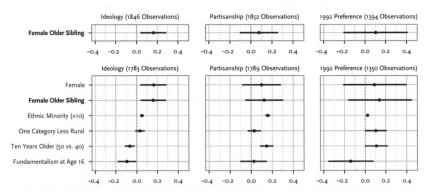

Figure 3.1 Measures of political beliefs, in baseline (top panel) and expanded (bottom panel) models. Bars indicate 95% confidence intervals. Positive numbers indicate more left-leaning attitudes.

a next-older sister implies that those with a next-older sister are two per-centage points (= 0.12 divided by 6) more likely to have voted for Clinton rather than Bush.

In all six models, having a female next-older sibling has the expected liberalizing effect: Those with a sister before them in birth order are more left-leaning than are those who followed a brother. Strengthening support for this expectation, being female oneself also takes a positive coefficient when it is included in the model, so that the effect of being a particular sex matches the effect of being influenced by a sibling of that sex. Although the coefficients imply a modest effect of sibling sex—the estimated dif-ference between those with female and male older siblings is between 0.1 and 0.2 points on the 7-point ideology and party-identification scales—these are comparable in magnitude to—indeed almost identical with—the estimated gender gap itself. The effect of sibling sex also is substantial in comparison to other important influences on political preferences; for example, the sex of the next-older sibling has a larger estimated effect on the dependent variables than does a one-decade shift in age. Statistically, the coefficients are most significant for self-declared ideology itself, as might be anticipated from that being the most direct measure of the concept involved. Although the point estimates for the more partisan variables also suggest that elder sisters associate with more Democratic leanings, this suggestion does not nearly attain the usual standards of sta-tistical significance: The 95% confidence interval extends well across the zero line.

Meanwhile, the control variables also have plausible coefficients. Older people call themselves more conservative yet are more likely to support and vote for Democrats, while people who grew up in more densely popu-lated areas and (especially) minorities tend to be more on the left across all measures of ideology. Conversely, those who were more religious at sixteen years old and those with higher incomes tend to be more conservative by these measures.

SIBLINGS AND DESIRE FOR GOVERNMENT INTERVENTION

As noted above, gender gaps characterize not only overall ideological pre-disposition but also positions on more specific issues, in particular with regard to relative confidence in the state rather than the market. Women generally are more comfortable with a larger degree of government involve-ment in the economy than are men. The GSS also includes several questions related to this variable.

One of these questions asks respondents to rate the extent to which they agree with the idea that private enterprise is the best way to solve America's problems. While this statement does not explicitly identify government as the alternative possible source of solutions or that market-based mechanisms (rather than nonprofit efforts) are what "private enterprise" means, the phrase is most commonly interpreted to mean profit-seeking business.[55] Men are also more likely to agree with the statement than are women in this survey. It therefore connects to previous studies of state versus market control of the economy and demonstrates the gender-gap characteristics necessary to motivate younger siblings to receive gender-inflected impressions.

Another relevant question inquires whether the respondent thinks the government should be doing more or less to solve national problems instead of leaving things to the private sector. Specifically, the question text reads, "Some people think that the government in Washington is trying to do too many things that should be left to individuals and private businesses. Others disagree and think that the government should do even more to solve our country's problems. Still others have opinions somewhere in between. Where would you place yourself on this scale?" This question more explicitly points to the government—indeed, the federal government rather than state or local governments—as the solution. By explicitly invoking "individuals" as a category separate from businesses, on the other hand, it pulls slightly away from making the opposing choice corporate. The question therefore complements the strengths and weaknesses of the previous one for examining the government–business trade-off. Responses to the two questions are related but only moderately: While women do again give more government-friendly answers on average, the correlation between answers to the two questions is only 0.29, where –1 represents a perfect inverse relationship, zero indicates no relationship, and 1 shows that the responses track each other perfectly.

Two further variants of this latter question concern whether the federal government should do more to help particular subgroups, namely the poor and the sick, or whether people should fend for themselves. While preserving the general theme of government involvement, these questions add an extra spin by bringing in particular other issues. Helping the poor ties into attitudes not only toward the government but also toward whether poverty is a personal failing—that is, whether the poor are deserving or undeserving (an issue that connects to family; see chapter 6). To the extent poverty is seen not as an issue of unfairness but as an earned consequence of bad choices, it may not be seen as a cause for public intervention even among those who generally think of the government as a more efficient or appropriate means of solving problems: This is perhaps especially likely given the importance of welfare reform to the political debates of 1994. With helping the sick, deservingness is usually a less prominent concern (though health issues from AIDS to adult-onset diabetes to emphysema have behavioral roots that some would certainly criticize). Given the climate of 1994, when the fight over President Clinton's proposed health-care reform had turned into a highly partisan controversy, the question of federal involvement in health care also offers something of a bridge to the more explicit partisan issues of Figure 3.1.

Answers for each of these four questions are on a 5-point scale, with higher values expressing greater preference for a larger, more interventionist government. Figure 3.2 reports the models considering these attitudes. Like with the models in Figure 3.1, then, those with a sister as next-older sibling are expected to give higher-valued answers than are those whose next-older sibling is a brother (just like those who are themselves female are expected to provide higher-valued answers to these questions, on average, than are men).

Across all four dependent variables, survey respondents who follow a sister in birth order are consistently more likely to welcome state intervention. This effect matches expectation in direction, and once more it also matches the direction of effect of being female oneself. With these survey items, unlike those studied in Figure 3.1, the effect of a female sibling is appreciably smaller than that of being female. This is plausible enough, given the theory here of indirect socializing influence.

Despite this similarity across the four variables, there are also differences. Most distinctively, government action on behalf of the poor sees a markedly weaker effect of sibling sex. With the other dependent variables, a female older sister has about one-half of the predicted effect of

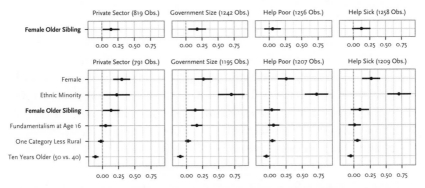

Figure 3.2 Measures of support for the welfare state. Bars indicate 95% confidence intervals. Positive numbers indicate greater support for government intervention.

being female; with helping the poor, the effect of sibling sex is less than one-fifth that of the respondent's own sex. Nor is the effect of a sibling statistically distinguishable from zero at any supportable level of confidence. This uncertainty about the actual effect size does not imply that the effect is completely trivial; the model's best guess implies that the difference between an older brother and an older sister roughly equals the effect of having grown up in a place one category more rural. The anomalously smaller effect of sisters in promoting government intervention on behalf of the poor may be a fluke, but it may also stem from other effects of older siblings. For example, it could perhaps relate to older brothers' greater tendency (compared to older sisters') to use aggression and violence against their younger siblings.[56] This could induce more of a sense among younger siblings that unfortunates, such as the poor, do not deserve their fates but are simply unlucky or victims of an unfair system, which on this issue might partially counteract brothers' socialization toward limited government.

Regardless of the cause, sibling sex has a stronger effect for the other attitudes concerning government intervention. Those with next-older brothers tend to give answers 0.1 to 0.2 points more market-friendly than do those with next-older sisters. The effect is always statistically distinguishable from zero with standard levels of confidence for the questions concerning the general competence of government and private enterprise; for the more issue-specific case of helping the sick, there is somewhat greater uncertainty about the real effect, although the 95% confidence interval only just crosses the zero line. Control variables are also plausible in direction and effect. Women and racial or ethnic minorities tend to be more favorable to government intervention; older people, the wealthier, and the better educated, are generally less favorable.

SIBLING CLOSENESS

While the results generally support the idea that the sex of a person's next-older sibling may influence that person's own preferences, they provide little detail into how reliably this process applies across individuals. Has the effect of sibling sex diminished among recent generations as gender roles have become less distinct? Are some individuals more susceptible to sibling influence? If the above effect of siblings in practice applies only in some cases—or applies more strongly in those cases—it would illuminate the mechanisms by which sibling socialization occurs.

Perhaps the most theoretically pressing dimension of the sibling relationship is the closeness of the siblings. Siblings who have a deeper emotional connection and those who have spent more time together are more likely to be conduits for ideological influence: That was the whole basis for looking at the next-oldest sibling rather than, say, the oldest sibling overall. Thus closeness is conceptually relevant. If we assume closeness matters in this way, we can examine the mechanism considered here by seeing if closer siblings associate with stronger effects from their siblings' gender: People who feel close to their next-older siblings should have their ideology more strongly influenced by those siblings' sex than would those whose relationships their siblings are more distant. It is accordingly worth testing whether sibling closeness intensifies the ideological effect of sibling sex.

Unfortunately, the GSS does not contain usable direct measures of a particular sibling's influence. The closest available measure concerns how frequently the respondent spends an evening with a sibling, but this variable does not distinguish which sibling is involved or even whether the same sibling is consistently involved. It thus may inflate the apparent closeness of respondents from large families (since there are more potential siblings with whom one could spend an evening) or indicate closeness to a younger rather than to the older sibling. In addition, this question is asked only of a small fraction—less than one-sixth—of the sample, resulting in very small numbers of respondents and commensurately low reliability in measurement.

Still, measures of sibling closeness are available that are usable even if they are less explicitly relevant. One indirect measure of sibling closeness is the difference in age between the respondent and the next-older sibling. Siblings closer in age tend to interact more and to have deeper emotional bonds, as might be expected from their increased likelihood of shared interests and typically longer shared residence in the parental home.[57] This suggests that the relative leftward influence of sisters compared to brothers will be largest when the siblings are close in age, progressively fading as the age gap widens. This measure has drawbacks besides its doubtless imperfect correlation with actual sibling closeness: Large age gaps are selected, not randomized, and parents who choose to space childbirths out further tend to differ from other parents. Some of these differences could change the ways that siblings interact as well as the general household environment. In addition, the age gap itself may allow parents to devote more resources to children or otherwise differently treat those born closer or further from their siblings.[58] When studying the effect of age differences, then, the natural-experiment characteristic of the basic research design falls apart. Additional control variables such as those included in the fuller, bottom-panel models of Figures 3.1 and 3.2 should, however, take into account the effects of likely confounding factors.

Using the age gap itself as variable is tricky, because its distribution fits poorly with the usual assumptions that statistical models require. There are in particular extreme outliers, with respondents being up to thirty-one years younger than their next-older sibling. As a first cut at measuring the effects of larger or smaller age gap, then, the sample is divided into two. One group contains those whose next-older siblings are within five years of age of the survey respondent; the other group comprises those for whom the next-older sibling is at least five years older.[59] Because Americans typically start school at around the age of five, this separates those who were more likely to have spent time being cared for full-time together with their next-older sibling before that sibling went to school—a somewhat arbitrary benchmark but one that generally correlates with time that the siblings will have spent together. Once the survey respondents are categorized in this way, the models can look for interactive effects, that is, those where the effect of sibling sex interacts with the size of the between-sibling age gap to affect respondents with different age gaps differently.

The expectation that follows most naturally is that siblings who are closer in age will see more convergence than will those who are more separated. Thus the difference between having a sister and a brother should be larger when the siblings are nearer in age. The direction of expected effect does not change; sisters should associate with more leftism and more support for government programs, even if the expectations are for stronger associations when the siblings are close in age. Figure 3.3 reruns the full models of Figures 3.1 and 3.2, disaggregating sibling effects by the age gap between the respondent and the next-older sibling.[60]

As before, older sisters consistently associate with more liberal-leaning or larger-government policy than older brothers do: The estimated effect is virtually always to the right of the zero line in the figure, though the confidence interval often stretches across it. Even the one exceptional case, regarding helping the poor among those who are much younger than their next-older siblings, is only slightly to the left of zero. The interaction, too, generally follows the predicted pattern. In six of the seven attitudes, the result is as predicted, with elder siblings who are closer in age having a larger estimated effect on the respondent's preferences: This can be seen because the top-panel estimate, involving sibling pairs closer in age, is farther to the left (more negative) than is the analogous bottom-panel estimate. The exception is the variable concerning help for the sick. Respondents whose next-older sibling is at least five years of age older see almost twice the effect from having a sister rather than a brother than do those who are nearer to their sibling in age. It could be that those with much older siblings are more likely to have observed those siblings having health troubles, so

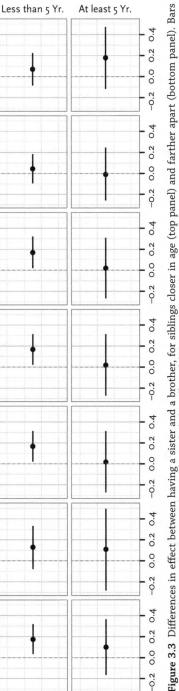

Figure 3.3 Differences in effect between having a sister and a brother, for siblings closer in age (top panel) and farther apart (bottom panel). Bars indicate 95% confidence intervals; control variables included in all models but unreported.

that issues of sickness resonate differently. Why this would play out differently for older sisters than for older brothers is obscure, though the two sexes' different biologies do mean they tend to face different health risks and life expectancies.

Even allowing for this exception, younger siblings do tend to express beliefs more along the lines of their sibling's gender when the two groups are closer in age. These differences never achieve very high levels of statistical confidence; this may be unsurprising, given how minutely the data is being parsed and subdivided. But the result still hints that an older sibling's effect on political preferences might diminish as that sibling grows relatively older compared to—and presumably more distant from—the respondent. This is consistent with the model of sibling socialization presented above. Although much older siblings probably have better-formed political beliefs and more ability to articulate explicitly political information to their brothers and sisters, their effect on ideology appears weaker, at least in this rough measure and in these specific issue areas.

CONCLUSION

Siblings, especially older siblings, serve as important socializing influences for many people. Most often, siblings provide influences similar on average to those of other family members and peers, since they themselves experience many of the same conditions and frequently travel in the same social networks. Perhaps as a result, their potential for independent influence remains masked. Yet some siblings are far from average in some ways. A sibling in prison, or one with disabilities, may exert a profound, observable effect, in directions yet to be studied—and so, in more everyday ways, might an otherwise unremarkable sibling of a particular sex.

Here, as in chapter 2, the models considered both broad ideology and specific issues. Like ideology, the particular issue area in question here, state activism, has a gender gap in preferences, which translates into divergent effects of sisters and brothers. Women tend to be left-leaning and have more faith in the value of the public sector; so, as seen in the results, do their younger siblings. Other questions with sex-linked differences may see similar effects, if the findings here reflect broader trends in political psychology and public opinion. Nor need these processes be restricted to beliefs and preferences: Siblings' different propensities to participate in politics (or engage in other forms of political behavior) may similarly set an influential example. As sociologists have intensively studied, siblings also affect behaviors such as educational attainment, which has its own broad influence on outcomes of political interest.

In pursuing the effects of siblings, many questions remain open. One surrounds the role of biology. Many analysts find that biological older brothers are particularly important in determining younger brothers' sexual orientations, and this effect's failure to carry over to nonbiological brothers raised in the same household suggests that socialization may not be the only way siblings shape socially relevant outcomes.[61] Pinpointing the extent of such biological outcomes is a task to which political science has only recently turned. Another set of questions for future research deals with other mechanisms by which sisters and brothers influence outcomes relevant for political science and economics. As a first cut at the many possible effects of siblings, this chapter focused on one small and relatively simple issue, the influence of the next-older sibling as suggested by that sibling's sex. But the full complement of siblings surely matter in their ways, and they are more than their sex.

The next chapter takes up this thought by moving beyond the next-older sibling and considering influences beyond the effect of sibling sex; more precisely, it changes the sense of "sex" at issue.

CHAPTER 4

Birth Order Revisited: Attitudes Toward Morality

Birth-order effects have lurked at the fringes of social science for a very long time. It makes such intuitive *sense* that having older or younger siblings would make for different experiences, shaping all manner of psychological properties from self-confidence to intelligence—and, by extension, altering political attitudes regarding leadership or ideology. Yet despite decades of searching, a whole slew of studies have failed to find much by way of systematic relationships between birth order and psychological or sociological outcomes.[1] Occasional studies do find seeming patterns of birth order, to be sure: Frank Sulloway's controversial *Born to Rebel*,[2] for example, tried to make a Darwinian argument that firstborn children would be more conservative while their younger siblings would be more rebellious. Other studies have suggested that younger siblings may be less intelligent[3] and, as noted at the end of chapter 3, more likely to be gay.[4] Many promising initial results along these lines have eventually been debunked,[5] however, and one set of authors likened birth order to a vampire that cannot be killed:[6] No matter how furiously rigorous empirical studies have contradicted the ideas of birth-order theorists, their ideas inexorably rear up again, especially in pop psychology. In more academic studies, the demotion of birth-order effects is of a piece with the recent broader trend in which scholars have tended to see childhood and family influences as involving primarily genetic rather than environmental factors.[7]

The rather dismal record of finding psychological or behavioral consequences of one's age relative to one's siblings has one notable exception, though: breaking the rules in adolescence.[8] Even thoroughgoing detractors of the whole birth-order argument grudgingly concede that firstborn children tend to be less likely to drink, smoke, or have sex during their teenage years and that when they do move in these directions they tend to do so later.[9] Indeed, no matter how forceful parents may try to be about these matters, siblings often seem to be more important influences in determining relevant behavior.[10] Laterborns' (meaning those who are not the eldest children in their families) distinctive choices extend from "problem" behaviors such as early sexual activity into outright delinquency and criminality.[11] The most central of these dubious behaviors to public policy, and to present-day political debates, is sex, which is accordingly the focus here.

A variety of studies have shown that younger siblings are typically more sexually active at an earlier age than are firstborn children.[12] Some of the reasons follow the logic in chapter 3. Younger siblings tend to try to imitate their elder siblings and so get pulled into many activities, wholesome or otherwise, once their elder siblings are involved. Even if the older siblings did not engage in early sexual activity themselves, the younger siblings are by definition at a lower age when the oldest siblings do start experimenting, which tends to hasten the laterborns' initiation. Elder siblings thus have a direct influence, and since they generally convey positive attitudes toward sex—especially if they are older brothers—this tends to encourage less restrained behavior by younger siblings.[13] Alternatively, the socializing influence may not be the elder siblings as such but, instead, broader social networks. If parents find it more convenient to enroll younger siblings in the same extracurricular activities as the elder siblings, the younger sibling may end up thrown into social situations that tend to include older teenagers. These older youth may then pressure or encourage more sexual precocity in that younger sibling.

Another plausible source for younger siblings' propensity for early sexual activity stems not from the older siblings as such but from parents. Several forces seem to push parents to supervise their firstborn child more closely than subsequent siblings.[14] For one thing, parents are simply older when they deal with their laterborn offspring; they may have less energy by the time their younger children reach adolescence, leaving less time and cognitive attention available to dealing with childcare issues. Depending on the age gap between their children, they may already have their hands full with the eldest sibling's negotiation of adolescence, leaving less time to supervise other children entering that phase of life. Even if parents do have the wherewithal to supervise children directly, they may feel they can delegate some of the supervision to the laterborn's elder sibling(s), or they may have the resources but adopt a less micromanaging parenting strategy if they found that much of their supervisory effort at the first child was unnecessary.[15] Any of these mechanisms could mean younger siblings face less parental scrutiny, allowing them more freedom to try behaviors that their parents might, if they noticed, oppose and punish.

This discussion makes no distinction among different classes of later-borns—those with one older sibling are lumped together with those having six, each equally "laterborn." Nor does the analysis have any cause to discuss what effect, if any, having younger siblings might have. These sorts of distinctions may certainly matter for some political questions. However, for the particular topical question studied here, the central effect identified in previous studies relates to the mere presence of an older sibling—any older sibling—as a model and as a moderator of parental behavior.

Whether because younger siblings observe and mimic their elders' activities or because parents are less prone to monitoring deviant behavior by their later teenagers, younger siblings seem to be generally more apt to engage in controversial activities from earlier on in adolescence. The question remains whether this behavioral difference translates into politically relevant attitudes. There is reason to believe that it might, despite the negative findings of most previous studies of birth order. Certainly, to the extent that behavior reveals beliefs, the repeated finding that laterborn children act in distinctive ways with respect to sex (and drugs) suggests that they could have systematically different opinions regarding related issues. More theoretically, much of the logic that led scholars to look for more delinquency among laterborns also suggests that firstborn children would have different attitudes regarding those potentially delinquent behaviors. This is because the logic and process of socialization into beliefs is similar to that concerning socialization into behaviors. Indeed, part of the story above is that younger siblings engage in different behaviors precisely *because* they have different attitudes. Elder siblings tend to socialize their younger siblings into more openness to sexual activity, while reduced parental supervision reduces the centrality of any parental socialization that might tend to discourage sex, allowing increased peer influence (through social network effects).

The adoption of these less restrictive attitudes toward sexuality could then shape relevant political attitudes—and evidence suggests that it does. Sexual tolerance tends to associate with a preference for abortion legalization,[16] so that blaming people for their sexual activity, for example, tends to reduce acceptance of abortion.[17] Moreover, politically charged attitudes during adolescence tend to be relatively stable into adulthood.[18] Any relatively acceptant attitudes encouraged by being a laterborn thus have the potential to influence beliefs into adulthood at the time people are eligible to vote or to respond to surveys. It has been proposed along these lines that firstborns' general inclination toward the status quo causes them to be more likely to pursue monogamous relationships throughout life, while laterborns are relatively more inclined to play the field.[19] All of this suggests that firstborn children would be less likely, everything else equal, to accept nontraditional behaviors relating to sex—and accordingly less supportive of liberal policies in relevant issue areas.

This smooth conflation of attitude and behavior glosses over some potential complications. The translation from earlier experimentation with various behaviors and subsequent attitudes toward those behaviors need not be automatic. If those—disproportionately younger siblings— who dabbled more readily in sex or alcohol regretted having done so, there might be a negative relationship between having older siblings and having acceptant attitudes toward such behaviors or policies that allow for them. Still, studies most commonly find that earlier experience associates with more related behaviors in later life,[20] suggesting that the more common pattern would be for younger siblings to continue to resist stringent regulation of conduct instead of turning against the behaviors with which they experimented so freely.

Another complication of drawing attitudinal inferences from behavior is that not all adolescent problem behaviors are alike. Some things teenagers do, such as drink or have sex, arouse far less censure when done by adults; other potential outcomes, such as abortion, remain controversial and even illegal at any age. Different behaviors also vary in their immediate ramifications for adolescents' lives. It may consequently be that having taken more risks during youth—or simply being a laterborn who was socialized to be more acceptant of such risk-taking—plays out differently in attitude formation across different issues. The following discussion takes up these differences when considering specific behaviors and policy preferences. Despite these potential differences, the logic outlined here suggests that, in general, younger siblings may have more tolerant attitudes to the behaviors they were more likely to try young.

Note that nothing in the above discussion necessarily implies that people in different birth-order positions show very different overall ideologies, or even that they would tend to choose different parties. Most of the issues where younger siblings behave noticeably differently make for a relatively small part of most people's broad ideologies: Few people primarily classify themselves as liberal or conservative on the basis of their attitudes toward, say, premarital sex. Nevertheless, differences between older and younger siblings in their attitudes toward policy in these realms would be of interest. Not only would it help explain beliefs and preferences for anyone interested in the specific issues in question, it would also illuminate a pathway by which family and childhood environment might shape political behavior (and vindicate some of those persistent, popular claims about the importance of birth order).

MEASURING THE CONCEPTS

Unfortunately, unlike the general sibling effects explored in the previous chapter, birth-order effects do not easily allow for quasi-experimental study designs, at least not within ethical bounds. People with a greater number of older (or younger) siblings obviously tend to occur in larger families, which, since family size is to some extent a conscious choice by the parents, complicates comparisons across families. It could be that parents who have lots of children—and who thus raise a disproportionately large share of younger siblings—are also likely to otherwise provide different environments and circumstances for their children, for instance if they are also richer or poorer and hence associated with different homes, neighborhoods, and schools. If this were the case, then any seeming differences observed between younger siblings (mostly drawn from larger families) and firstborns (disproportionately coming from smaller families) might actually reflect family-size effects, not birth order as such. The basic research problem thus is more similar to chapter 2's than to chapter 3's, even though the former did not directly consider siblings at all.

Even within families, siblings face differences of environment. The parents' being inherently older when their later children are born means that any effect of parental age—including indirect effects, for example if parents generally gain workplace experience and hence income as they age—will vary across siblings. Because of these unavoidable complications, studying the effect of birth-order forces the use of a nonexperimental, observational research design. This limits the certainty that any observed effects actually stem from birth order, but with careful control of alternative explanations that could have produced the observed outcomes and a theoretical story supporting the claimed effect, a reasonably confident causal claim can be advanced (though with the acknowledgement that unknown and unaccounted-for factors could invalidate the results).

To test the theory that firstborn children will be less acceptant of the controversial behaviors—and likely to want policies that crack down on them—I turn to the same 1994 General Social Survey (GSS) data used in chapter 3. This is not only because, as the discussion in that chapter noted, this is a rare data set with information about both siblings and political attitudes. It also happens to be a survey that, as befits a sociological study interested in family dynamics, has several questions relating to the acceptability of various relevant behaviors, ranging from birth control to homosexuality to abortion. Naturally, these are quite different behaviors despite their common substantive link to sexuality, so the effect of being an eldest sibling is analyzed separately for attitudes regarding each of these issues.

As always, testing the relevant hypotheses requires coming up with measures for several relevant variables. Most centrally, it necessitates determining who counts as a firstborn child. The most problematic issues resemble those in the chapter 3 discussion of elder siblings: Do stepsiblings and half-siblings count? How about siblings who died young or were raised separately from the survey respondent, thereby creating what is sometimes called a "functional" birth order different from the natural one? What is the best way to handle twins or triplets—can a family have multiple "firstborn" children?

For consistency, the answers to these questions generally follow those used in chapter 3: Anyone who did not have a defined elder sibling there counts as a firstborn here. That is, step- and half-siblings are treated as equivalent to full siblings, while anyone born in the same year as the family's eldest sibling counts as firstborn. Since the survey lacks precise data on when siblings came into or left the household, anyone whom the respondent gave information about as a sibling is taken as having been one from the time of the younger sibling's birth. Note, too, that this coding rule counts children without any siblings—"only children"—as firstborns: Only chlidren similarly lack the influence of an older sibling yet are presumably subject to at least the same rigors of parental attention as are firstborns in larger families. To put it another way, the theories and empirical tests in this chapter look only at the effects of older siblings, not younger ones, for the same reasons given in chapter 3.[21]

The coding of the necessary "family size" variable also follows these guidelines: For the reported results, all people the respondent chose to report as siblings, stepsiblings, or half-siblings are counted as siblings. There is one additional caveat. As mentioned in the previous chapter, the GSS reports only information on the first nine siblings the respondent mentions. As a result, some people from very large families have their family size underestimated, though they still end up on the top of the family-size scale.

While family size is a necessary control variable, it is unlikely to be sufficient. As usual, any other factor that influences respondents' probability of being a firstborn child as well as their attitudes toward the issues considered here may produce the false appearance of a relationship if not taken into account.[22] As with many family questions, the factors that could cause an increased likelihood of being a firstborn child are somewhat unclear. Prior research in birth order is inconclusive about what these factors might be, with different authors pointing to quite distinct variables as necessary controls. Furthermore, since factors that increase the likelihood of being a firstborn child must have arisen by the time of the respondent's childhood, this problem poses the same data-availability difficulties encountered in chapter 2 when thinking about parental influences: surveys contain relatively little data about factors that held during respondents' childhoods.

Despite these challenges, a few relevant factors stand out as things that we might want the models to control for. Religiosity is a central driver of political attitudes on moral issues,[23] so it is an obvious control-variable candidate. So, too, is age. Both because of social changes over time or other generational issues[24] and because of changes in personal circumstances, older people tend to have different, most commonly more conservative, attitudes than do younger people.[25] Finally, consider parental education.[26] Mothers' and fathers' educational attainment influence the choices they make about the size and upbringing of their family, even as it offers another potential source for their thinking about moral issues. It also serves as a proxy for the educational experiences the children themselves have during their youths, given the association between parents' educational attainment and that of their children.[27]

The logic for including these control variables is arguably simply an indirect means of getting at family size. As the models include a direct measure of number of siblings, this may suggest that the additional variables are superfluous at best. They may be worse than that, given the potential that these factors *result* from family size. A mother who has children early and often may have fewer opportunities to get years of education; as is discussed in chapter 6, parents' ideology and concomitants such as religious outlook may also be affected by their number of children. The retrospective nature of the measurements also leaves an opening for family size to affect memories of the childhood home, which could skew the measure of, say, childhood religiosity. These complications can add some extra uncertainty to the richer models: Even as such models reduce the potential that omitted variables are producing spurious results, they are more likely than usual to introduce other forms of bias, muddying the logic of causation. Still, this potential is worth hazarding for several reasons. As pointed out in chapter 2, such endogeneity bias would tend to be conservative, meaning that it reduces the likelihood that the results will show a significant effect of being firstborn. Moreover, having an additional set of models offers some assurance that any observed results extend beyond one precise configuration of variables and measurements. Including control variables also facilitates interpretation of effect sizes. While it may not be clear whether a hypothetical difference of 0.08 points is large enough to care about when comparing two populations, an intuitive sense that, say, "age is important for determining attitudes toward abortion" makes it clearer that an effect of being firstborn that is of comparable size to the effect of age might be worth paying attention to.

PREMARITAL SEX

Simply having sex before being married is in many ways the least controversial of the activities considered in this chapter—unsurprisingly, given that premarital sexual activity is widely prevalent and was at the time of the survey in 1994.[28] By some accounts, it is a nearly universal experience.[29] Yet even widely accepted practices sometimes become political issues. Prominent politicians have incorporated issues surrounding birth control and the value of policy that discourages cohabitation and premarital sex into their rhetoric and campaigns.[30] State and national politicians have (despite a dubious reaction by the public) also pushed for "abstinence-only" education policies that emphasize the virtue of refraining from sexual activity before marriage.[31]

The GSS includes questions on three topics of particular relevance here: One concerns the acceptability of premarital sexual activity in general. The question wording is, "If a man and woman have sex relations before marriage, do you think it is always wrong, almost always wrong, wrong only sometimes, or not wrong at all?" Another question concerns cohabitation, implicitly including a sexual relationship, asking for agreement on a 5-point scale (strongly agree, agree, neither agree nor disagree, disagree, strongly disagree) with the statement "It is all right for a couple to live together without intending to get married." A third relevant question concerns the acceptability of teenagers obtaining birth control pills. In particular, the survey asks "Do you strongly agree, agree, disagree, or strongly disagree that methods of birth control should be available to teenagers between the ages of 14 and 16 if their parents do not approve?" While this is not explicitly concerned with premarital relations, the overwhelming tendency for Americans to not marry until after age sixteen effectively makes it relevant. All of these variables are coded so that greater acceptance of the behavior in question gives a lower score: higher values mean more restrictive attitudes.

The different question wordings, though variations on a theme, do speak to somewhat different situations and social issues. Cohabitation, for instance, implies a commitment to monogamy that can inflect attitudes to a premarital relationship, so that those who value stability in social relations may find cohabitation more acceptable than premarital sex more generally. The cohabitation and premarital sex questions differ in several other notable ways. The cohabitation question does not specify that the couple is heterosexual, perhaps relying on the invocation of marriage to imply this given the unavailability of same-sex marriage at the time of the survey. The availability of the fifth, neutral choice in answering the cohabitation question (but not in either of the others) may also affect answers, given survey respondents' frequent penchant for anchoring themselves toward the center of a set of answers. The birth control question brings in other issues alongside premarital sex, implicating parental control and autonomy more directly than do the others. By focusing on oral contraception, it may be less applicable to boys than to girls, whereas the others are more gender-neutral. It also specifies a particular age range, a point worth keeping in mind when comparing results across questions.

Firstborn siblings' behavior, along with the theories discussed above, suggests that younger siblings will tend to be more acceptant in each of these issues. That is, firstborn children should be less likely to condone premarital sexual activity or cohabitation and more likely to oppose children having access to birth control pills.

The top panel of Figure 4.1 explores these hypotheses in the simplest possible model, given the inherent need to control for family size when considering birth order. One variable in these models looks at whether or not the particular survey respondent is a firstborn child; the other considers the effect of having an additional sibling in the family. These models, like all models reported in this chapter, treat each additional child in a household as equally influential: Adding a seventh child to a family that

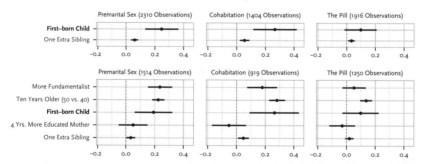

Figure 4.1 Attitudes toward premarital sex, in baseline (top panel) and expanded (bottom panel) models. Bars show 95% confidence intervals. Positive numbers indicate more restrictive beliefs.

already had six is treated as equivalent in effect to giving an only child a brother or sister. This is, of course, a debatable proposition. Richer models that look at the effect of each possible family size separately produce similar results for the birth-order effects that are of central interest here, however, so I use the simpler models for easier presentation.

Considering first the acceptability of premarital sex in general, seen in the leftmost graphs in Figure 4.1, the best estimate in the baseline model is that firstborns have a score around one-quarter of a point higher (which is in the direction of premarital sex being wrong) on the 4-point opinion scale. This easily clears standards of statistical significance and is roughly comparable to the effect of coming from a family with four more siblings. Given the distinctive sociological characteristics attendant with larger families—and the fact that the effect of additional siblings is itself statistically significant—this suggests a substantial influence on attitudes. Moreover, the pattern of firstborns being more restrictive in their moral attitudes holds up with the additional control variables added in the bottom row of Figure 4.1. The estimated effect size of being a firstborn child falls somewhat, to slightly under one-fifth of a point, as would be expected from bringing in variables that might themselves be partly the result of firstborn status. Even with this smaller effect, though, the difference between firstborns' and laterborns' attitudes comfortably attains statistical significance. The estimated effect is only just smaller than the effect of being born in 1944 rather than 1954, or to the difference between someone whose religious upbringing was "moderate" and one whose upbringing was "fundamentalist." With the importance of age and religion in determining attitudes toward sex, this reinforces the case for believing that firstborn status makes an appreciable difference in moral sentiments.

A similar story holds for the question about the acceptability of cohabitation, modeled in the center column of Figure 4.1. The estimated conservatizing effect of being firstborn is ever so slightly larger than with premarital sex more broadly, though in practical terms this probably implies a slightly smaller effect, since the cohabitation question is on a 5-point scale instead of the premarital sex question's 4-point scale. Regardless, the model predicts with high confidence that being firstborn is in fact associated with conservatizing on this question, as indicated by the confidence interval lying wholly to the right of zero. The estimated effect is again the same as that of adding approximately four extra siblings to the respondent's family. Also like the responses concerning premarital sex, the model including additional control variables preserves the gist of these results. In these results, shown once more in the bottom panel of Figure 4.1, the difference between a firstborn and an otherwise identical laterborn is comparable to that between people 1 point apart on the fundamentalism scale or between a forty-year-old and a fifty-year-old. These are respectable effect sizes, and the statistical significance of being a firstborn child remains.[32]

The rightmost column of Figure 4.1 presents the results for the question concerning fourteen- to sixteen-year-olds having access to birth control pills. The results here, though continuing to associate firstborn children with more restrictive positions, are smaller and do not attain comparably high levels of statistical significance. In particular, the effect of being firstborn is almost exactly one-tenth of a point (on a 4-point scale, just as with the premarital sex question in the left column), roughly the same estimate as that for adding three additional siblings. When the additional control variables come into play, the smaller sample size means that the level of statistical significance falls accordingly. Nevertheless, the expected difference between firstborns and laterborns is estimated at slightly larger than that between people a point apart on the fundamentalist-background question, a not insubstantial effect even if the confidence in the precise value is low.[33]

The three measures considered in Figure 4.1 thus tend to find a systematic tendency for firstborn children to be less acceptant of premarital sexual activity. These are not the survey's only indications of a link between firstborn status and premarital sexual mores. Other attitudes point in the same direction. For example, the GSS includes a question asking not just about premarital sex but about premarital sex specifically among those who are fourteen to sixteen years old—the same age covered by the question about birth control pills. There, too, firstborn siblings are notably less acceptant than are younger siblings, although the difference is only about a third the size of that seen in the general premarital sex question. Intriguingly, this difference shrinks to essentially zero in a slight variant of that question asking just about those "in their early teens, say under sixteen years old" (hence, implicitly, thirteen to fifteen years of age). Hence, when asked about premarital sexual activity at any age, laterborns take a decidedly more relaxed attitude than do similar firstborns; when asked about fourteen- to sixteen-year-olds, there is a smaller, marginally significant difference; when asked about thirteen- to fifteen-year-olds, no difference appears at all. This suggests that there may be a consistent trend toward people of any birth order converging on rejection of sexual activity as the age of those involved falls low enough. This pattern may also contribute to the weaker results for the birth control question, which specified a youngish age range, than for the other opinions considered in Figure 4.1.

ABORTION

While most Americans have an almost casual acceptance of premarital sex, they are much more divided in—and much more likely to bring into the explicitly political sphere—their attitudes toward abortion. Some have even traced increasing political polarization of the American public to divisons over abortion, and the issue has remained politically prominent for decades.[34] In many ways, this intensity of belief should be expected to reduce the influence that matters such as birth order have on attitudes. Strongly held beliefs should by definition be harder to alter, and the constant presence of abortion in media coverage and public discussions give survey respondents greater access to perspectives beyond their own personal experiences when formulating opinions. Even so, the role that having older siblings seems to play in shaping sexual mores opens the possibility that birth order may still hold some sway, and previous, glancing looks at the relationship between abortion attitudes and birth order have provided suggestive evidence toward this conclusion.[35] Recall that studies cited earlier indicated that general permissiveness regarding bedroom behavior tended to spill over into attitudes toward abortion. With the results in the previous demonstrating a link between being a laterborn and being more willing to countenance various sexual activities, could it follow that abortion attitudes also systematically differ with birth order?

The GSS has several questions relevant to abortion, closely related but different in important ways. The bluntest question asks for a simple yes/no response as to whether "it should be possible for a pregnant woman to obtain a legal abortion if the woman wants one for any reason." Those who agree that women should be able to have the abortion show, obviously, more acceptant attitudes concerning abortion. Having only two possible answers, this question produces a binary measure of relevant attitudes. It is coded here so that those who agree with the statement get a more positive coding: Higher values associate with more permissive attitudes toward abortion.

A different question asks survey-takers for their degree of agreement or disagreement with the statement, "A pregnant woman should be able to obtain a legal abortion for any reason whatsoever, if she chooses not to have the baby." This question allows respondents to give one of five answers: "strongly agree," "agree," "neither agree nor disagree," "disagree," or "strongly disagree." This is used as the basis for a 5-point abortion scale variable, with more agreement indicating more acceptance of abortion.

The most detailed measure can be put together as an index from the responses to more specific yes/no questions using the same "It should be possible for a pregnant woman to obtain a legal abortion" prompt as in the binary measure but inquiring about a variety of more specific circumstances: one, for example, if the pregnancy was the result of rape; another if the woman's health is endangered by the pregnancy; a third if her family has a low income and cannot afford to raise additional children; and so on. The survey contains six such questions other than the "under any circumstances" one used as the binary measure.[36] Counting the number of conditions under which the respondent agrees that abortion should be legally acceptable thus produces a 7-point scale of abortion attitudes, which serves as a third alternative measure of abortion attitudes.

Even more than the various surveys items considered in the last subsection, these questions all get at the same underlying issue. Still, they serve as useful cross-checks against each other. Small differences in the wording or design of survey questions often produce quite different results, so comparing the results from two different wordings enhances confidence in the predictions. Even aside from any systematic bias introduced by question wordings, having multiple measures should cancel out any randomness brought about by miscodings or respondent inattention. For example, twelve respondents strongly agreed that women should be able to obtain legal abortions under any circumstances yet said no when asked the straight up–down question about the same topic. Similarly, over 100 respondents indicated on the binary measure that women should be allowed to have legal abortions at their discretion yet disagreed that women should be allowed to have abortion under at least one of the six more specific conditions raised.[37] While some of these responses may indicate very particular interpretations of the questions, others probably reflect simple transcription error. In addition, the questions were asked of different subsamples of the GSS respondent pool. While 802 respondents have valid data for all three questions, an additional 1,396 survey-takers have data only for some fraction of the questions. (The 5-point question, in particular, had a quite different sample from that of the other questions.) This provides for semi-independent sets of people who have information for each measure, so that consistent results across the three variables reduces the likelihood that the results were a fluke of the particular sample of people surveyed.

Figure 4.2 looks for evidence of these theories in the GSS data. As with Figure 4.1, each column of graphs represents a different question whose answers are statistically predicted, while the rows represent different combinations of variables used to generate those predictions.

The upper left graph in Figure 4.2 shows that, taking into account the size of the respondent's family, laterborns are about five percentage points

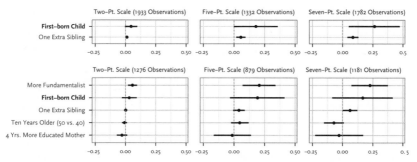

Figure 4.2 Attitudes toward abortion, in baseline (top panel) and expanded (bottom panel) models. Bars show 95% confidence intervals. Positive numbers indicate more restrictive beliefs.

more likely to agree that women should be able to have abortions for any reason they see fit. The 95% confidence interval on that figure does cross the zero line but only by a whisker. It does attain a relatively high degree of statistical significance. It is also comparable to the effect of adding three extra siblings to the respondent's family, and adding a sibling *does* meet the 95% benchmark for statistical significance. Moving to the bottom row of the table, adding the control variables reduces the size of the estimated effect, so that once the other factors in the model are accounted for, only about three percentage points more laterborns profess to believe that women should be able to have abortions under any circumstances. This effect falls well short of the standard levels of statistical significance, although it still manages to represent about half the estimated effect of a 1-point increase in fundamentalism of upbringing.

A similar picture emerges in the other two columns of Figure 4.2, looking at attitudes on the 5-point abortion scale instead of the simple yes/no question and on attitudes toward abortion's legality under specific circumstances. In the upper, baseline model, firstborns' average answer is slightly under 0.2 points more antiabortion than was laterborns' average answer on the 5-point question. Just as with the binary question concerning abortion, this effect sits just at the cusp of 95% confidence even as it signifies a predicted effect larger than that of coming from a family with three more siblings. The lower, richer model has, with its smaller sample size, a less precise estimate of the effect of being firstborn, though the coefficient barely budges in magnitude. In the rightmost column, not having older siblings associates with saying abortion should be illegal in 0.26 more conditions out of the set of six. This effect falls somewhat in size and statistical significance when the control variables are added in the bottom panel, though the point estimate is still for firstborns to tend toward the side of more restrictions.

Considering attitudes toward the different possible motivations for abortion provides further evidence that firstborns' distinctive political attitudes reflect differing perceptions of the acceptability of sexual behavior. The six individual questions comprising the 7-point index of abortion attitudes include some that vary in potentially relevant dimensions. For instance, in three cases—where she is unmarried but does not want to marry the father, is married but does not want more children, or has a low income and cannot afford more children—the woman voluntarily risked pregnancy under circumstances that imply she would not want any potential children. If respondents think this carries with it a heavier responsibility to avoid pregnancy in the first place, they may be less tolerant of resultant abortion. Allowing abortion in these sorts of circumstances might be expected to thoroughly depend on attitudes toward sexual behavior in general, which in turn suggests that firstborns and laterborns may be more likely to diverge in their attitudes. For the other three conditions that the GSS asks about—pregnancy that involves rape, a fetal defect, or a serious threat to the mother's health—the mother's agency and sexual conduct may be seen as less relevant to bringing about the condition that triggered the desire for abortion. In this case, there is less reason to think that firstborns' judgment of conduct will be more stringent than laterborns'.

The survey responses do mostly conform to this expectation. While in all six cases firstborns are less likely to say that abortion should be allowed, the size and statistical significance of this effect varies. The two cases that consistently see the smallest difference (of around one percentage point) in average attitude between firstborns and others are when the mother's health or birth defects are at issue; these are also the cases where firstborns' attitudes can never be statistically distinguished from laterborns' with any degree of confidence. By contrast, attitudes in the other situations—including rape, contrary to the prediction sketched in the previous paragraph[38]—differ more between firstborns and laterborns, with estimated effects typically suggesting that younger siblings are three to five percentage points more likely to voice support for the acceptability of abortion.

All told, then, being firstborn does consistently associate with having lower tolerance of abortion. Any conclusions drawn from this must be tentative: There is some uncertainty in the estimates, with a reasonable probability that effects as large as those observed could have arisen from a sample that flukily happened to have tighter firstborn only moralism links than most. Still, the similarity of the results across different questions (involving different subsamples of the GSS respondent pool) and the pattern of responses toward questions concerning abortion in more specific contexts point to laterborns tending to be more willing to have abortion be legal in cases where the woman involved did not want to have a baby yet chose to engage in sexual activity.

HOMOSEXUALITY

Gay and lesbian sex, while controversial (especially in 1994, at the time of the survey used as a data source here, when American AIDS deaths were near their peak), has a somewhat different relationship to sexual attitudes than does abortion. Although many of the same moral traditions that condemn abortion also condemn homosexual activity, the two play out quite differently in the sphere of public opinion, whether because of abortion's connection to ending a potential life, the fact that different segments of the population are likely to be involved, or some other reason.[39] The difference extends to basic prevalence of acceptance: In the 1994 GSS, 68% of the sample replied that homosexual relations were "always wrong," whereas a large majority—92%—of respondents allowed that abortion should be legal in at least some circumstance among the set discussed in the previous subsection.[40] This is obviously not a like-to-like comparison, since respondents may have found abortion wrong yet still believed it should be a legal choice, and the large battery of questions regarding abortion afforded many more opportunites to express nuance or acceptance. Still, it points to a potentially different structure for relevant public opinion.

The models below focus on two variables relating to attitudes toward homosexuality. One, looking at sexual behavior, parallels the earlier questions concerning premarital sex. This contains the response to the question, "What about sexual relations between two adults of the same sex—do you think it is always wrong, almost always wrong, wrong only sometimes, or not wrong at all?" with, as the wording indicates, four choices available. This purely moral formulation is complemented by questions about the rights of a hypothetical "man who admits that he is a homosexual" (without any explicit statement as to whether that man simply has homosexual impulses or in fact acts upon them): Should such a man be eligible to make a public speech, to teach at a university, to have "a book he wrote in favor of homosexuality" available in the public library? The measure used here counts the number of these opportunities for expression that the respondent thinks homosexuals should have. Thus someone who says that the homosexual should not be allowed to teach, give speeches, or have his books in the library would get a score of zero, while someone with the opposite position on all three questions would get the maximum possible score of

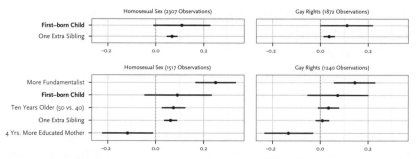

Figure 4.3 Attitudes toward homosexuals and homosexuality, in baseline (top panel) and expanded (bottom panel) models. Bars show 95% confidence intervals. Positive numbers indicate more restrictive beliefs.

3. While this does not directly get at some of the more recent touchstones of gay rights such as same-sex marriage, it speaks to concerns that were still topical in 1994, the year of the survey. For example, more than a quarter of respondents at that time felt that the hypothetical gay man should not be allowed to teach in a college. Figure 4.3 shows the models predicting these variables.

Starting as usual with Figure 4.3's upper-left graph, firstborn children prove to be just over 0.1 points less acceptant of homosexual sex than are laterborns. The 95% confidence interval only slightly overlaps zero, indicating a relatively low likelihood that an effect this large could have arisen through random sampling variation, yet the effect is still small compared to that seen in other figures in this chapter. For example, it implies that being firstborn has less impact than does having two additional siblings, whereas most other differences seen were more in line with having three or more added siblings. The firstborn-laterborn difference is furthermore less than half the size of that seen in the analogous model of Figure 4.1, looking at a very similarly worded and identically scaled question about (presumably heterosexual) premarital sex. This already small effect size decreases still further in the lower part of Figure 4.3; while the estimates continue to find firstborns to be less acceptant of gay sex than are laterborns, the wider confidence interval wrought by the reduced sample size further reduces confidence that the seeming effect of being firstborn was not an artifact of chance correlation.

With the more policy-oriented question considered in Figure 4.3's rightmost column, the best estimate for the effect of being a firstborn is again about 0.1 points on the 4-point gay-rights scale. This difference is in the expected direction, so that firstborns are less inclined to grant open homosexuals the rights in question, and approximately the same predicted effect as having three extra siblings. The now-familiar fall in effect size with the additional control variables is less severe than with attitudes toward homosexual activity itself. The predicted effect size with the control variables can only doubtfully be distinguished from zero given the large uncertainty about the estimate, though it is still comparable to about half the effect of increasing fundamentalism of upbringing by one category.

The overall gist of the results for homosexuality then resembles that for abortion: when only family size is controlled for, the firstborns seem somewhat less tolerant of the behavior in question. This holds even though most laterborns, even in their periods of adolescent experimentation, would not identify themselves as homosexuals (especially given the stigma of doing so in 1994). Having an older sibling, and therefore having more latitude for traditionally frowned-upon sexual activities, seems to extend tolerance to other groups who, as consenting adults, defy conventional mores. The GSS data does not estimate these effects very precisely, though, and so leaves open the possibility that the apparent connection derives from the vagaries of sampling rather than from an actual causal effect.

CONCLUSION

Overall, then, being firstborn associates with less lenient attitudes toward premarital sex, especially when the participants are past their early teenage years. Firstborns also appear less tolerant of abortion and homosexuality and more likely to prefer policies that limit or outlaw relevant behaviors. The statistical significance of these results is, however, somewhat sensitive to the measurements used, as well as to the particular configuration of variables controlled for. Given the past findings that younger siblings quite commonly have greater experience with premarital sex but the lesser likelihood that any particular younger sibling would have had to grapple seriously with issues of abortion or homosexuality, it makes sense that the statistically strongest results would occur with that issue. Nonetheless, even these individually less significant differences showed a consistent tendency for laterborn children to be more permissive than were firstborns.

Moreover, this persistent tug pulling individual younger siblings' attitudes in a more sexually liberal direction can add up to much larger, macrohistorical outcomes. For example, while many factors—technological, sociological, economic—played into the occurrence and timing of the sexual revolution of the 1960s through 1980s, it notably emerged in the wake of an upsurge in family sizes. The post-WWII baby boom saw fertility rates (the number of children per woman) in many Western countries rise to levels not seen since the 1800s, an era when infant and child mortality was far higher. This meant larger families, and larger families inherently mean a greater preponderance of laterborns in the population. As these baby boomers reached adolescence, then, there was suddenly an unusually large fraction of the population whose experiences as younger siblings predisposed them to sexual openness. In this way, the conservative, family-oriented mores of the 1940s and 1950s might have indirectly led to the opposite reaction in ensuing decades.

All this reinforces chapter 3's idea that even having the same parents and growing up in the same household may not always mark the limits of household influence on children's political socialization. Siblings, too, can inflect the formation of each other's political consciousness—and not only by their particular characteristics, as in chapter 3, but by their mere presence. While, as the failed results that litter the birth-order literature warn, these sibling influences may be more potent for behavior within the family than for general personality, conduct, attitudes, or at times behavior in the privacy of the home enters the political arena. When these worlds collide, the formative influence of siblings may be particularly influential in life-long political beliefs.

The findings here point to other possibilities of birth order that may help influence relevant political behavior. The discussion alluded to the possibility that older brothers may have different effects than do older sisters, and it could further be that mixed-sex siblings have a different influence than do same-sex siblings. Another possible direction, following chapter 3, might look at the size of the age gaps between siblings; this could influence both how the siblings interact and the extent to which parents were able to supervise child behavior. With fuller information about siblings, even richer, more complex relationships would be open to study.

Still, as large as sisters and brothers loom in the lives of most who have them, they typically do not assume the all-consuming emotional importance that parents and children often attain. This gives children a different entrée into the world of their parents' political preferences than siblings have: Children are known much later in life than siblings are but with a unique dependence on the parent. It is time, then, to turn to children and see how this different sort of kinship relation can influence politics.

CHAPTER 5

Girls Are from Mars, Boys Are from Venus: Children and Militarism

As noted in chapter 1, most discussion of the political worlds of parents and their children has involved a one-way flow of information, opinions, and ideas from parent to child. Children have typically been seen as having far less influence on their parents' politics. Parents might gain access to new and distinct information sources from children who are grown-up enough to think and act independently, but by that time, decades of personal experience and information have deeply entrenched the parents' political views, and so any new information is unlikely to shift attitudes. As for younger children, how often could a six-year-old formulate a thought that would challenge or redirect parents' beliefs? Perhaps greater attention to issue areas relevant to children and adolescents, such as education and childcare, might change relevant parental attitudes,[1] but children's potential broader political effects are not much thought of. The studies that have considered the possibility have often found a "parenthood gap" in attitudes toward domestic politics: Those with children may differ from the childless in their political and policy preferences.[2]

While keeping the focus on the family, this chapter moves the analysis away from the domestic sphere in the political sense. It instead focuses on foreign-policy preferences, especially those relating to security and war. This is less common ground for the study of the family; it is no coincidence that, to this point in the book, international affairs have appeared only as a foil, in the placebo test of chapter 2. Yet several factors bring together these seemingly disparate concepts of family and national security; one of the most important is how much people care about the future—their "time horizons," wherein they weigh present gains against potential future gains. This is a ubiquitous trade-off in economic, social, and psychological life: Should I spend money now or save it to have it for some future occasion instead? Is it worth completing a chore now rather than procrastinating and having to bear the costs of doing it later? Should I take the momentarily gratifying step of telling off my boss, if doing so leads to the future unhappiness of unemployment? Different people vary greatly in how much they consider the future when they make plans: A drug addict or young child tends to be very fixated on the present, while some cultural traditions strongly emphasize sacrifice now in order to save for the future. Attitudes toward payoffs that come only long in the future are an important consideration when dealing with children—and when dealing with war, which of necessity imposes immediate costs in blood and treasure even when it might hold out the prospect of better outcomes in the future.

Time horizons cut both ways with children, however—they can be a cause rather than an effect. In particular, long time horizons could encourage people to have more children: If the inconveniences of pregnancy and childbirth are not sufficient to deter those concerned with immediate payoffs, the prospect of spending the next several years changing diapers rather than sleeping might be. Consequently, to show that children really can cause changes in political views rather than that the people who are less demanding of instant gratification are more likely to become parents, it is useful to have a causal variable other than simply having children. To that end, this chapter proposes to look for differential effects when the child is a boy instead of a girl. This sex-of-child research design echoes that used in chapter 3.

Luckily, there is reason to believe that these sex differences may matter for attitudes to foreign policy, particularly militarism. This produces an array of hypotheses to examine, concerning both whether parents' potentially longer time horizons lead to distinctive foreign-policy preferences and whether the guardians of girls respond more hawkishly to the world than do guardians of boys.

PARENTHOOD AND THE WORLD

The same widely acknowledged mechanisms that influence parents' views of domestic policy issues also have the potential to shape their foreign and military policy preferences. This connection is less studied but is a basic extension of the underlying theories. The main ways by which children affect parents' views of domestic policies, after all, are time horizons and self-interest—each of which also are likely to matter for foreign-policy preferences.

There are straightforward reasons why children might change their guardians' time horizons.[3] In the contemporary developed world, children have a much longer life expectancy than do adults, so any concern for the child's welfare involves something that will most likely last longer than the adult will. This provides reason to more heavily weigh points in the distant future when making calculation. In the most literal form, those without living children may have less reason to try to reserve funds to leave a positive bequest rather than debt,[4] but the same principle extends to other sorts of decisions that have costs now but may provide benefit in the future.

This is not simply a matter of theory. Analysts across the social sciences have long found that parenthood is associated with an increased willingness to pay for policies and public goods whose benefits arise only in the future and sometimes in the distant future. For instance, parents can be more supportive of environmental policies requiring expensive technology or the willpower to avoid exploiting resources so that later generations may enjoy a cleaner environment.[5] These findings could support the possibility that parents feel the shadow of the future more than the childless do and that such concerns shape policy preferences. At the same time, individuals with long time horizons may be more likely to have children, whether because they more greatly anticipate the nonmaterial benefits of children or in order to ensure material support in their own old age. While this possibility that time horizons affect propensity to have children muddles the direction of causation, it also serves to emphasize the potential empirical link between children and the future.[6]

This concern for the future speaks directly to foreign-policy attitudes, especially those concerning war and conflict. Military action almost inevitably imposes short-run costs on a country through lives lost (or damaged), money spent, and moral compromises made; those preoccupied with national welfare only in the near future may shrink from these outlays regardless of the longer-term consequences.[7] If the longer-term consequences are also negative—breeding more conflict in the future, for example—then time horizons do not matter: People have cause to oppose the war regardless of how they weigh the present against the future. Attitudes toward these sorts of conflicts should then not differ much between those with shorter and longer time horizons. But, though it need not be the case, the longer-term consequences of military intervention can be positive despite high short-term costs.[8] Wars that head off a rising international threat, or that provide access to an otherwise inaccessible resource, or that build national credibility can make the future cheaper to negotiate. Moreover, over the decades countries can often recoup some of the direct monetary losses of war,[9] though obviously this does not apply to the unrecoverable human costs.[10] Among the set of wars in which different time horizons will matter for attitudes, then, the distribution of benefits across time will tend to present costs now and possible benefits later. Hence, those who value the future more heavily compared to the present would tend to be more receptive to the possibility of international conflict potentially being worthwhile.

If children lengthen time horizons because costs borne in the present will more likely redound to the benefit of the young, and longer time horizons lead to more willingness to accept war, then those with children, especially young children, should be more likely to support going to war.[11] This suggests several testable hypotheses. Individuals with responsibility for children are more likely to support foreign military intervention than are individuals without. They should additionally be more supportive than are others of policies or priorities that pay off longer in the future.

Time horizons, though, are not the only way in which wars might touch parents especially. Even if parents valued the future to exactly the same extent as others did, certain policies are simply more or less beneficial for parents. These different concerns, or a distinctive self-interest, could motivate policy preferences. In the foreign-policy realm, this may be most immediately true for the parents of soldiers, who have obvious reasons to care about the state of the military.[12] But guardians of children not serving as soldiers, or who are too young to serve, may receive distinctive rewards from issues of war and peace. For one thing, spending on the military may crowd out expenditures on public services like education, health care, and income redistribution—all of which are disproportionately consumed by children and families—or, conversely, may serve as a channel to provide these welfare benefits to society.[13] For another, involvement in international conflicts, especially protracted conflicts, has the potential to imperil future soldiers. Military actions undertaken today may last into the adulthood of those currently underage, particularly in a security environment that seems to have made wars more likely to devolve into longstanding quagmires.[14] Even if the particular military intervention in question ends swiftly, foreign military intervention can induce a sense of commitment that may impel a government to again intervene in the future or may serve as a precedent allowing intervention to occur more readily in the future. When children's guardians take the longer-term view, the benefits of current and potential future interventions must weigh against the possibility that future conflicts may imperil those children.

This suggests that one major determinant of parents' opinions is their perception of how likely it is that their children might end up in the line of fire. Because this requires assessment of future events, parents naturally cannot know this probability with any precision. An additional complicating factor is that many of the predictors of likelihood to join the military—socioeconomic status; regional, ethnic, and cultural influences—are household characteristics that directly influence the parents' assessments of the war's costs and benefits. That is, the same factors that make a child more likely to enlist in the military also tend to affect parental attitudes toward war in general. Furthermore, the parents have relatively explicit, conscious control over several of these contributors to military enlistment. Thus selection effects mean these child characteristics are not clearly distinct influences on guardians' behavior: Even if we observe that people in a particular group are both more likely to have children who end up in the military and that they have distinctive opinions about war, it may not be that the prospective military career is what causes the opinions.

However, there is at least one factor most often outside parents' control that remains very pertinent to military careers: the child's gender. Although children of either gender can become soldiers, boys have always been more likely than girls to enlist.[15] In recent years, less than a fifth of those on active duty in the US military have been female, and this figure is at its historical peak. While other factors ranging from regional culture and racial/ethnic group to socioeconomic status affect individuals' propensity to enlist, men are consistently more likely to enlist than are women across all these groups.[16] Further, even when women do enlist in the armed forces, they are less likely to complete training and actually serve.[17] Parents can therefore reasonably expect that male children are far more likely to someday serve in the military than are female children. Also, under current law many societies, including the United States, subject only men to (front-line) military conscription, so that even boys who do not have militaristic dispositions or who have many career alternatives may face greater risks of bearing costs—service, injury, or death—of future military operations. Even in the volunteer military, men are more likely than women to be assigned positions that directly expose them to combat.

This suggests that guardians of boys might have more incentive to be wary of military intervention than guardians of girls. Other causal mechanisms also point in the same direction. For example, most military casualties in current conflicts are male, and people with sons of their own may feel with particular empathy the loss suffered by a family whose son dies.[18] These differences between men and women allow a variant of the natural-experiment design seen in chapter 3 using gender to provide more evidence that children are having causal effect on their parents' preferences.[19] In particular, it suggests a hypothesis that should be, by the standards of the messy world of social science, relatively easily to test cleanly: Individuals with responsibility for girls are more likely to support foreign military intervention than are individuals with responsibilities for boys. This accords the evidence noted in chapter 1 that sex of children affects parental political preferences, though previous studies have tended to focus on more explicitly gender-related issues.

Considered together, the two hypotheses—one comparing parents to nonparents, the other considering parents of girls in contrast to parents of boys—push policy views in various directions for different individuals. The implications for guardians of girls is unambiguous: Girls should induce preferences more open to military action than either childlessness (because the children induce longer time horizons) or boys (because of the differential probability of military involvement). More complicated is the distinction between those not caring for a child and those raising boys. Parenthood may enhance the perceived value of long-run benefits of a military action, but for parents of boys it also increases the potential costs of military action—with the potential for the costs to be highly concentrated, rather than the much more diffuse national benefits that the international engagement may offer. In the end, then, the difference between these two groups derives from which effect is stronger. If the time-horizons argument dominates, parents of boys would be more hawkish than nonparents (though still less militaristic than parents of girls). If the sex-of-child argument dominates, parents of boys would be more dovish than nonparents.

"Parents," in all this discussion, may be restrictive. The arguments above make no reference to, and need not derive from, biological parenthood. Just as in chapter 2, the logic of parenthood-based policy preferences mostly reflects an attachment to or concern for the welfare of children that may stem from stepparenthood, simple guardianship, or other close relationships with children. This is worth considering not only when thinking through the logic of the theory but also when measuring the relevant concepts, the next task.

TESTING THE ARGUMENT

Testing these hypotheses—and the theory that underpins them—requires showing several connections. Supporting the first hypothesis entails demonstrating that parents have distinctive foreign-policy concerns regardless of the sex of their children, particular when the policy in question pays off in the future rather than immediately. Supporting the second hypothesis involves showing that these parental concerns translate into differing policy preferences for parents of girls than for parents of boys.

The 2004 iteration of the American National Election Study (NES) contains information that speaks to these points. This data set, familiar from chapter 2, does not contain a direct indicator of parenthood. Instead, it offers as substitutes various measures of household composition. Specifically, the survey contains measures of the total number of children under the age of eighteen in the respondent's household, along with the number of female children under eighteen in the household. The number of male children is then the difference between these two numbers. This measure thus fails to account for parents who do not have in-home custody of their children (as commonly happens through divorce), for adult children whether or not they reside in the respondent's home, and for minor children who have already left home. Parental concern for these unobserved children may of course affect the preferences of survey respondents. The measure may conversely include children such as foreign-exchange students, who would not have the hypothesized effect on respondents' military policy preferences. These cases inject some noise unrelated to the central theory.

Despite these drawbacks, this operationalization offers some compensating advantages as the independent variable of interest. By counting only those under the age of eighteen, this measure focuses squarely on children whose long expected life span encourages uniquely long time horizons. At the same time, adult children are far less likely to enlist in the military at any point in the future. After embarking on other career or educational paths, individuals are far less likely to enlist; in the United States, more than two-thirds of new enlistees have historically been under the age of twenty-one, and an eighteen-year-old is almost ten times as likely to enlist as a twenty-four-year-old.[20] Hence, survey respondents' children excluded because of their age are less likely either to induce very long time horizons in their parents or to ever face military service in the future. In any event, to the extent that this variable is mismeasured and adult and out-of-household children do affect parental preferences in the same way as minor in-household children, the bias works against finding the hypothesized results: The groups of seeming "parents" and "nonparents" actually bleed into one another, reducing differences between the groups and thus the likelihood of observing significant disparities.[21] Meanwhile, measuring children in this way also allows for nontraditional family structures and examines those whose personal and household utility functions include the welfare of one or more children despite the absence of any biological relationship. While some studies have found that stepparents may be less emotionally involved in the raising of children and that they might accordingly be less likely to shift positions based on their stepchildren,[22] other studies have found nonbiological guardians hard to distinguish in terms of involvement.[23] Thus differentiating between biological parents and others who live with a child may be questionable. As a cross-check, the survey also contains questions asking only about the respondent's children in the household—that is, excluding stepchildren, grandchildren, foster children, or other nonbiological relationships. Using these measures instead of the broader conception of guardianship does not appreciably alter the reported results; unless otherwise specified, then, any use of "parent" or "parental" below also includes nonbiological adults living in the same household as the child.

The reported regressions use as their primary causal variable of interest a simple count of the number of boys and number of girls in the household. This way of measuring data suggests that additional children of one gender reinforce the effect of the first child. So, for example, if there are two boys (who might someday join the military) in the household instead of one, the conjectured aversion to foreign military intervention is twice as large. This accords with the logic of the hypotheses: Multiple children, after all, make it more likely that at least one child will be alive in the distant future or may enlist. (It is also parallel to the measure of number of siblings in chapter 4.)

Yet there are many other possible assumptions about how multiple children change the effect in question. It could be that a child's effect on household preferences is sufficiently drastic that additional children of the same gender have no appreciable effect. Concern for a son who might join the military is so overwhelming in this telling that it is effectively infinite, and additional sons cannot increase the effect; contemplating the death of a child, even in the distant future, might be so psychologically undesirable that people discount it and think of their child's lives as extending indefinitely. This sort of process would argue for measuring the presence of boys and girls in the household with simple binary variables, with one variable equal to one if the household includes any nonzero number of girls and another equal to one to indicate any nonzero number of boys.

Alternatively, there could be diminishing marginal effects to additional children, for example if children's influences on their siblings or the shared environment mean the children's lives, life expectancies, and behaviors correlate. This sort of correlation implies that if an issue was relevant for two children, it was more than likely already relevant with one. In this case, the best means of getting at the underlying process would involve a model that responded more strongly to the first few children of a particular gender but less fully incorporated subsequent children, as for example something involving the square root or logarithm of the number of children of the relevant sex. As a check to make sure any findings are not dependent on which measurement is used, the models were run with these alternative assessments of how many girls and boys are in the household. Generally, all measurement choices produce substantially similar results.[24]

In addition to measuring the children that could shape preferences, of course, we must also measure the preferences that might be shaped. Consider first the question of time horizons. The NES contains several questions about what the government should prioritize in foreign policy. Two of these possible priorities are particularly relevant to the story above linking children to foreign-policy preferences, offering as they do a complementary pair of security issues with contrasting time horizons.[25] One of these involves nuclear war, asking how important it is for much the government to stop the proliferation of nuclear weapons. Since the future spread of nuclear capabilities is not about the immediate prospect of violence but the potential for more cataclysmic violence later, this issue holds more risks for those with longer time horizons. Combating proliferation involves slowing down the (relatively slow) spread of nuclear weapons, which may (after some further time) collapse into war. The costs of further nuclear proliferation are mostly borne in the relatively distant future, putting a premium on longer time horizons, so the expectation is that those who care for children will weigh nuclear issues more heavily. As real-life substantiation of this line of thought, politicians have long tied nuclear war to anxieties about children.[26]

The other potential foreign-policy priority considered here is the prevention of terrorist atrocities. This is a much more immediate security threat—and one that might have seemed especially immediately urgent in 2004, when the survey occurred. While terrorism might pose longer-term threats as well, the important contrast with nuclear proliferation is the relative potential for present and future costs; the greater potential for more imminent gains suggests that longer time horizons are not as important for prioritizing terrorism prevention. In consequence, parents are less likely to be appreciably distinctive with regard to their emphasis on stopping terrorism.

Thus models considering the time-horizon problem involve two opinion questions. The wording of the proliferation question is, "Should preventing the spread of nuclear weapons be a very important foreign-policy goal, a somewhat important foreign-policy goal, or not an important foreign-policy goal at all?" The terrorism inquiry is the same except for substituting "combatting international terrorism" in for "preventing the spread of nuclear weapons." With the three possible answers,[27] this produces a 3-point scale for answers, with "very important" coded as the maximum and "not at all important" as the minimum value. Note that these questions, as separate survey items, do not force respondents to compare the two priorities directly; respondents can identify both (indeed, every potential priority presented) as "very important" or "not at all important" if they so choose.

The theory above suggests few reasons for differentiating between the sexes when considering these questions. Nuclear war and terrorism are both things that almost by definition kill and injure civilians, so that the female–male difference in military duties does not come directly into play. As such, the logic does not strongly suggest that girls and boys will have divergent effects on parents' priorities over these issues: Household exposure to children—boy or girl—will tend to raise the perceived importance of the nuclear issue. In the context of 2004, when the government's framing of counterterrorism efforts focused on a military "global war on terror," one might expect parents of boys to be more hesitant about prioritizing terror. Nevertheless, the primary logic here sidesteps the quasi-experimental design looking for differences in effect between children of the two sexes and leaves open the possibility that any observed association between foreign-policy attitudes and children is spurious.

Bolstering the case that children really are driving foreign-policy preferences, then, requires questions more explicitly invoking military participation. The models below again use two different measures. One is simply a yes/no measure of isolationism, the response to the question: "Do you agree or disagree with this statement: 'This country would be better off if we just stayed home and did not concern ourselves with problems in other parts of the world'?" This question is interesting not simply because isolationism is historically central to American foreign-policy debates. As many Americans associate "staying home" with "keeping troops at home" rather than with anything involving trade or economic issues (indeed, those who advocate staying home sometimes also advocate nonmilitary measures such as increasing foreign aid), this question begins to implicate putting troops in peril, the source of gender differences when thinking about children's effects on attitudes.

Another NES variable gets at this even more directly. This question asks respondents to place themselves on a 7-point scale on the relative utility of diplomatic versus military intervention in world affairs, with higher values associated with more hawkish, military-oriented positions.[28] Higher-valued answers, by advocating more military intervention, are likely to impose short-run costs on military families. Those living with male children are accordingly expected to be more isolationist and more in favor of diplomatic solutions, while female children should provoke relatively less isolationism and more willingness to support military action.

While these questions relate to the underlying trade-offs of international conflict, they are somewhat abstract in their framings. This is especially dangerous in survey questions about foreign affairs, which usually has a low enough political salience that survey responses can be somewhat forced and arbitrary (although the centrality of foreign affairs to political debates in 2004 may mitigate that problem).[29] Supplementing these more general philosophical statements of position are two more concrete measures of willingness to use the military to achieve foreign-policy goals: questions about whether the Iraq and Afghanistan wars were "worth the cost." Both these conflicts were ongoing at the time of the survey, though neither had yet reached its peak ferocity as far as American casualties were concerned. These questions pose the short-run costs of war at their most explicit. While having children would not obviously affect evaluations of the benefit of toppling the previous Afghan and Iraqi governments, the relative value of the war's cost should shift according to both time horizons and sex of respondents' children. At the same time as they show very clearly and starkly the costs of international involvement, they also reflect the reality of policy decisions being tied to other political and policy debates rather than a simple response to war. If these more specific considerations trump generally hawkish or dovish sentiment in practice, then concrete, immediate conflicts and their diverse consequences may obscure or eliminate the effects that children appear to have in the more hypothetical questions. Nevertheless, the central theory here suggests that the expectation is that those in households with girls will be more likely to say the wars were worth it, while those in households with boys will be more likely to say the wars were not worth it, when compared to a childless person.

Of course, many other factors influence both foreign-policy preferences and the propensity to have children in the household, and these influences must be controlled for. Age, for example, determines many of one's past experiences of conflict and military action even as it influences the likelihood of having children in the household. Other demographic and cultural features are similarly important for both foreign-policy preferences and household exposure to children. Hence the models also incorporate controls for education, sex, income, religiosity, being in the South or an urban area, whether the respondent had been in the military, and partisan identification. This last control variable does pose some reverse-causation problems, since respondents' foreign and military policy views presumably influence their choice of and attachment to political parties; one might identify as Republican *because* of one's support for the Iraq war, for example, even though the model is looking for people supporting the Iraq intervention because of their Republican attachment. If this reversal of causation exists, it should make it less likely the models will estimate a significant effect for the other independent variables. Excluding the variable from the models does, in fact, tend to increase the size and statistical significance of the coefficients on the variables relating to children, though the difference is never particularly large.[30]

RESULTS

The first task, as noted above, is to establish that children change—or are at least systematically associated with changes in—foreign-policy preferences in those around them, as this is a central idea in all the discussion above. To this end, Figure 5.1 shows two models for each of the two questions of foreign-policy priorities (preventing nuclear proliferation and fighting terrorism). The first model, presented in the upper model of the figure, focuses on the quasi-experiment, leaving out control variables to focus on the effect of having more girls and having more boys in respondents' households—the difference between the two effects then shows the relative effect of exposure to daughters compared to that of exposure to sons. When considering the effect of having children in general, however, more control variables are necessary; the bottom panel of the figures supplies the models including those additional controls.

Either sex of child proves to increase the estimated degree to which nuclear proliferation is perceived as a priority. The effect size is slightly

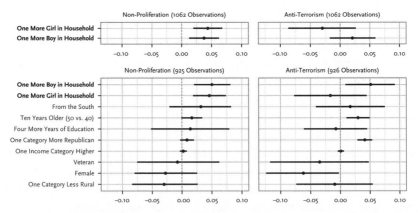

Figure 5.1 Feeling that issues are important foreign-policy priorities, in baseline (top panel) and expanded (bottom panel) models. Bars show 95% confidence intervals. Positive numbers indicate a feeling that the issue is more important.

larger when the additional control variables are included, but the effect is around 0.04 to 0.05 points in either case. This is not large, but the high priority that most respondents gave to nonproliferation (the average answer on the 3-point scale was 2.86, because so many people gave the answer of 3) means that even a modest effect size captures a relatively large proportion of the variation seen across respondents. This may be why that unprepossessing effect of 0.04 is larger than that seen with most of the other variables. Having an additional child in the house has a larger effect than does being twenty-five years older or being five categories more Republican (the difference between a "strong Democrat" and a "Republican"). That last, partisanship-related point is perhaps particularly noteworthy, since much of the controversy surrounding the Iraq conflict involved the claims that it was launched to fight the spread of weapons of mass destruction, including nuclear arms.

Just as important, the difference between the effect of sons and that of daughters is very small—essentially zero. This suggests that child gender has no effect in shaping attitudes toward prioritizing proliferation, and in fact the models are not even consistent as to whether girls or boys have a larger effect on their co-householders' attitudes. As expected, then, children seem to relate to the evaluation of the nuclear threat, but the sex of those children does not appear relevant.

The story is slightly different when looking at terrorism, shown in Figure 5.1's rightmost column. Without control variables, neither sex of child has an effect that can be distinguished statistically from zero, nor can the two effects be confidently differentiated from one another, even though girls are associated with less, and boys with more, parental concern with fighting terrorism. Once the control variables enter the model, on the other hand, those living with boys assign a substantially higher prioritization to terrorism. While this can be distinguished from the effect of girls with only moderate levels of statistical significance,[31] it is a large enough effect (0.05 points) to be statistically distinguishable from zero.[32] An effect of this magnitude is again larger than that of changes in most variables, although it is smaller when compared to the now larger effects of age and partisanship.

This effect of boys goes against the prediction of no effect made earlier: Although terrorism has immediate effects and so children have less cause for triggering systematic opinion shifts, having more children in the household does sometimes appear to shift attitudes. This is not wholly surprising, since terrorism implicates more than just time horizons, and the results did not indicate any general difference between parents and nonparents. The models do fulfill the prediction of seeing less systematic effect of

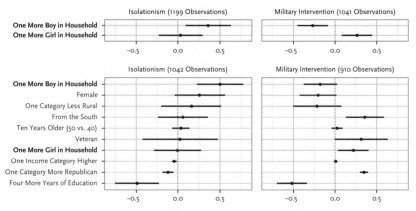

Figure 5.2 Attitudes toward international intervention, in baseline (top panel) and expanded (bottom panel) models. Bars show 95% confidence intervals.

children than did proliferation, and the effects seen—with boys' and girls' co-householders appearing to respond in opposite directions—anticipate in miniature the predictions made for military interventionism. Figure 5.2 turns to analyses speaking more directly to that point, isolationism and militarism. To the extent the hypotheses are borne out there, it suggests the effects of children in support for counterterrorism may be bound up with broader foreign-policy views.

Figure 5.2's left column looks for isolationist attitudes. Since avoiding engagement with the rest of the world presumably reduces the risks to prospective conscripts or enlistees, the expectation is that members of households with boys will tend to isolationism. Girls, by contrast, have a lower risk of bearing these costs and so are less likely to inspire the isolationist turn.

Those living with boys do appear to be more isolationist. Recall that, though the underlying question is binary, Figure 5.2 rescales the isolationism question so that it is on a 7-point scale to improve comparability with the military intervention variable considered in the right-hand column. Thus the effect of around 0.36 per additional boy suggests that each boy in the household increases the probability of giving the more isolationist answer by almost exactly six percentage points. Having a girl in the house, however, has no evident effect on isolationism: Those living with girls are essentially indistinguishable from the childless in their tendency toward isolationism.

These effects continue in a richer model of the figure's bottom panel. In fact, the expected effect of a boy in the household increases by over a third, increasing the size and statistical significance of the difference between girls' and boys' expected effect on isolationism. Several of the control variables also prove significant in predicting isolationism. Higher levels of income or education, more frequent church attendance, and a tendency toward Republican identification all are associated with lower levels of isolationism. In addition, female respondents are more likely to voice support for isolationism in some situations, though the 95% confidence interval does overlap zero in the reported model. Regardless, the included control variables provide substantive benchmarks for the effect sizes of having children: Boys turn out to have an effect comparable to three to four fewer years of education, or to being four categories more Democratic (the difference between a "Strong Republican" and a "Democratic-leaning Independent").

The different levels of enthusiasm for international engagement that boys and girls produce might complement divergent preferences over the form of foreign interventions when they occur. Once again, the more military-oriented engagements are, the more likely it is that boys and those concerned for boys' welfare will end up bearing the related costs. But a willingness to apply military pressure increases the government's leverage in international affairs—perhaps especially in issues such as nuclear proliferation, which deal explicitly with national security. This suggests that members of boys' households will tend to shrink from military intervention, while girls' households will be more open to its use. Figure 5.2's rightmost column considers this issue using the 7-point scale of preference for military (higher values) rather than diplomatic (lower values) foreign interventions.

The top panel gives baseline results without control variables. As can be seen, both boys and girls have strongly significant effects on the diplomatic-military scale. More boys in a household are associated with lower values of the dependent variable and hence a greater emphasis on diplomatic efforts, while households with girls tend to be more ready than others to use military force. The average effect is of about one-quarter of a point per child of the relevant gender. In addition to being distinguishable from zero, the effects of the two sexes of child can also be distinguished from one another with high confidence.

These effects largely continue even with the introduction of control variables in the bottom panel of the figure. The predicted effect of having a girl proves to be comparable in size to that of being a veteran, while the effect of having a boy is roughly the same as the effect of being female. The 95% confidence interval for boys slightly crosses the zero line, suggesting less certainty that boys pull family members toward preferring diplomatic interventions. This reduced confidence, however, stems mostly from the inclusion of the household income variable. Although this does not itself have any sort of significant predicted effect on foreign-policy attitudes, it results in the loss of over 100 observations from the sample: Many people refused to answer the question about their income, so data is unavailable for their self-reported income. This result notably depends on how income is measured; using the more widely available interviewer's estimate of household income instead of the respondent's report restores the significance of household boys while maintaining the significant effect of household girls.

Looking at the coefficients on the control variables themselves, education and partisan identification strongly affect opinions regarding the form of interventionism, with more educated and more Democratic-leaning respondents tending to favor a less military approach. In addition, Southern, veteran, and rural respondents are significantly more open to military action. Even taking these effects into account, both boys and girls have a substantial impact, albeit slightly diminished in size and statistical significance, on the preferred instruments of foreign policy.[33]

Figure 5.3 tests whether the child-inflected policy preferences are strong enough to translate into support for actual military interventions, considering opinions over whether the ongoing military conflicts in Iraq and Afghanistan were thought to be "worth the cost." In the case of both conflicts, the measure of boys in the household consistently received negative coefficients, while the measure of girls in the household consistently took positive coefficients. But, as the figure suggests, the coefficients were not all significant at the same level as they were in the general

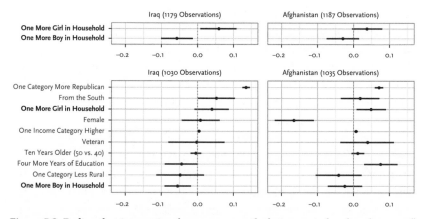

Figure 5.3 Feeling that international wars were worth their cost, in baseline (top panel) and expanded (bottom panel) models. Bars show 95% confidence intervals. Positive numbers indicate more support for the relevant war.

diplomatic-versus-military question of Figure 5.2. As suggested above, this may reflect that actual conflicts bring in other complicating issues that can be set aside when contemplating the clean, purely theoretical question of war versus diplomacy.

Most often, boys consistently significantly alter opinions only about the Iraq war, while girls' effect is consistently significant only with regard to Afghanistan. The reasons for the stronger effect that girls appear to assert on Afghanistan war opinions are less obvious, but the finding for boys accords with intuition. At the time of the survey, many more soldiers (over-whelmingly males) had lost their lives in Iraq compared to Afghanistan, making the cost side of the question especially salient in Iraq.[34] Moreover, the larger number of personnel involved in Iraq had greatly increased discussions of the possibility of reinstating conscription. It therefore stands to reason that social ties to boys would influence feelings about the Iraq conflict more strongly than those about Afghanistan.

The estimated effect sizes on the child-related variables are consistently appreciable. In the models without control variables, having a daughter rather than a son is associated with a nearly twelve percentage-point change in likelihood of supporting the Iraq war. While the difference is smaller regarding Afghanistan, it still is around seven percentage points.

The effects of control variables again accord with intuition. The most important predictor of opinions on both conflicts was partisan identification; in both cases, more Republican-oriented individuals were far more likely to say the wars were worth the cost. For the Iraq war, Southerners and more frequent attenders of religious services were also more likely to find the net benefits of the war to be positive. Concerning Afghanistan, males (strikingly, given their comparability to females when looking at Iraq) and those with higher incomes were significantly more likely to think the war worth the cost. Interestingly, education came up significant in both cases—but with opposite signs. More education was associated with a more positive assessment of the Afghanistan conflict but a more negative assessment of the Iraq situation.

The effect of respondent gender—that striking tendency for women to oppose the war in Afghanistan—is especially of interest for the broader sex-of-child literature. Almost universally, past studies of child gender have suggested that daughters tend to take parents' views toward the average position of adult women. That is, women tend to be more feminist and more supportive of abortion rights than men are, and daughters' "feminizing" influence means that parents of a girl also take on some of those attitudes. In the case of Afghanistan, though, adult women and parents of daughters tend to pull in opposite directions. This suggests that the effects

of children may be richer and more interesting than some traditional analyses have considered.

CONCLUSIONS

In a variety of contexts, those in households with boys have more dovish or
isolationist foreign-policy preferences, while those in households with girls
have more hawkish preferences compared to those in households without
children. These patterns may arise because concern for children generally shifts individuals' foreign-policy priorities, while attachment to male
children increases the perceived risks of military engagement and thereby
outweighs the sex-neutral effect. This is particularly interesting in that it
cuts against multiple conventions of the child-gender literature. First is the
substantive issue in question, which is not as explicitly gender-related as
the issues (abortion policy, affirmative action) more commonly considered.
Second are the results, which differ from many other results. The effect of
having a child of a given sex in the household has, atypically, the *opposite*
effect of being of that sex. Men are generally more acceptant of conflict and
military intervention than are women, yet girls associate more with household members' militarism while boys associate with pacifism. Relatedly,
the overall ideological tilt of the results also goes against the grain in that
girls are associated with the more traditionally right-wing (military interventionist) position, even though most studies of child gender find that
having daughters associates with leftism.

More broadly, these findings provide a micro-level, public-opinion perspective on the newly resurgent field of political demography in international relations.[35] This chapter emphasizes two points that relate to and
build on that literature. First, the age distribution of a society, in particular the proportion of young people, may shape reactions toward major
foreign-policy issues. Second, the sex ratio of youngsters may have more
subtle consequences than sometimes supposed. The classic fear connecting
young people and war is that having a disproportionate number of young
males may make society more warlike and prone to conflict as the young
men's heightened competition for mates spills over into violence.[36] While
direct extrapolation from a US survey to the mores and societies of, say,
developing Asia is obviously fraught with peril, the relative abundance of
young males in certain parts of the world may not simply make the societies more belligerent. To the contrary, the results here suggest that the presence of young males may influence significant portions of society to be less
warlike: Even if the surplus of men may themselves be more aggressive,

those young men's relations may try to act as a brake on conflict. To the extent that young men do not have the final say in policy, this brake may be effective. With the tendency for young people to not participate politically and therefore to be underrepresented in many social institutions, this is possible.

The results here also suggest pathways for future research. To take the most obvious route, this raises questions about whose foreign-policy preferences are being influenced by having children around. Traditionally, in Western society, female adults have borne a disproportionate share of child-rearing; thus one might expect that women would be most influenced by having a child in the household. Conversely, cultural or biology may more sensitize women to the costs that children and caregivers face even if they are not themselves currently living with a child. By this logic, women are not so dependent on the state of their own household, and the effects of children in the household are more likely to be seen among men. As a first-cut look at this question, Figure 5.4 addresses this question by repeating the analyses of the bottom panels of Figures 5.2 and 5.3, restricting the sample[37] to first women (in the top panel) and then men (in the bottom). This provides a rough approximation of how mothers and fathers may differentially react to their children's gender.[38] To improve readability and comparability across the panels, Figure 5.4 reduces the 7-point scale of the military versus diplomatic intervention variable down to having the same range as the other, binary, variables.

As the figure shows, the general direction of the predicted effects holds regardless of the adult household member's gender: Compared to girls, boys lead to more support for isolationism and more diplomatic forms of international engagement but decrease acceptance of wars' costs. Nevertheless, there are differences between men and women in the size and significance of the effects. Where specific wars are involved, the significant effects are mostly driven by children's effects on men. This holds through the models: Even when, as is often the case, women see a significant effect of having

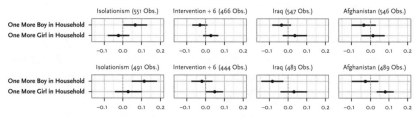

Figure 5.4 Effects of child gender on attitudes to international engagement, for female (top panel) and male (bottom panel) guardians. Bars show 95% confidence intervals. Models include the other control variables from bottom panels of Figures 5.2 and 5.3.

children in the household, the effect tends to be substantively larger and still more significant for men. Children, that is, seem to matter more for the foreign-policy opinions of the men in the household than for the women. As the questions turn away from wars per se to questions of different types of international intervention, though, the gaps narrow. When the question involves contrasting military and diplomatic action, fathers show effects of child gender only about a fifth larger than mothers do. When the question is simply about isolationism rather than any international activity (without specifying whether that activity is military), the difference falls to virtually nothing. That is, fathers' stronger reactions to child gender seem closely tied to specifically military questions.

By no means is guardian's gender the only potential source for interesting interaction with the child-based effects considered here. This chapter examined how child gender mattered in the broadest possible context in order to demonstrate that the effects were significant to the population at large. Still, the underlying causal story proposed here suggests that the effects may be even stronger for certain subgroups. For example, the gender-based differences might not apply even among groups where enlistment is relatively unlikely—religiously based pacifists or those from better-off families that can broaden career options outside the military.[39] Or, consider the question of how the hypotheses discussed here apply at different ages of the child: Does a teenager have the same effect on parents as a toddler for whom most of the relevant risks are more distant?[40] Clarifying these points may also shed further light on some of the curious anomalies of the results presented above, such as the asymmetry between girls and boys in their relative effect on Iraq and Afghanistan opinions. The explanations proffered here also raise questions about the extent to which these phenomena arise in other contexts: countries more likely to face direct war on their territory so that civilians as well as soldiers may be directly exposed, isolationism between the world wars in the United States, and so on.

While gender serves as a relatively forceful way of showing that offspring really have influence on their parents' attitudes—even when those children are likely too young to formulate their own independent ideologies—it is only a small part of how children can influence their parents. The next chapter turns to another mechanism, uncertainty, that all children can impose on their parents and looks at how this might play out in policy contexts other than war and foreign policy.

CHAPTER 6

Children, Economic Security, and Support for Big Government

Children expose parents to all sorts of new risks. Many of these risks are largely outside the scope of government; regulations do not, as yet, cover the danger that one's dinner companion will suddenly start shrieking in the middle of a previously enjoyable restaurant meal. More macro-level risks, however, do fall in the public sphere: Think of the insurance that governments provide against national disasters, or the way that publicly provided police forces seek to reduce the hazard of crime. Parents who worry that crime or disaster may befall their children may, consequently, have distinctive preferences on public issues.

One such risk that is particularly central to political life is the problem of economic uncertainty. Even in rich societies where the odds of outright starvation or other catastrophic outcomes are low, economic insecurity is a protean force. It has been linked to everything from obesity[1] to major policy shifts.[2] As a result, factors that create or dampen a sense of economic threat have broad interest for politics and society—and children offer one likely source of heightened fears of economic volatility.

Children have the potential to raise fears of economic insecurity through multiple pathways. One is that taking care of children sometimes involves time commitments that may interfere with the successful completion of work and accordingly increases the likelihood of unemployment. For example, if parents periodically have to stay home from work to care for a sick child (or because they have caught illnesses from their children), the increased absenteeism may attract employers' ire or harm job prospects if a position cannot be found to accommodate the need for flexible scheduling.[3] Job performance may also suffer because of sleep deprivation produced by childcare responsibilities.[4] Even if children's guardians are in fact just as able to make workplace commitments, employers may perceive them to be less reliable and therefore groundlessly discriminate against them. This possibility seems particularly acute for mothers, who are less likely to be hired[5] and often receive lower wages for comparable work than do nonparents.[6] Discrimination of this sort may contribute to mothers' tendency to become more liberal on social welfare policies.[7]

It is also the case that children's guardians may have a smaller economic nest egg on which to draw if bad luck should happen to strike. Raising a child is, simply put, an expensive proposition. As a result, those with children in the household may have to draw down savings, or, equivalently, fail to accumulate wealth, under circumstances when the childless have greater reserves to store away money or invest for the future. This means that those with children may objectively have more to worry about from an economic shock of a particular size; all else equal, they will have a smaller asset base on which to draw if economic insecurity befalls them. Wage discrimination against mothers could further exacerbate this problem of relatively low savings.

Alongside these objective risks, the psychology of modern American parenthood and guardianship may also push for a greater perception of threat. Parenthood tends to involve an array of psychological consequences, many highly rewarding but others costly.[8] One of the less positive turns is the potential for an increase in anxiety: One is responsible not only for one's own welfare but also for others', so economic deprivation has costs not only materially but also in self-image in failing to provide as a parent. This pressure to be a breadwinner for a dependant—and minor children are particularly dependent dependants, since they have fewer outside resources to draw on than might, say, a healthy retiree—applies to both men and women and may increase the amount of worry associated with any one particular negative economic consequence. In consequence, those caring for children may feel a greater sense of insecurity, all else equal, than do those who do not.

The perception of risk from any of the above mechanisms has implications for many aspects of politics and elections. Fear and uncertainty, for example, are widely associated with particular ideological predispositions and with voting for extremist politicians.[9] They also may change politically salient behavior, for example by providing more motivation to seek out information about politics and to act on that information by voting or other forms of participation. Here, though, I focus on the implications for attitudes concerning policy, especially economic policy.

Previous studies have found that increased sense of insecurity does not automatically lead to increased demand for government policies that insure against risk.[10] This follows the general rule seen in previous chapters that positions on policy, even economic policy, do not always flow directly from self-interest; it also points to the fact that threat and anxiety do not always correlate.[11] Yet feelings of insecurity do tend to move together with support for government-provided economic insurance.[12] This is natural and intuitive: Those who are concerned about the prospect of job loss gain not just potential future returns from government payments but also some immediate reassurance about what should happen if their fears come true. Those at risk economically could sometimes increase their own savings rate to offer themselves more security through entirely private means (though this would be difficult for those already struggling). But a public insurance scheme effectively subsidizes this behavior, both because it spreads the risk across more people—the pool of taxpayers—and because it is likely that the people who are less worried about needing economic assistance probably are in fact less likely to ever require that public aid. These individuals' being compelled by the government to put aside funds in case of future unemployment will implicitly then transfer funds to those whose economic position is less stable.

The focus on risks in the argument above tends to militate against some of the potential avenues for reversed or spurious causation. Those who have custody of children would be more likely to perceive risk or to want government to insure against those risks if people who are most exquisitely sensitive to downside risks are also the ones more likely to choose to have children. Yet childrearing is a hazardous enterprise, and having children would not be an obvious strategy for someone looking to avoid risks. It seems unlikely that anxiety about the perilousness of the world would predispose one to have children who would then have to face those perils. Moreover, past studies have observed that economic insecurity as such does not seem to reduce the number of children people have in real-world data,[13] further suggesting that causation is not reversed from the story given here. These points reduce the probability of a few potential confounding factors, even as other potential sources of spurious causation remain for research design to address.

Note that the mechanism here is not simply that those raising children are getting handouts through these programs. There are, of course, government expenditures and tax breaks that do directly go into the pockets of people with custody of children: education spending including college financial-aid programs, for instance, or public provision of childcare (even if American governments have generally not gone as far in this direction as have most northern European countries). These sorts of programs could test whether those raising children were narrowly seeking expenditures on their immediate government programs. Other public programs, such as environmental protections, might speak to the longer horizons explored in chapter 5, but this is also distinct from the matter at issue. The mechanism examined here suggests that even when child-rearers value the future just as much as those not caring for children, even in policies that will benefit neither group immediately, those with children will have differing outlooks and preferences.

To get at these possibilities, this chapter explores the connection between having custody of children and supporting the sorts of welfare-state institutions that could insure against economic risks—not unrelated to those considered in chapter 3. Building this case empirically involves several steps. Based on the most immediate logic of the argument just presented, the initial question is whether taking care of children connects to greater feelings of insecurity. The first set of data tests takes up that task. The subsequent sections then expand the causal chain, linking child-rearing to broader political beliefs about economically insecure groups in society and the trustworthiness of government before ultimately looking at the ties between having children and supporting specific policy initiatives (such as expanding welfare spending) that could reduce the threat of economic misfortune. Before estimating these models, though, the next section discusses the measures used and some of the potential alternative causal stories that the models take into account.

DATA AND MEASUREMENTS

The trusty American National Election Study (NES), now familiar from its use in chapters 2 and 5, offers the information needed to test hypotheses relating the raising of children to perceived risks and concomitant policy expectations. Although the bulk of the questions and responses here come from the past thirty years, some data is available stretching as far back as the 1950s.

The primary variable of interest in looking at attitudes surrounding economic risk is the number of children that the respondent helps care for. As in the previous chapter, the most frequently available measure here is the number of children in the respondent's household. The advantages and disadvantages of measuring concern for children in this way mostly carry over from the discussion there to the situation here,[14] though one additional wrinkle is worth emphasizing: This variable was not collected in the

1970, 1994, and 2000 administrations of the NES. This was less relevant in chapter 5: The relevant questions of war and about child gender were not asked in years other than 2004, so the fact that parallel data was unavailable for other years was immaterial. Here, however, this constraint appreciably reduces the sample sizes available. Fortunately, alternative data is available in the years for which the standard information is absent. Most obviously, all three years include information on how many children the respondent had, whether or not those children lived with the respondent.[15] Supplementing the children-in-household data with this alternative measure when it is the only one available does not substantively change any of the conclusions of the analysis here; I use the smaller data set for consistency across chapters.

Another issue raised by this measurement is how risk and policy attitudes might be expected to change for different numbers of children. It could plausibly be that the important circumstance is whether or not a respondent has (any number of) children in the household but that once children were around, the precise number of children was unimportant; that is, parents differ from nonparents, but parents with large families and those with small families are fundamentally similar. Some family processes do operate like this, as with the birth-order discussion in chapter 4 (where the theory and prior literature emphasized the importance of having *any* older-sibling model but did not imply that additional older siblings pushed the effect further). But in this case, many of the arguments suggest that having more than one child may compound the effect. The expense of having additional mouths to feed and the need for flexibility in work scheduling are likely to increase when there are more children to take care of. Even the psychological pressure from having more people depending on one's income may increase with additional children. Following this logic, the analyses below report models counting the number of children in the household, not simply a yes/no indicator as to whether there are children. An alternative possibility might allow for nonlinear effects. For example, possible economies of scale in raising children, so that twins do not double the added cost to the family budget that a single child does, would suggest that the difference in perceived economic insecurity would be relatively smaller when comparing five- and six-child households than it would be when comparing zero- and one-child households. While not reported below, alternative models allowing for such possibilities generally produce similar results to those given; I stick with the simpler models for ease of interpretation.

Number of children is not the only thing to be measured, to be sure. The observational nature of the data here obliges us to factor in other circumstances that might have determined both economic risk and the likely number of children that would be in the household. When explaining the number of children, the causal factors are again likely to parallel those from chapter 5 (and, for that matter, the family-size discussion of chapter 4): The same demographic and socioeconomic considerations that came up in that analysis will pertain here. Thus the discussion here focuses more on who is likely to face economic risk—or to presume greater risk even when faced with actually similar circumstances.

Demographic factors are obvious starting points when considering factors that influence economic risks. Younger workers, lacking seniority, are traditionally more likely to be dismissed from their jobs when layoffs occur,[16] while older workers may worry it will be difficult to find an acceptable new job, with the higher health-insurance costs they typically present to employers and new technologies that render established skills obsolete.[17] Fears of discrimination may similarly heighten economic insecurity for racial or ethnic minorities, as well as women. Even without having to worry about future discrimination, these groups may have less access to the social connections that expedite the finding of a new or higher-paying job: Certainly, women and minority groups are in practice disproportionately likely to end up relying on many welfare-state programs.

Conversely, even independently of children's expense reducing the size of one's savings, individuals vary in how much savings they would have. Those with higher incomes are likely to be able to squirrel away more money, since a smaller proportion of their income will go to necessities. The costs borne and skills obtained through education, similarly, are likely to shape savings behavior even independently of education's potential effect on income. Contextual factors also influence economic prospects. Geographically, more diversified urban or regional economies can reduce the riskiness of their economic lives, while temporally the prosperous 1950s present a different environment from the stagflation of the 1970s or various deep recessions.

Finally, consider the role of religion. People of more intense religious faith may differ in their assessment of economic risks, whether because economic considerations are less important in their contemplations or because they have confidence that a higher power will provide even in the worst of times. Deep religious belief may then soften the psychological blow of unemployment.[18] Social connections through formal organized religion may additionally provide insurance against hardship, which further modifies the grounds for concern about potential uncertainty.[19] Religiosity is tricky as a potential causal variable because it poses the danger of getting causation backward. Put another way, it may be that attitudes toward risk *cause* religion, either because personality types that choose risky life trajectories are systematically less likely to be religious[20] or because a feeling of uncertainty may cause one to turn to religious certainties or consolations as a balm.[21] While religion is worth controlling for, then, some caution is required when interpreting relevant results.

With the stage now set for the models, the next sections turn to discussing specific variables that children may affect by way of economic insecurity—and to testing to see whether those effects actually hold.

ECONOMIC INSECURITY

As discussed above, establishing the first step in the causal mechanism leading from having children to specific preferences over economic policy requires assessing respondents' confidence in their own economic position. The NES most directly covers this concept with a question concerning employment risks. Since wages derived from employment are the primary income source for most American households and, along with ancillary benefits of employment such as pension plans, the linchpin of their overall economic security, this is a plausible means of getting at how certain people feel about their economic prospects. Better still, this question focuses squarely on negative shocks to their economic prospects, which are particularly relevant to reliance on the welfare state (compared to positive shocks to income such as lottery jackpots or sudden increases in salary) and likely, given people's tendency toward loss aversion, to weigh most heavily when respondents respond to uncertainty.[22]

The basic question text is "How worried are you about losing your job in the near future: a lot, somewhat, or not much at all?"[23] As this wording suggests, the NES offers three choices for how worried respondents are about their employment: "a lot," "somewhat," or "not much at all." These are coded here so that higher levels of uncertainty mean higher values of the variable. That is, those who say they worry "a lot" receive 3 points on the uncertainty scale, while those who report "not much" worry get a score of 1.

Although this question about employment directly gets at a substantial portion of economic security issues, it touches on other dimensions of economic security less directly. As an alternative measure, then, the models below also consider another potential source of economic insecurity: health issues. In particular, other models consider responses to the question "In the past year did you (or anyone in your family living here) put off medical or dental treatment because you didn't have the money?"[24] This speaks to respondents' having faced unexpected expenses that they were unable to cover, which may indicate greater likelihood of future costs the respondent cannot afford (or the fear of such outlays). It is a simple yes/no question, coded here so that those answering "yes" have a higher score: As with the other question, higher values of the coding associate with greater economic insecurity. It correlates positively but relatively weakly[25] with the job-insecurity measure, indicating that the two variables pick up on some of the same concepts yet also reflect different processes.

Figure 6.1 shows the model estimates. The top panel shows reduced models controlling only for year of survey in looking at the effect of the variable of interest. Using either measure of economic insecurity, those with children appear to be in a more parlous economic state: Each additional child corresponds to a 0.06 units (on a 3-point scale) increase on the job-insecurity scale. Though this difference is not large on its face, it is statistically very easy to distinguish from zero and adds up across many children.[26] A similar pattern holds for the likelihood of delaying medical treatment. There, the model predicts that each additional child raises by around four percentage points the probability of having had to postpone medical treatment for economic reasons. This estimated effect, too, is easy to distinguish statistically from zero.

Figure 6.1's bottom panel brings in the control variables. Beginning as usual with the graph on the left, additional children in the household continue to be associated with expected increase in expressions of worry about having a job. Each extra child in the household raises the predicted average feeling of job insecurity by a little over 0.03 (on the 3-point scale), about half the effect in the top panel. Even this smaller coefficient estimate is

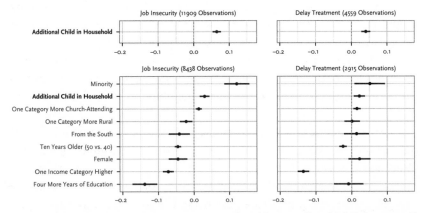

Figure 6.1 Indicators of economic insecurity, in reduced (top panel) and full (bottom panel) models. Bars show 95% confidence intervals. Positive numbers indicate greater sense of insecurity.

precise enough to have its entire 95% confidence interval on the positive side of zero, however. The 0.03-point coefficient is also substantively significant; it implies that the effect of having an additional child on job security is roughly the same as having one less year of formal education, or that having two additional children increases job insecurity by as much as does falling by one income category on the 5-point scale.

The results for the control variables themselves are generally as would be expected. Race and ethnicity have a very strong effect on feelings of insecurity, with non-Hispanic whites far less concerned about their job-market prospects than others. Richer and better-educated respondents are also less worried. Regional differences also turn up, with those in the South and in rural areas feeling more confident about their jobs. Those who attend church more frequently, however, feel less confident (perhaps because, as suggested above, people turn to religion as balm and solace when they have economic anxieties).

Finally, the bottom-right panel of Figure 6.1 shows results from the models predicting the alternative measure of economic insecurity, delaying medical treatment for financial reasons. Fewer of the variables attain standard levels of statistical significance, as might be expected with the much smaller sample size, but having more children in the household is one of the exceptions still having an effect statistically distinguishable from zero. As with the other three graphs in the figure, having more children associates with reduced economic security; as with the job-insecurity measure, children's effect falls somewhat upon the introduction of the control variables. Still, the effect compares respectably in size to those of the control variables; two additional children, for example, have roughly the same predicted influence as does being a non-Hispanic white.

While this higher propensity to delay medical care could be because the inherently larger household wrought by having more children around simply means it is more likely that someone required medical care to begin with, the end result is still that children increased one measure of household economic inadequacy. Potentially increased medical costs themselves are, in other words, part of the insecurity that comes with children. In any case, circumstantial evidence suggests that the effect of children on this measure of insecurity is not simply a matter of household size, as increasing the number of adults in the household has a smaller and far less statistically significant effect.

Whether economic insecurity is measured as worry about job loss or as inability to pay for important services, then, it appears to be more common among those with children. The next step is to see how, if at all, this effect of children carries over into insecurity-linked political attitudes.

POLITICAL ATTITUDES

While perceptions of economic insecurity can be of interest in their own right,[27] typically their relevance for political discussions is less direct, coming from their implications for other attitudes and preferences. This section focuses on two kinds of attitudes that have more prominent roles in political discourse. The first of these is attitudes toward economically disadvantaged groups, and the second concerns trust in government institutions, in this case the American federal government. These general preferences can naturally reflect a relatively broad set of factors, but increased economic insecurity could plausibly play an important part in shaping them.

Attitudes toward those suffering economic distress is a key determinant of many political beliefs.[28] The NES includes many questions explicitly probing respondents' sympathy toward all sorts of major social groups, from Catholics and Democrats to policemen and the women's liberation movement (as distinct from feminists, who are covered by a separate set of questions). The NES's favored form of this question is a "feeling thermometer," which asks respondents to rate how warmly the respondent feels toward the group in question on a scale from zero to 100. Respondents were prompted to give a score of 50 to those groups about whom they had no strong feelings either way, with scores above 50 indicating a progressively more favorable attitude and scores below 50 indicating progressively more intense dislike.[29]

Two of these thermometers are especially pertinent to economic risks. One asks about attitudes toward welfare recipients ("people on welfare," as the NES typically deems them). Those who worry about their own propensity to suffer economic reverses may be less apt to disdain those taking state aid; those facing few economic risks, by contrast, may find it easier to believe that welfare recipients require assistance only because of their own laziness or failure of character. As a result, if those taking care of children expect to face more chance of lean economic times, they might also be less likely to condemn welfare recipients.

A similar logic may hold for the feeling thermometer seeking respondents' opinions about "poor people," which was asked somewhat more frequently.[30] Alternatively, the logic may not be the same at all: Though this question closely resembles that about welfare recipients on the surface, there is reason to suspect it might produce rather different responses. For one thing, "welfare" has taken on racial overtones in many Americans' minds;[31] it is less clear that poverty and being poor have done so to the same extent. Alternatively, the observed difference in attitudes toward those perceived as "deserving" and "undeserving" poor may connect with the different terms, either because the poor who do not rely on government programs are considered more honorable and independent or because respondents assume that welfare programs' eligibility requirements weed out the less deserving that might fall under the general rubric of poor. The two attitudes, then, might differ despite their undoubted overlap.[32]

A separate consequence of increased economic security may be a turn toward the government as a refuge. Much of the broad economic debates between left and right hinges on the tendency for those dubious about market outcomes to put more faith in the government. States and markets are not always in opposition, of course: One could have confidence in all social institutions, or conversely be skeptical about all sorts of human arrangements. Still, it is psychologically comforting in times of uncertainty to have a rock on which to lean, and the government offers one possible repository for faith. This is hinted at by the increased clamor for tariffs and other government trade barriers in time of recession or when the global economy is seen to be volatile. The potential for such a turn toward the government is further worth exploring because of the association between trust in government and other core political beliefs.[33]

The NES measures trust in government through an index that equally weights responses toward each of four questions:

- "How much of the time do you think you can trust the government in Washington to do what is right?"
- "Would you say the government is pretty much run by a few big interests looking out for themselves or that it is run for the benefit of all the people?"
- "Do you think that people in the government waste a lot of money we pay in taxes, waste some of it, or don't waste very much of it?"
- "Do you think that quite a few of the people running the government are crooked, not very many are, or do you think hardly any of them are crooked?"

The average of these scores is on the same zero to 100 scale used in the feeling thermometers, with higher values indicating more trust that the government will do what is right, be run for the people, and have little waste and graft. If the risks incumbent on raising children increase trust in government, then, there should be a positive association between children and this measure.[34]

One striking feature of the attitudes covered here, most pointedly on the feeling thermometers, is the stark variance across racial and ethnic groups.[35] Indeed, the difference in attitudes across these groups looms so large that it is hard to display on the same diagram as are other variables' effects: Any scale that accommodates that effect size in the coding used for the other models in this chapter tends to make other effects and confidence intervals illegibly small. To make the models more readable, then, the indicator of being from a non-white or Hispanic group is coded as being on a 2-point scale (those who deem themselves white take a value of zero; everyone else gets a score of 2), which has the effect of halving the estimated effect size.[36] With this coding peculiarity in mind, Figure 6.2 presents the model results.

In the upper panel of the figure, each additional child in the household consistently has effects that can be distinguished from zero with great confidence. The predicted effect size is approximately a half-point increase in respondents' feeling thermometer toward welfare recipients, a two-fifths point increase in feelings toward the poor, and a four-fifths point increase in government trust. In all three cases, then, the tendency for those with children to have more sympathy for those who suffer, or offer insurance against, economic insecurity.

The story is different when looking at the bottom panel. Although the direction of the effect always remains the same as in the top panel, the size and statistical significance of that effect varies more. For attitudes toward welfare recipients, the effect of having children more than doubles when compared to the model without control variables. For the attitudes toward the poor, however, the control variables tend to reduce the predicted effect of children in the household. These two results, moreover, are statistically distinguishable from zero only with relatively lenient standards of confidence.

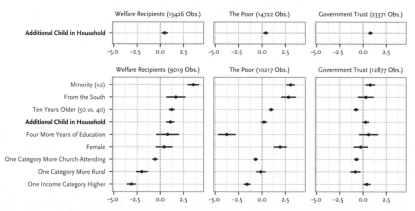

Figure 6.2 Indicators of insecurity-influenced political attitudes, in reduced (top panel) and full (bottom panel) control variables. Bars show 95% confidence intervals. Positive numbers indicate a more positive attitude toward the social group or government.

Child-rearing is not the only factor whose effects on sentiments toward welfare recipients and on sentiments toward the poor diverge. While several variables do have relatively constant effects across the two attitudes—non-white groups, older respondents, and Southerners are consistently more positive, while the rich and more frequent participants in religious services are consistently more negative—other variables seem to reflect differently on welfare recipients than on the poor. Women, for example, feel relatively warmly toward the poor but are hard to distinguish from men when considering welfare recipients; rural residence, by contrast, makes little difference in feelings about the poor but associates with harsher judgments toward welfare recipients. Increasing education is more striking still, tending to produce a slightly more positive view of those on welfare but a starkly worse view toward the poor. While it is thus reasonable that children might have differential effects on parents' views of the poor and on welfare recipients—and, to foreshadow the results of the next section, the difference will reverberate into different attitudes toward spending on the two groups—the reasons for the precise difference seen is unclear. It could be perhaps because the several welfare programs that are targeted toward families and children create associations where the typical welfare recipient is more likely to be seen as having children, producing a sense of affinity between respondents who care for children and welfare recipients.

Finally, Figure 6.2's lower-right graph, considering respondent trust in the government, produces results like those seen in attitudes toward the poor. Having more children does continue to relate to having more trust in government when control variables are added to the model, although the effect is slight in substantive terms and only marginally statistically significant. The model predicts that each child in the household increases government trust by about one-quarter a point on the 100-point scale. Still, this difference is not so negligible given the limited effect of many other predictors of trust. Two additional children would have a larger estimated effect on government trust than would three additional years of education or a one-category increase in income.

Possibly as a result of the greater sense of economic insecurity, people with children tend to demonstrate both more sympathy for the downtrodden and a greater faith in the government. Bringing these two strands together suggests that caring for more children might lead to increased willingness to allow the government to attempt to tackle problems of poverty and inequality. The next section turns to attitudes toward these sorts of initiatives.

The NES asks several questions about specific policy initiatives that might alleviate problems of economic insecurity or otherwise respond to concerns about the market. The ideal question might follow directly from the perceptions of risk noted above by asking about attitudes toward unemployment insurance, but unfortunately no such question is available in this survey. Three others, though, are present and speak to the same set of issues. Two of them closely follow the thermometer questions reviewed in the previous section. Where those simply asked how people felt about welfare recipients or the poor, though, the set of questions looked at here takes the next step and translates those into attitudes about government spending. How much should the government spend on programs targeting those groups of people? Those questions were not frequently asked in surveys with relevant data on the other questions, but they are supplemented by a model considering respondents' answers to a more frequently asked question about food stamps, a quintessential program targeting those suffering from a patch of economic hardship. All of these follow the traditional logic that increased economic risk—or feeling that such risk is heightened—will increase demand for redistributive, welfare-state institutions.[37]

Just as with attitudes toward the group, these policy preferences should relate to one another yet may show certain differences. Any differences in attitudes between spending on welfare and spending on the poor probably follow the same logic as differences in general opinion of the respective groups. Indeed, the level of correlation between the answers on the two spending questions is almost identical to that on the feeling thermometers: The two do have a positive correlation but only a moderate one. Feelings about food-stamp spending tend to correlate somewhat more closely with spending on welfare than with spending on the poor.

The question text was "Should federal spending on welfare programs be increased, decreased or kept about the same?" with appropriate wording substituted in for "welfare programs" when asking about "aid to poor people" or "food stamps." The responses are all coded so that higher values indicate a preference for greater spending on the associated program (and so, by the logic sketched above, should correlate with having more children to take care of). Although these questions closely interrelate in their substance, the samples who faced the variants are quite different. The NES included the food-stamps query throughout the 1980s and 1990s but discontinued it after 2000, while the other questions only started in 1992 and continued through 2008.

The question's explicit invocation of *federal* spending bears some emphasis. While the logic and evidence of the previous sections implied that child-rearers might be more willing to accept government intervention in economic outcomes, very little of the discussion pointed to a specifically federal focus. The logic held more generally to public spending by any sort of government, and the data only lightly touched on the federalism issue (with a single one of the four questions comprising the government-trust index specifying "the government in Washington"). There is little reason to believe that the mechanisms under discussion do not apply to specifically federal spending, and so it is reasonable to suppose that these questions should reflect underlying attitudes toward the poor and to government institutions. The specification of federal spending nevertheless has the potential to bring in other issues, injecting some noise into these policy questions as measurements of the concepts at issue.

Figure 6.3 presents the model results. When considering welfare spending as such, living with more children associates with a small uptick in the preferred federal spending level for both the model with and without control variables. That uptick measures in each case between 0.03 and 0.04 points (per child) on the 3-point scale. The 95% confidence interval on this estimate does very slightly spill over into the area below zero when control variables are included,[38] although the low confidence stems in part from the relatively small sample size—the estimated effect size is actually larger than in the model without control variables.[39] In substantive terms, the effect of each additional child is around one-third of the size of the gender gap or the effect of changing income by one category.

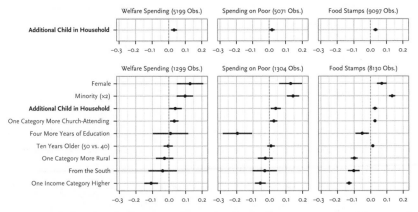

Figure 6.3 Indicators of insecurity-influenced policy preferences, in reduced (top panel) and full (bottom panel) models. Bars show 95% confidence intervals. Positive numbers indicate greater willingness to spend more on the policy in question.

The effect of children in the middle column of the figure, looking at spending on the poor, is almost identical to that on welfare spending. The estimated effect once more implies that having more children correlates with preferring higher levels of spending. Both with and without control variables, the effect clears, if not by much, the threshold for 95% confidence. These estimated effects do diverge somewhat in size; including control variables causes the effect of each additional child to roughly double, from 0.02 to 0.04 points. The effect is sizable compared to that for some other significant attitudinal influences; an additional child is, for instance, expected to change opinions on spending on the poor by approximately as much as would a two-thirds unit increase in income.

Opinions about food-stamp spending, considered in the final column of Figure 6.3, yet again show an association between more children and more willingness to countenance relevant expenditure. The effect holds steady at 0.03 points per child, which the much larger sample sizes than in other columns of the table carry easily past benchmarks of statistical significance. Here, each additional child has roughly the same effect as two more years of education, so that two additional children have a comparable effect to being female rather than male.

The underlying substantive relationship among Figure 6.3's variables is reflected in the stability of effect of many of the predictor variables, not just the number of children. Minority groups, especially racial or ethnic minorities, as well as more frequent attenders of religious services are apt to want greater spending across all these issues, while the rich consistently prefer less spending. More centrally relevant to the argument here, though, is the remarkable consistency by which children appear to affect preferences over social welfare policies. Across all three outcome variables, those living with children saw virtually identical increases in their estimated average support for relevant federal spending. Although this change is relatively small, especially on a per-child basis, it is large enough to be appreciable.

CONCLUSION

Those taking care of children, then, seem to report greater feelings of economic insecurity. They also, perhaps in consequence, express relatively more sympathy for some classes of those who struggle economically and often voice greater support for welfare-state spending. Like the birth-order results in chapter 4, this effect of family composition finds a suggestive echo in large-scale historical and policy trends: The social consensus favoring welfare spending was at its strongest in the immediate postwar decades, just when the baby boom meant that the number of children was at its twentieth-century peak. The expansions of the American welfare state in that era—reaching their peak of ambition in Lyndon Johnson's Great Society programs—may have been more politically palatable at that time, precisely because there were so many children around to stoke concerns about economic insecurity. Conversely, as families have grown smaller over the ensuing decades, support for welfare programs has receded.

One interesting undercurrent about the central finding of this chapter is that it pulls against an oft-mooted theory that parenthood tends to pull people politically rightward,[40] which would typically associate with less support for funding the welfare state. However, it is possible to reconcile the two ideas: Like support for social insurance, conservatism is often associated with a feeling of threat.[41] This may suggest that parents' increased welfare liberalism might be canceled out in their overall ideology by increased conservatism in other issue areas, so that in broad measures of political alignment parents may look similar to nonparents even though that average similarity conceals dimensions of difference.

Hence the ideas under discussion in this chapter do not merely have relevance for welfare and its concomitants. They also connect to several other aspects of political decision making. To consider a link to the questions taken up in chapter 5, if those rearing children are more sensitive to threats more generally and not simply in the economic sphere, they may have distinctive perceptions of war, terrorism, and foreign policy questions. Threat and security are central to these issues, after all, and circumstances that predispose people to an anxious psychology shape relevant attitudes.[42] The challenges confronted when raising children can shape adults' outlooks across the field of politics.

CHAPTER 7

Conclusion: It's All Relatives

The analyses in the previous chapters have touched on a wide range of potential effects that parents, siblings, and children might have on political attitudes. One aim of this is to push studies of family effects further beyond predictions of simple convergence toward parents' and spouses' personal political views. It is time to take stock and review some of the other familial effects explored throughout the book.

WHAT HAVE WE LEARNED?

Parents do more than talk to their children about political beliefs. They also take actions, and those actions affect children both by serving as a model and by affecting the choices available to those children. Chapter 2 suggests that this sort of less direct shaping of political preferences can matter, even when allowing that parents' political orientations may explain their actions. The results found when looking at mothers' labor-force decisions tend to support this idea: Those whose mothers worked outside the home express more left-leaning policy preferences in domestic policy areas. While this finding must be tentative, with the data available having only very blunt measures of parental attitudes, it indicates the childhood environment, whether inside or outside the home, might be a promising place to look for things other than the explicit messages and opinions that parents hold.

Chapters 3 and 4 look at one of those childhood-environment characteristics: siblings. Of course, siblings are more than mere childhood appendages; they are usually an important presence in people's lives into adulthood, for better or worse. To show that siblings can really matter for political preferences, chapter 3 used the quasi-experiment of the next-older sibling's sex as an influence on ideology. It did indeed turn out that female older siblings systematically associate with more left-wing views, although this did not translate into statistically significant effects on partisanship or candidate preference. Siblings' effects similarly shade opinions over the more specific issue of the desirability of government intervention in the economy. Particularly on the basic public–private trade-off, those whose next-older sibling is female are more likely to express preferences aligning with the female side of the gender gap. There is some provisional evidence that these effects are stronger when the two siblings are closer in age, though with the data available this can be at best speculative.

With some reassurance that siblings actually can drive effects, chapter 4 turns to birth order and attitudes toward issues relating to sexuality. Firstborn children have long been found to be less adventurous in their adolescences, starting sexual activity later and more cautiously. As this hints, firstborn children are also less acceptant of nontraditional sexual activities and policies: They are less tolerant of premarital sex—and possibly homosexual activities as well—and generally more supportive of policies regulating abortion, teenage access to contraception, and gay rights.

Chapter 5 moves on to look at how children influence their parents and other guardian figures. It in particular looks at attitudes toward war and foreign policy, considering whether parents have the greater appetite for war that their putatively longer time horizons might suggest, and whether the differential exposure to overseas conflicts of men versus women cause guardians of boys to shy away from militaristic attitudes. These patterns do seem to be the case, especially for father figures. Parents are generally more concerned about nuclear proliferation than are nonparents, while differences between parents of the two sexes emerge in several places—even in the prioritization of fighting terrorism, where the basic theories laid out in the chapter did not obviously lead to an expectation of difference. Less surprisingly, parents of boys were more inclined to isolationism, more keen on diplomatic intervention if there was to be overseas involvement and more skeptical about the net benefit of the wars in Iraq and Afghanistan.

Chapter 6 continues the focus on children while turning back to the domestic sphere, considering how children affect their parents' economic insecurity and hence their support for social insurance. With the multiple channels through which children increase the precariousness, real and psychological, of their parents' economic positions, it seems possible that parents, regardless of their current financial position, might demand greater protection from economic reverses than do the otherwise similar childless—and so it seems, with parents being slightly more likely to demand income-security programs such as food stamps or welfare spending. These spending preferences move with broader attitudes as well, as parents express more sympathy for welfare recipients (if not for the poor more broadly) and more trust in the government.

As noted in chapter 1, the theories considered in these chapters aim for mostly modest extension of ideas that are either well grounded in the literature (younger siblings' tendency to engage in more early sexual behavior, women's propensity to be more supportive of government intervention in markets, the way that gender can reveal children's effects on parental opinions) or rest on conventional intuitions (such as the increased caution of those who care for children). This aims to demonstrate that family variables can enhance many literatures and interests that are already widespread. But equal, perhaps even greater, potential exists for more creative thinking about how families affect behavior. Given that there are things one might not do where one's parents can see, do politicians—whose political acts are often of necessity performed in full view of the public—behave differently after their parents are dead?[1] Perhaps this applies to only less religious politicians or those from religions with less personalistic views of the afterlife, who may be less concerned with parental monitoring even from the grave. Does having longer-lived grandparents increase people's willingness to support spending and public health care for the elderly? Not only would the longer lives increase the likelihood of grandparent–grandchild interactions (the grandparent is more likely to be alive to participate), thus providing a direct-influence motivation for changing attitudes, but any genetic component of life expectancy would mean that the grandchild may also have more cause to draw on resources devoted to the elderly, creating a complementary self-interest motivation for supporting old-age programs.

Then there is the specter that has lurked throughout the book, especially when looking at data unprotected by a quasi-experimental design: What if the stories here are backward, so that it is politics that is causing the family characteristics rather than the other way around? While it is perhaps unlikely that a mother might observe her child to be conservative and so decide to drop out of the paid workforce, there is ample reason to think that some family forces are, in fact, driven by politics.

POLITICS AND THE MAKING OF FAMILIES

Exhibit A in this case is the evidence, discussed in chapter 1, as to how important political orientation seems to be in choosing a mate. While many couples do get together despite political disagreements, it is more common for views to align—so much more common that many sociologists point to political ideology as one of the most powerful characteristics people match on when picking spouses and long-term partners. But it is not simply potential spouses whose treatment responds to political views. Some studies have suggested that political conservatives are more likely to discriminate against their overweight daughters, for instance,[2] and conservatives may also be more likely to spank their children.[3] Political views may be still more deeply related to people's relationships with their children: Those views may partly determine whether they choose to have children to begin with.

The decision to have a child can reflect many psychological states. Of course, not all births are intentional; some may not reflect a conscious decision-making process. Studies find that up to one out of three births in the developed world are unintended or "seriously mistimed" (i.e., born to parents who intended to have children but not for several years).[4] But for those births whose occurrence and timing are planned, the willingness to have children suggests several possible conditions. They may reflect a sense of preparedness, given the considerable commitment of time and resources that will be necessary to care for a child. They may also require a certain optimism: Bringing a child into the world is a more attractive prospect when the future, and hence the child's opportunities, seem brighter. This suggests that conditions driving the demand for children reflect not merely events within the family but also broader social and political life.

For example, many community characteristics appear to influence birthrates. Some of these reflect the returns to having a child. A child born in a context with more opportunities or stability has a greater chance of success in life and so may offer more material or nonmaterial rewards to the parents.[5] Other important community factors seem to indicate social norms, so that associating with others who are having children increases one's own propensity to have children: These sorts of contextual effects may be especially strong in certain subpopulations, such as unmarried parents.[6] These effects of the broader community echo themes seen in individual-level determinants of childbirth. While biological imperative makes parenthood its own reward to some extent, prospective parents are more likely to choose to conceive when they feel that the available resources—financial, temporal, emotional, or community—are sufficient to support a new child.[7] But natality decisions are not deterministic results of economic or sociological circumstances; people vary in their tastes for parenthood, and these variations often reflect political or ideological sentiments.[8] Most previous inquiries into such variation have focused on opinions concerning the proper role of women in society. Nevertheless, there is reason to conjecture that other political opinions and attachments may also influence decisions regarding fertility.

A strong association with a group, and the feeling that one is part of a broader, supportive whole that may come with it, may be part of the psychological support that allows people to take the risk of having children.[9] The psychological benefits of belonging affect several crucial life outcomes: People who belong to and identify with groups tend to live longer and report being generally happier.[10] If these connections are causal, it suggests that people who associate with an organization may have more resources available by being able to draw on the products of group effort. As important, they may *feel* themselves to have those resources, with the psychological reinforcement of having a group of common-minded people as a potential to support. A political party could be one such group, especially with how closely bound many people's identities are to their politics. Strong attachments to and belief in a political party may accordingly forge social connections that encourage fertility. This is especially likely because political parties have several characteristics that enhance group identification even for informal members, such as explicit definition in opposition to other groups.[11]

A political organization may be especially useful in promoting childbirth since it is not merely a group but a group with a vision. One role of political parties is to articulate goals for policy and the country. Committed belief in such shared social goals reduces the prospect of anomie, which is associated with reduced fertility.[12] This suggests that strong ideological commitment to a political party may predispose people to have more children. This holds regardless of the family values or policy position of that party, as seen with the higher fertility rates among intense believers in belief systems that do not explicitly encourage childbearing.[13] Taken from another perspective, political parties typically express at least some views on ideas, policies, and desired outcomes for the future—and an interest in the future is a strong predictor of parenthood.[14]

Alternatively, family life could be a retreat from the world. In this case, it is not clear that membership in a group or investment in particular political outcomes would spur childbearing. Indeed, people could devote more time to the family precisely because no outside organization is providing a sense of community and belonging: Home life could serve as a refuge from indifferent or hostile political circumstances. Alienation from mainstream political groupings, by this theory, may cause people to build private relationships as a substitute for public affairs. This set of ideas connects to various previous observations of politics and society. Some scholars have seen investment in children as a form of social capital building that could substitute for other forms of social capital such as group membership.[15] This is a more moderate version of the marked tendency for family to become a more central part of life in many dictatorships: With limited other outlets for social energies, more resources are available for children and other family activities. Household concerns accordingly come to the fore.[16]

Potential mechanisms thus connect degree of partisan identification to both higher and lower propensities to have children: higher because intense partisan orientation promotes a sense of belonging and a feeling of representation and lower because political involvement may distract from, or substitute for, family life. What happens when these theories collide in the real world? Resolving the direction of the actual effect, if any, of partisan intensity becomes a question that only data can answer.

Figuring out any such relationship calls for political beliefs at the moment of conception—but the moment of conception is a difficult time to quiz people for their political preferences, because (among other reasons) survey-takers have no way to anticipate when that moment is. All most surveys can observe is whether people have children[17] and what their views are *if* they already have children—that is, well after the moment of conception. The time gap raises serious questions about any possible inference that the views were in place before the birth of the child, for some of the reasons reviewed in previous chapters: Observing that one has had a female child, for instance, might change partisanship per the mechanisms seen in chapter 5. A slightly less precise way to study the relationship between partisanship and fertility would use data over time. If surveys ask respondents in successive years what their political beliefs are and whether they have children, we can compare the political beliefs in one year with having newborn children in the following years. This requires a large data set, since relatively few households have children in most years, but it can speak to relationships between partisanship and fertility.

Large data sets that track both political sentiment and household structure are, as repeatedly despaired about in previous chapters, somewhat uncommon, but one that does is the British Household Panel Survey (BHPS) data set. This study surveys households every year from 1991; the data used here runs through 2007. As members leave households—for example, through teenagers leaving the family home or divorces—the survey tracks them and their co-householders in their new residences in addition to the people who remain in the original households. Panel data has an additional advantage for examining how partisan identification affects behavior: People whose party feeling is unstable over time may react differently to partisan cues than do those with more stable orientations, even if both currently claim the same level of attachment to their party. Those who, over time, consistently feel a very strong attachment to a party may differ from those who profess that strong attachment only fleetingly. With around 10,000 individuals surveyed each year, the BHPS data provides enough observations to distinguish these sorts of effects and to see appreciable numbers of births in any particular year.

When bringing this data to bear on the question of whether partisans are more likely to have children, the first task is figuring out whether the surveyed individual had a child in the past year. The data here does not actually report all new children but only those within the respondent's household. This does overlook a notable fraction of new births. Around 7% of newborns in the sample have one parent (mostly fathers[18]) outside the household, suggesting that a sizable number of adults have new children even if those children would not show up in a survey structured like the BHPS: At least some of the missing parents of those 7% are likely to be alive and know of their children, even though they are not in the survey sample. In addition, adults in the sample could have conceived any number of children that were stillborn or dead as young infants, given up for adoption, or otherwise out of the household of both biological parents. However, if the households sampled here are typical of the contemporary British population, the proportion of such children is fairly small.[19]

The independent variable of interest is how strongly the respondent identifies with a particular political party. In the BHPS, this corresponds to a question in which respondents that have conceded a feeling of greater closeness to one party than to others are asked whether their support for that party is "very strong," "fairly strong," or "not very strong." This produces a 3-point scale of intensity of partisan preference.[20]

As is now thoroughly familiar, several socioeconomic and demographic factors that influence both disposition toward partisan and the likelihood of having children must be controlled for. Perhaps the most important is age (in years). Age is strongly associated with entrenched partisan preferences.[21] In addition, both biological and sociological factors strongly affect the ages at which people are likely to have children. Adolescents and most very young adults do not yet have the interest or independence to support a child.[22] Even starker effects appear among older subpopulations: Many women are unable to conceive children, and relatively few men do so after their forties. In fact, the oldest new parent in the sample is fifty-seven years old. Including older adults in the data set—and there are many, with even some centenarians participating in the BHPS—therefore includes a great deal of data where there appears to be no prospect of childbearing. As an arbitrary cut-off, those sixty years and older are left out of the models (other cut-offs produce similar results).

Other particularly relevant demographic factors include household income, which increases the ability to comfortably provide for a new child and the resources available to devote to political commitments; education, which especially among women is associated with both lower fertility rates and higher political engagement;[23] and whether the individual is in a permanent, long-term relationship (marriage, cohabitation, or civil partnership), which allows more opportunity to have a child and may indicate a social predisposition toward family ties.[24]

In the models reported below, these variables are "lagged," or measured from before the year the new child appears in the survey. The ideal length of the lag is unclear. For most childbirths, one year is the obvious length, since attitudes in 1998 will be the ones most relevant for a 1999 birth. However, in some cases a conception within a few months of the 1998 survey would not show up until the 2000 survey, especially as the timing of the survey sometimes varies from one year to the next. For these cases, a two-year lag would better reflect the actual sequence of events. Models below allow for either possibility by reporting results with lags of either one or two years on the predictor variables.

Figure 7.1 presents the resulting models. Intensity of partisan preference either one (left panel) or two (right panel) years previously has a positive effect, suggesting that the probability of conceiving a child is greater for those who feel closely attached to a party. The result is slightly larger for the model with only a one-year lag. This is foreseeable in the context of the theory, since the one-year lag probably better fits the actual time of conception than does the two-year lag. In magnitude, the effect is more appreciable than it may at first appear. Because having a baby is such an unusual event,[25] even relatively small changes in the probability (such as the changes of around two percentage points [0.02] seen with being married or partnered) translate into substantial increases in the odds of having a child. For example, for a person with average levels of income, education, age, and partnership status and whose partisan affiliation is "not strong at all" has a 2.0% predicted chance of having a child in a year, while someone

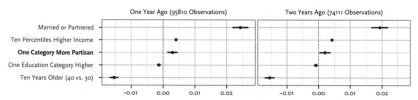

Figure 7.1 Probability of having a new baby in a given year, based on respondent characters one year (left panel) and two years (right panel). Bars indicate 95% confidence intervals.

with maximum attachment to a political party has a 2.6% chance, almost one-third higher. As might be expected, this is smaller than the effect of being in a permanent relationship or of a large swing in age. It does compare to being several percentage points higher on society's income scale, however, or to having a few more categories of education.[26]

This evidence is necessarily open to multiple interpretations. It may indeed be that partisan identification directly enhances people's willingness to have children. It might alternatively (or additionally be) that certain personality types or genetic makeups may be wired to be both more partisan and more interested in having children. It could even be that causation is somewhat backward, where it is not that being partisan makes one have children but it is being pregnant that makes one partisan. Given the hormonal and other biological shifts that occur during pregnancy—and sometimes spill over into affecting the father's blood chemistry[27]—partisanship seeming to precede childbirth may in fact stem from still earlier changes in household arrangements. No matter which story holds, though, it suggests connections between the family and having children that bear further study.

MOVING FORWARD

The conclusion to the partisanship–fertility question is therefore open. So, too, are many of the analyses throughout the book—and other promising possibilities not considered here, such as possible effects that family might have on behavior (such as voting) as well as on attitudes.[28] The plaints that relative data were not often seen in surveys have by this final chapter become almost an incantation. This is not entirely the irrepressible scholarly reflex to conclude that "further research is needed," even for topics that are already exhaustively studied. It is simply the case that relatively few surveys cover the intersection of family and political opinion. Sociologists and developmental psychologists considering family structure are generally unconcerned with broader political attitudes, while economists' and political scientists' treatment of family tends to be perfunctory, with a question about marital status often being the only appearance of kin in a questionnaire. Obviously, not every study needs to gather a great deal of costly data about sisters and cousins and aunts, since researchers can pursue questions for which those relations are not relevant enough to be worth the cost of information gathering. The results from the previous chapters might caution, though, that the range of substantive questions for which family members are "not relevant enough" may be smaller than previous research has assumed.

With so few alternative data sources to serve as a cross-check, all of the questions throughout this book must remain unsettled. While many of the results are suggestive, and at times there are whole constellations of findings that provide circumstantial evidence in favor of some deeper pattern, the paucity of available data always allows for flukes to determine result. While the confidence intervals presented throughout can give some sense of the likelihood that the findings are simply the result of a lucky random sample, other contaminating factors can undetectably creep in. It is impossible to know if results hinge on a particular question wording, to take one obvious hazard, unless one has multiple question wordings across which to compare results. While the analyses here tried to allow for these sorts of possibilities by considering related questions and wordings (e.g., attitudes toward premarital sex *and* cohabitation, questions about whether the war in Iraq *and* the war in Afghanistan were worthwhile), the limited palette of survey items in one survey or two will always allow more scope for alternative explanations than would having more surveys. Diminishing marginal returns have not yet set in when looking at how politics and family interact.

A possibly larger reason for better understanding of that interaction is that family may in fact underpin other, seemingly unrelated phenomena across the social sciences. The judgment of the scholarly community could well be that potential links between family and political attitudes do not inspire curiosity—that would be an obvious reason why they have received relatively little study in the past. Even if they do not hold direct interest, though, the political effects of family structures and relatives' behavior matters. With all the other opportunities and beliefs that come with being a member of a particular family, with connections to particular kinfolk, relatives contribute to many life outcomes. If those relatives are also through their actions creating particular political outlooks, then apparent links between the life outcomes and the political outlooks may be masking the real, underlying effects of family.[29] Relatives—and not just parents and spouses—have unexplored potential as the source of many real-world regularities in political attitudes.

APPENDIX: STATISTICAL MODELS AND TECHNICAL DETAILS

As mentioned in chapter 1, all presented models in the text are linear (ordinary least squares) models. This sort of model, by simply assuming straight-line relationships, treats the variables that are being predicted as though they can take any possible value—as though they are "continuous." Many of the variables predicted throughout this book, though, are "discrete," taking only a limited number of possible values. For chapter 4's question inquiring whether women should be allowed to get an abortion on demand, respondents really have only two possible substantive responses, "yes" or "no."

When social scientists try to make predictions about this sort of variable with only two (or, more generally, a limited number of) choices, the standard statistical approach frowns on linear models, for two main reasons. One is that fitting a line to a variable that can only take a limited number of values almost always makes impossible predictions. If a survey question can only be answered with "yes" (traditionally coded as 1) or "no" (zero), any straight line that allows for values of both zero and 1 will necessarily make predictions that are in between those two values (a single line cannot jump between the two points). These values, though not possible answers on the survey, can perhaps be read as probabilities: A prediction of 0.5 indicates a 50% chance that the answer is zero and a 50% chance the answer is 1, while a prediction of 0.1 means that there is only a 10% chance the answer is 1. But this solution breaks down, given that lines extend infinitely. A line, being infinite, will also extend beyond those two possible values: Any line[1] that gets from zero to 1 over some distance will eventually get to 2, then to 3, and so on. A predicted 200% probability of answering 1 is nonsensical, so it is not obvious how to read these sorts of predictions if the only possible answers on the original question were zero and 1. In consequence, social scientists often prefer models that constrain predicted values to be between zero and 1, which guarantees that no absurd predictions of negative or overlarge values can arise.

The second standard reason for preferring nonlinear models is somewhat more technical. The underlying argument is that when we think in terms of probabilities, an effect of a fixed size can have quite different meanings depending on the context. If something is a rare event that happens only one time in 100, an increase of two percentage points (0.02) in that probability is a dramatic change, tripling the likelihood of the event happening (from 0.01 to 0.03). But that same 0.02 change has much less impact for more common events; the difference between a 40% probability and a 42% probability does not represent a tripling of likelihood.[2] If something is so substantial as to triple the likelihood in one context, the traditional intuition is that it should have a more than piffling influence on the odds of the outcome occurring in other contexts too. This logic recommends finding mathematical functions that rise more slowly at 0.01 than at 0.40 and which flatten out again at 0.97 (where a two percentage point increase would decrease the chance of something *not* happening by a hefty two-thirds).

Alas, functions with this "S-shaped" characteristic tend to be complicated, hard to interpret, and daunting for the uninitiated.[3] Still, if a model produces more accurate, useful predictions, it is worth battling through technical complications. Statisticians have formulated several readily available varieties of model that both stay within prescribed ranges and have the desired S shape. Standard statistical software makes it very easy to implement these models, most frequently logistic ("logit") or probabilistic ("probit") regressions or, when the predicted variable has more than two categories, their "ordered" variants. Models of these forms have been standard throughout the social sciences since computing power developed to allow them instead of linear models.

Why, then, do this book's models flout this easy to implement, standard model form in favor of linear models? The answer stems from the (in practice) very limited benefits and substantial costs of adopting nonlinear models. First, consider the benefits. The S shape of classic nonlinear models may mimic a plausible trajectory with the largest effect sizes occurring in the middle parts of the distribution, but in practice, few predictions typically cover both the middle and the extremes of a range. Unless a predictor variable has an extraordinarily large effect on the outcome being predicted, its predictions will cover only a range where the nonlinear estimator has a relatively constant slope: in other words, where it is nearly linear. In fact, the transformations like those in a logit or probit model typically change predicted values and effect sizes by very little from those produced by a linear model.[4]

To make this more concrete, consider the example of chapter 6's variable about the predicted likelihood of delaying medical treatment for financial reasons. As one might expect, this is mostly an issue for poorer segments of the population. Across the five income groups in the data, the proportion of respondents who report having postponed treatment falls successively from 49.2% in the lowest income group to 41.1%, 30.0%, 15.8%, and 7.6%. This is an unusually powerful relationship, and one centered around one of the most nonlinear parts of an S-curve, where the curve goes from the relatively low slope of the range near zero to the maximally steep curve around 50%. Nevertheless, predicting this variable as a function of income produces quite similar results using either a linear (which would produce predictions of 50.9%, 39.8%, 28.6%, 17.5%, and 6.3%, respectively) or a logistic model (53.0%, 39.3%, 27.0%, 17.5%, and 10.9%). The largest divergence between the two predictions, in the top income category, is possible because this category is much the rarest, with less than a third of the observations of the second smallest category. Note, too, that predictions of the logistic regression model have a larger error for *every* income group. That poor performance by a logistic model is not a general result but simply the happenstance of this particular model. Yet the supposed technical superiority of the logistic model does not guarantee or even necessarily encourage better or more accurate predictions; in cases like this, it produces markedly worse predictions.

Note, too, that these predictions are all between zero and 1 and so straightforward to interpret as probabilities. This is typical: While it is true that a model that produced large numbers of predictions outside the range of possible values would be suspicious, standard linear models tend to do little of this. By mathematical construction, average estimates lie close to the average observed value in the data, and linear models tend to bias predicted effects downward,[5] keeping predictions disproportionally within the possible range. Hence, while it is certainly possible to produce implausible results with linear models, it tends to be a relatively minor problem. (Confidence intervals more often extend to impossible values, but interpreting them substantively as extending only over the possible range is not difficult.)

It is in any event unclear why the precision of individual predictions matters greatly. It may be true that we can extrapolate to implausible conditions to produce ludicrous predictions (where the regression predicts that a variable that can only be zero or 1 is, in fact, 6.7), but the primary aim in this book, like in most social science, is to test hypothetical *relationships*, not to forecast individual values. That is, the concern is for the effect of a *change* in a particular predictor variable. For this purpose, neither linear nor nonlinear models make inherently impossible predictions, so the benefit of restricting possible predicted values is minor.

What about the costs of nonlinear models? One consideration is that models like logit and probit function poorly when confronted with batteries of categorical/discrete predictor variables, especially if there are large numbers of categories and so relatively few observations in any one category. If all observations in a particular predictor-variable category also belong to the same outcome category, the nonlinear models cannot be estimated, and so they simply discard any affected observations. For example, in chapter 2's models, there are many possible categories of father's occupation or of place of childhood residence. When all respondents whose father had a given occupation also share feelings about women's proper role, they will be systematically excluded from any ordered logit or probit models. This not only throws away information but does so in a way that raises possibilities of selection bias. Models with many such categories are also simply difficult to estimate: Algorithms that calculate the likelihood of a particular set of predictions often fail to converge, leading to dubious predictions.

Besides this, nonlinear models are notoriously murky in making predictions where one predictor variable is allowed to influence the effect of another—models with "interactions," in the usual social-science jargon. (These are seen in various chapters of the book, as when in chapter 3 the models explore whether siblings who are several years apart in age see similar effects to those who are less widely spaced.) Methodologists have long warned that nonlinear models often produce inconsistent results regarding interactions—to the point where even within an individual sample different observations will be predicted to have diametrically opposed effects.[6] Nor does dividing the sample into subgroups and running separate nonlinear models on each subgroup circumvent this problem: This, too, typically produces inconsistent, noncomparable results, unless models are constructed to avoid these problems instead of to test the substantive hypothesis they were originally meant to.[7] These are extreme examples of the general opacity of nonlinear models, extending beyond the general difficulty in interpreting their coefficients. Linear regressions sidestep most of these issues. Even when dealing not with interactions but with simple effects, the assumptions built into models like logit and probit are often more questionable than the assumptions of a standard linear regression.[8]

For all these reasons, the supposed superiority of nonlinear models is doubtful at best. Nor is this a wholly idiosyncratic conclusion; other (though by no means all) analysts, including some very sophisticated methodologists,[9] are also adopting an approach of reporting linear results even when recent convention would dictate using a nonlinear model. This does not imply that nonlinear models have no value. They serve as a valuable check as to whether models are sensitive to the precise specification and assumptions imposed by linear models. Accordingly, though all the reported models in the main text's figures are ordinary least squares regressions, the following tables also provide parallel (ordered) logistic regressions for each model.

Throughout, coefficients in bold are statistically distinguishable from zero with 95% confidence (two-tailed). For variable definitions and descriptions for the key variables of interest in a table, see the main text; measurement of control variables, however, is explained more thoroughly below. Note that for reporting purposes age squared is always divided by 1,000 so that its coefficients are on a comparable scale to those of other variables.

CHAPTER 2 CONTROL VARIABLES (IN ORDER OF APPEARANCE)

Age is measured using the respondent's self-reported age in years and, to accommodate the possibility that the relationship between age and conservatism may not be linear, the square of the respondent's age. The age variables can be replaced with measures of year of birth without substantively altering the results.

Female, the included control variable for respondent sex, is a simple indicator variable equal to 1 for female and zero for male.

Minority accounts for the influence of different racial or ethnic cultures; its reported specification is an indicator of ethnic (including racial) minority status, equal to 1 for those self-identifying as nonwhite or Hispanic. Breaking the racial categories down further does not make an appreciable difference to the models' estimates on the variables of interest.

Childhood ruralness measures, on a 3-point scale, the urbanization of the respondent's locality of childhood. This is constructed from two separate yes/no questions asking whether the respondent grew up in a rural area and, separately, in a major city. Those who grew up in a rural area and not in a major city get a score of 2; those who grew up in a major city and not in a rural area get a score of zero. Those answering "no" to both questions— who hence grew up in neither a rural area nor a major city—get a score of 1. No respondent is listed as having grown up in both a rural area and a major city, notwithstanding the urban prairies of Detroit.

Survey year is a binary indicator of the election year with which the survey associated. The small proportion of respondents (around 5% overall) who were surveyed early in the calendar year following that of the election are coded as having been surveyed in the prior year.

Place of residence during childhood, to capture the effect of different regional cultures, is a battery of indicator variables, one for each state or country where at least one respondent grew up.

Father's occupation involves a set of thirty-five indicator variables, one for each description of father's job included in the survey. This number of variables is considerably inflated by inconsistency in the coding of paternal occupations across the survey years. Although the data set always groups jobs into broad thematic categories—"executives" or "laborers," say—the number and description of categories changed after the 1976 survey and again (less radically) after the 1982 survey. To allow full flexibility in controlling for the effect of paternal careers, the models below preserve these distinctions and include separate binary indicator variables for each of the coding schemes. That is, one variable indicates those whose fathers in the 1970–1976 surveys were deemed "craftsmen, foremen, and kindred workers," a separate variable indicates those in the 1978–1982 surveys whose fathers were in the substantially similar "craftsmen and kindred workers" category, and so on. Merging similar occupation groups across the survey coding schemes does not substantially affect the reported results, however.

Father Independent, Father Republican, Father other/no party, Mother Independent, Mother Republican, and *Mother other/no party* are six separate zero or 1 variables aiming to capture parental ideology/partisanship. Democrats are the omitted category for each parent and hence serve as the baseline against which the other coefficients should be read. A single battery of indicator variables indicating both parents' partisan identifications, allowing for interaction between mothers' and fathers' political affiliations, produces very similar results.

Nativeborn parents is an indicator noting whether both parents were born in the United States. Accordingly, foreign origins are measured with an indicator variable showing if either parent was born abroad.

Ruralness of residence, like *childhood ruralness*, is measured on a 3-point scale but is constructed differently. In adulthood, the National Election Study bases place ruralness on objective characteristics of the place where the respondent resides, not through any sort of subjective question put to the respondent. In decreasing order of population density, places are coded as one of "central city," "suburban areas," or "rural, small towns, outlying and adjacent areas." Reported results treat the various levels as ranked in order as listed, even though suburbs might not be halfway between central cities and rural areas in their effects. Using a more flexible coding scheme with indicators for each category generally produces similar results.

Income is a five-category measure, based on the respondent's self-reported family income, of position in the survey-year's income distribution. The middle category includes the middle third of the contemporaneous income distribution; the lower two categories equally split the poorer third of the sample, while the top two categories are split unequally such that the richest

5% of the sample is in the top category and the remainder of the top third is in the second-highest category. In dollar terms, category boundaries vary considerably over time; in 1972, for instance, the poorest category included family incomes up to $3,999, while by 1992 twenty years of inflation and economic growth put the upper limit of that same category at $9,999.

Education is a four-category measure, distinguishing those with grade-school educations, those with at least some high school, those with some college but no degree, and those with a college degree.

Church attendance, a proxy for religiosity, is measured in the reported models on a 5-point scale based on frequency of attendance at religious services as a widely available variable capturing both intense religiosity and social factors. A variety of other measures are available for smaller portions of the sample. These include what religion, if any, the respondent professes, measures of attitudes toward God and scripture, and how large a role religion plays in the respondent's daily life. Adding these, or replacing the measure of attendance at religious services with some combination of them, tends not to substantially alter the estimated effects of maternal work (although sometimes the number of observations plummets to the point where estimates become much more uncertain).

Time in community and *time in house* are each measured on a 6-point scale coding number of years of residence; converting these six categories into fractions of life produces similar results.

Table A.2.1.1. FIGURE 2.1 TOP PANEL[a]

	Reported, OLS Models		Ordered Logit Models	
	Ideology	Party ID	Ideology	Party ID
Stay-at-home mother	**0.137** (0.026)	**0.065** (0.030)	**0.188** (0.035)	**0.065** (0.027)
Age	**0.030** (0.004)	**−0.024** (0.005)	**0.044** (0.006)	**−0.024** (0.004)
Age squared/1,000	**−0.236** (0.041)	**0.205** (0.047)	**−0.350** (0.057)	**0.191** (0.047)
Female	**−0.066** (0.023)	**−0.110** (0.028)	**−0.112** (0.032)	**−0.095** (0.025)
Minority	**−0.509** (0.040)	**−0.998** (0.038)	**−0.698** (0.056)	**−0.943** (0.038)
Childhood ruralness	**0.101** (0.020)	**0.163** (0.023)	**0.141** (0.027)	**0.139** (0.021)

OLS = ordinary least squares.
[a] Robust standard errors in parentheses. All regressions also control for survey year, place of residence during childhood, and father's occupation (during respondent's childhood).

Table A.2.1.2. FIGURE 2.1 MIDDLE PANEL[a]

	Reported, OLS Models		Ordered Logit Models	
	Ideology	Party ID	Ideology	Party ID
Stay-at-home mother	**0.114** (0.036)	**0.101** (0.038)	**0.169** (0.051)	**0.109** (0.038)
Age	**0.041** (0.005)	0.001 (0.006)	**0.061** (0.008)	−0.004 (0.006)
Age squared/1,000	**−0.324** (0.056)	−0.025 (0.058)	−0.491 (0.080)	0.004 (0.064)
Female	−0.049 (0.032)	**−0.125** (0.034)	**−0.091** (0.046)	**−0.111** (0.035)
Minority	**−0.523** (0.060)	**−0.796** (0.053)	**−0.727** (0.085)	**−0.847** (0.059)
Childhood ruralness	**0.077** (0.028)	0.027 (0.030)	**0.102** (0.039)	0.010 (0.031)
Father Independent	−0.005 (0.078)	**0.651** (0.084)	0.019 (0.110)	**0.666** (0.079)
Father Republican	0.087 (0.056)	**1.180** (0.066)	0.142 (0.079)	**1.206** (0.068)
Father other/no party	−0.112 (0.097)	**0.369** (0.105)	−0.123 (0.137)	**0.403** (0.106)
Mother Independent	0.145 (0.075)	**0.543** (0.082)	0.198 (0.107)	**0.559** (0.078)
Mother Republican	**0.349** (0.057)	**1.104** (0.067)	**0.482** (0.080)	**1.129** (0.069)
Mother other/no party	0.144 (0.085)	**0.536** (0.091)	0.171 (0.121)	**0.581** (0.094)
Nativeborn parents	**0.117** (0.050)	**0.179** (0.054)	**0.153** (0.070)	**0.190** (0.057)

OLS = ordinary least squares.
[a] Robust standard errors in parentheses. All regressions also control for survey year, place of residence during childhood, and father's occupation (during respondent's childhood).

Table A.2.1.3. FIGURE 2.1 BOTTOM PANEL[a]

	Reported, OLS Models		Ordered Logit Models	
	Ideology	Party ID	Ideology	Party ID
Stay-at-home mother	**0.123** (0.026)	**0.092** (0.033)	**0.169** (0.036)	**0.096** (0.029)
Age	**0.015** (0.005)	**−0.045** (0.005)	**0.021** (0.006)	**−0.045** (0.005)
Age squared/1,000	**−0.115** (0.047)	**0.451** (0.057)	**−0.158** (0.066)	**0.439** (0.055)
Female	**−0.121** (0.025)	**−0.084** (0.031)	−0.196 (0.035)	−0.055 (0.028)
Minority	**−0.363** (0.039)	**−0.859** (0.043)	**−0.501** (0.055)	**−0.874** (0.039)
Ruralness of residence	**0.183** (0.019)	**0.264** (0.024)	**0.243** (0.027)	**0.235** (0.021)
Education	**−0.049** (0.015)	**0.159** (0.020)	**−0.058** (0.022)	**0.199** (0.018)
Income	**0.084** (0.013)	**0.155** (0.016)	**0.120** (0.019)	**0.148** (0.014)
Church attendance	**0.158** (0.009)	**0.061** (0.011)	**0.223** (0.012)	**0.041** (0.010)
Time in community	0.013 (0.009)	**−0.031** (0.010)	0.015 (0.012)	**−0.031** (0.009)
Time in house	0.003 (0.013)	−0.008 (0.015)	0.006 (0.018)	−0.013 (0.014)

OLS = ordinary least squares.
[a] Robust standard errors in parentheses. All regressions also control for survey year and state of residence at the time of survey.

Table A.2.2.1. FIGURE 2.2 REPORTED ORDINARY LEAST SQUARES MODELS[a]

	Woman's Role	Egalitarianism	Abortion Policy	Government Spending	Defense Spending
Stay-at-home mother	**−0.238**	**−0.563**	**−0.108**	**−0.188**	0.059
	(0.045)	(0.176)	(0.024)	(0.064)	(0.053)
Age	−0.006	−0.002	−0.003	**−0.041**	**0.024**
	(0.007)	(0.026)	(0.003)	(0.010)	(0.008)
Age squared/1,000	−0.106	−0.238	−0.024	**0.339**	**−0.211**
	(0.076)	(0.256)	(0.035)	(0.104)	(0.084)
Female	**−0.084**	**0.424**	−0.014	**0.367**	**−0.191**
	(0.042)	(0.163)	(0.021)	(0.059)	(0.049)
Minority	0.107	**2.993**	**−0.122**	**0.669**	−0.130
	(0.069)	(0.231)	(0.034)	(0.093)	(0.083)
Childhood ruralness	**−0.300**	−0.103	**−0.100**	−0.086	0.071
	(0.037)	(0.146)	(0.018)	(0.053)	(0.043)
Father Independent	0.013	0.405	**0.142**	0.159	0.013
	(0.095)	(0.417)	(0.051)	(0.141)	(0.114)
Father Republican	0.029	−0.207	−0.001	0.005	**0.179**
	(0.071)	(0.305)	(0.036)	(0.102)	(0.082)
Father other/no party	**0.229**	0.402	−0.018	0.045	−0.014
	(0.116)	(0.394)	(0.062)	(0.158)	(0.122)
Mother Independent	0.011	**−1.026**	**−0.100**	**−0.440**	0.007
	(0.089)	(0.410)	(0.050)	(0.134)	(0.113)
Mother Republican	−0.107	**−0.709**	0.003	**−0.295**	0.095
	(0.072)	(0.307)	(0.036)	(0.101)	(0.082)
Mother other/no party	−0.126	**−1.474**	0.024	0.048	0.118
	(0.108)	(0.367)	(0.053)	(0.149)	(0.111)
Nativeborn parents	0.048	−0.233	0.004	0.033	0.063
	(0.065)	(0.251)	(0.033)	(0.090)	(0.078)

[a] Robust standard errors in parentheses. All regressions also control for survey year, place of residence during childhood, and father's occupation (during respondent's childhood).

Table A.2.2.2. FIGURE 2.2 ORDERED LOGISTIC MODELS[a]

	Woman's Role	Egalitarianism	Abortion Policy	Government Spending	Defense Spending
Stay-at-home mother	**−0.206**	**−0.210**	**−0.220**	**−0.172**	0.060
	(0.043)	(0.068)	(0.044)	(0.074)	(0.061)
Age	−0.007	−0.011	−0.007	**−0.048**	**0.031**
	(0.007)	(0.010)	(0.006)	(0.012)	(0.010)
Age squared/1,000	−0.080	−0.028	−0.050	**0.370**	**−0.260**
	(0.070)	(0.098)	(0.066)	(0.124)	(0.096)
Female	−0.005	**0.135**	−0.030	**0.481**	**−0.246**
	(0.039)	(0.064)	(0.039)	(0.071)	(0.057)
Minority	0.065	**1.185**	**−0.342**	**0.982**	−0.035
	(0.065)	(0.090)	(0.063)	(0.111)	(0.093)
Childhood ruralness	**−0.348**	−0.083	**−0.289**	−0.090	0.087
	(0.031)	(0.051)	(0.030)	(0.055)	(0.045)
Father Independent	0.032	0.235	**0.327**	0.269	0.061
	(0.090)	(0.159)	(0.097)	(0.163)	(0.128)
Father Republican	0.049	−0.067	0.077	0.030	**0.217**
	(0.066)	(0.118)	(0.066)	(0.119)	(0.095)
Father other/no party	**0.220**	0.009	−0.142	0.128	0.116
	(0.112)	(0.154)	(0.117)	(0.184)	(0.141)
Mother Independent	0.027	**−0.448**	−0.180	**−0.609**	−0.032
	(0.086)	(0.160)	(0.095)	(0.155)	(0.128)
Mother Republican	−0.068	**−0.306**	0.020	**−0.472**	0.077
	(0.068)	(0.120)	(0.067)	(0.120)	(0.097)
Mother other/no party	−0.084	**−0.528**	0.135	0.053	0.083
	(0.101)	(0.144)	(0.098)	(0.174)	(0.128)
Nativeborn parents	0.047	−0.036	0.030	0.032	0.065
	(0.062)	(0.098)	(0.063)	(0.103)	(0.087)

[a] Robust standard errors in parentheses. All regressions also control for survey year and place of residence during childhood.

CHAPTER 3 CONTROL VARIABLES (IN ORDER OF APPEARANCE)

Female is, as in chapter 2, coded as a simple indicator variable.

Age is measured as age in years. For the same reasons as in chapter 2, age squared is also included whenever age is.

Minority is a binary measure noting whether the respondent claims to be of a nonwhite racial group or to be Hispanic.

Fundamentalism, age 16 is the self-reported measure on a 3-point scale as to whether the respondent's childhood religion was "fundamentalist," "moderate," or "liberal." Treating this as a nominal variable instead of ordinal does not significantly change reported results. In practice, this is a somewhat noisy measure, as the General Social Survey oddly codes all those raised Catholic as "moderate" on this scale and all those raised Jewish (or, more intuitively, in nonreligious households) as "liberal." Several variables concerning adult religion are available without the quirky treatment of Catholics and Jews. Using these alternatives produces similar results to those presented. I present results looking at the fundamentalism of the childhood home solely because of its better fit with the causal logic and the procedure in chapter 2.

Urbanness, age 16 is measured on a 6-point scale, ranging from "nonfarm location in the countryside" to "city of more than 250,000 inhabitants." Combining the nonfarm countryside category with the farm category does not appreciably alter the reported results.

Census division, age 16 is a battery of dummy variables indicating the various possible values of census division (that is, the Census Bureau's nine-part regional classification of US states, not the four-part classification that the Census Bureau calls "regions"). All respondents living outside the United States at age sixteen are grouped into a single category with its own indicator.

Table A.3.1.1. FIGURE 3.1 TOP PANEL[a]

	Reported, OLS Models			(Ordered) Logistic Models		
	Ideology	Party ID	1992 Vote	Ideology	Party ID	1992 Vote
Next-older sister	**−0.162**	−0.077	−0.018	**−0.223**	−0.065	−0.073
	(0.064)	(0.093)	(0.026)	(0.083)	(0.082)	(0.109)
Constant	**4.266**	**2.812**	**0.427**			**−0.296**
	(0.044)	(0.065)	(0.018)			(0.074)

OLS = ordinary least squares.
[a] Robust standard errors in parentheses.

Table A.3.1.2. FIGURE 3.1 BOTTOM PANEL[a]

	Reported, OLS Models			(Ordered) Logistic Models		
	Ideology	Party ID	1992 Vote	Ideology	Party ID	1992 Vote
Next-older sister	**−0.159**	−0.124	−0.023	**−0.237**	−0.103	−0.100
	(0.065)	(0.092)	(0.026)	(0.087)	(0.085)	(0.117)
Female	**−0.163**	−0.099	−0.015	**−0.213**	−0.081	−0.075
	(0.065)	(0.094)	(0.027)	(0.087)	(0.087)	(0.118)
Age	−0.000	**−0.036**	−0.001	−0.002	**−0.034**	−0.003
	(0.011)	(0.016)	(0.005)	(0.015)	(0.015)	(0.020)
Age squared/1,000	0.075	0.241	−0.012	0.109	0.217	−0.057
	(0.110)	(0.159)	(0.044)	(0.149)	(0.152)	(0.197)
Minority	**−0.490**	**−1.580**	**−0.374**	**−0.662**	**−1.512**	**−1.884**
	(0.099)	(0.119)	(0.030)	(0.133)	(0.127)	(0.197)
Fundamentalism,	**0.096**	−0.026	0.023	**0.117**	−0.027	0.104
age 16	(0.045)	(0.064)	(0.019)	(0.059)	(0.059)	(0.083)
Urbanness, age 16	−0.030	−0.029	−0.017	−0.050	−0.025	**−0.080**
	(0.023)	(0.032)	(0.009)	(0.031)	(0.030)	(0.040)

OLS = ordinary least squares.
[a] Robust standard errors in parentheses. All regressions also control for US Census division of residence at age 16.

Table A.3.2.1. FIGURE 3.2 TOP PANEL[a]

	Reported, OLS Models				Ordered Logistic Models			
	Private Sector	More Gov't	Help Poor	Help Sick	Private Sector	More Gov't	Help Poor	Help Sick
Next-older	**−0.141**	**−0.174**	−0.052	−0.123	**−0.253**	**−0.247**	−0.084	−0.161
sister	(0.067)	(0.070)	(0.065)	(0.071)	(0.128)	(0.102)	(0.103)	(0.101)
Constant	**3.650**	**3.185**	**2.992**	**2.622**				
	(0.046)	(0.048)	(0.046)	(0.050)				

OLS = ordinary least squares.
[a] Robust standard errors in parentheses.

Table A.3.2.2. FIGURE 3.2 BOTTOM PANEL[a]

	Reported, OLS Models				(Ordered) Logistic Models			
	Private Sector	More Gov't	Help Poor	Help Sick	Private Sector	More Gov't	Help Poor	Help Sick
Next-older sister	**−0.137**	**−0.140**	−0.036	−0.095	−0.246	−0.188	−0.078	−0.122
	(0.066)	(0.068)	(0.064)	(0.070)	(0.133)	(0.108)	(0.109)	(0.105)
Female	**−0.305**	**−0.269**	**−0.258**	**−0.272**	**−0.689**	**−0.448**	**−0.477**	**−0.388**
	(0.067)	(0.070)	(0.065)	(0.073)	(0.142)	(0.113)	(0.114)	(0.110)
Age	0.015	**0.040**	0.018	0.016	0.037	**0.063**	0.027	0.025
	(0.012)	(0.012)	(0.011)	(0.013)	(0.024)	(0.019)	(0.019)	(0.019)
Age squared/ 1,000	−0.046	**−0.335**	−0.148	−0.126	−0.143	**−0.540**	−0.216	−0.197
	(0.115)	(0.117)	(0.110)	(0.125)	(0.237)	(0.183)	(0.186)	(0.184)
Minority	**−0.226**	**−0.702**	**−0.726**	**−0.708**	**−0.462**	**−1.129**	**−1.230**	**−1.136**
	(0.104)	(0.105)	(0.092)	(0.096)	(0.212)	(0.166)	(0.160)	(0.162)
Fundamen- talism, age 16	−0.053	**−0.164**	−0.061	−0.013	−0.116	**−0.237**	−0.079	−0.018
	(0.047)	(0.047)	(0.044)	(0.048)	(0.097)	(0.075)	(0.075)	(0.071)
Urbanness, age 16	0.022	−0.026	−0.041	**−0.054**	0.044	−0.037	−0.070	**−0.098**
	(0.023)	(0.024)	(0.023)	(0.025)	(0.046)	(0.039)	(0.039)	(0.038)

OLS = ordinary least squares.
[a] Robust standard errors in parentheses. All regressions also control for US Census division of residence at age 16.

Table A.3.3.1. FIGURE 3.3 REPORTED ORDINARY LEAST SQUARES MODELS

	Ideology	Party ID	1992 Vote	Private Sector	More Gov't	Help Poor	Help Sick
Next-older sister	**−0.175**	−0.129	−0.018	**−0.167**	**−0.169**	−0.045	−0.069
	(0.073)	(0.105)	(0.029)	(0.074)	(0.077)	(0.073)	(0.079)
Five-year-plus gap	−0.025	−0.030	−0.005	−0.040	−0.185	−0.124	−0.108
	(0.109)	(0.155)	(0.045)	(0.110)	(0.121)	(0.107)	(0.126)
Next-older sister × Five-year-plus gap	0.076	0.021	−0.024	0.147	0.150	0.053	−0.110
	(0.155)	(0.222)	(0.064)	(0.165)	(0.166)	(0.149)	(0.171)
Female	**−0.164**	−0.099	−0.015	**−0.311**	**−0.268**	**−0.257**	**−0.268**
	(0.065)	(0.094)	(0.027)	(0.067)	(0.070)	(0.065)	(0.072)
Age	0.000	**−0.036**	−0.001	0.016	**0.040**	0.018	0.016
	(0.011)	(0.016)	(0.005)	(0.012)	(0.012)	(0.011)	(0.013)
Age squared/1,000	0.073	0.241	−0.011	−0.053	**−0.338**	−0.149	−0.122
	(0.111)	(0.159)	(0.044)	(0.115)	(0.117)	(0.110)	(0.124)
Minority	**−0.488**	**−1.581**	**−0.376**	**−0.221**	**−0.703**	**−0.728**	**−0.717**
	(0.099)	(0.120)	(0.030)	(0.104)	(0.105)	(0.092)	(0.096)
Fundamentalism, age 16	**0.096**	−0.026	0.024	−0.052	−0.165	−0.061	−0.014
	(0.045)	(0.064)	(0.019)	(0.048)	(0.047)	(0.044)	(0.048)
Urbanness, age 16	−0.030	−0.029	−0.017	0.022	−0.025	−0.041	−0.053
	(0.023)	(0.032)	(0.009)	(0.023)	(0.024)	(0.023)	(0.025)

[a] Robust standard errors in parentheses. All regressions also control for US Census division of residence at age 16.

Table A.3.3.2. FIGURE 3.3 (ORDERED) LOGISTIC MODELS[a]

	Ideology	Party ID	1992 Vote	Private Sector	More Gov't	Help Poor	Help Sick
Next-older sister	**−0.259**	−0.117	−0.078	**−0.316**	−0.222	−0.077	−0.087
	(0.098)	(0.097)	(0.132)	(0.150)	(0.122)	(0.123)	(0.116)
Five-year-plus gap	−0.058	−0.034	−0.017	−0.065	−0.263	−0.206	−0.172
	(0.144)	(0.145)	(0.197)	(0.217)	(0.190)	(0.180)	(0.191)
Next-older sister	0.102	0.068	−0.107	0.361	0.180	0.013	−0.144
× Five-year-plus gap	(0.207)	(0.204)	(0.285)	(0.332)	(0.260)	(0.253)	(0.262)
Female	**−0.214**	−0.082	−0.073	**−0.704**	**−0.446**	**−0.473**	**−0.385**
	(0.087)	(0.087)	(0.118)	(0.143)	(0.113)	(0.114)	(0.110)
Age	−0.001	**−0.034**	−0.003	0.039	**0.064**	0.027	0.025
	(0.015)	(0.015)	(0.021)	(0.024)	(0.019)	(0.019)	(0.019)
Age squared/ 1,000	0.107	0.218	−0.054	−0.166	**−0.544**	−0.217	−0.196
	(0.150)	(0.152)	(0.198)	(0.237)	(0.184)	(0.186)	(0.182)
Minority	**−0.662**	**−1.510**	**−1.890**	**−0.452**	**−1.130**	**−1.241**	**−1.151**
	(0.133)	(0.127)	(0.197)	(0.213)	(0.167)	(0.162)	(0.162)
Fundamentalism, age 16	**0.117**	−0.027	0.105	−0.111	**−0.237**	−0.080	−0.019
	(0.059)	(0.059)	(0.083)	(0.097)	(0.076)	(0.075)	(0.071)
Urbanness, age 16	−0.049	−0.025	**−0.080**	0.042	−0.036	−0.068	**−0.097**
	(0.031)	(0.030)	(0.040)	(0.046)	(0.039)	(0.039)	(0.038)

[a] Robust standard errors in parentheses. All regressions also control for US Census division of residence at age 16.

CHAPTER 4 CONTROL VARIABLES (IN ORDER OF APPEARANCE)

Fundamentalism, age 16 is measured as in chapter 3 on a 3-point scale ranging from "liberal" to "moderate" to "fundamentalist." Using richer alternative measures based on adult religion produces similar results to those presented as far as the firstborn variable is concerned (the predicted effect of education often changes).

Age is measured as age in years. As in previous chapters, age squared is also included whenever age is. Such nonlinear effects are especially likely to be relevant here both because the middle-aged are most likely to be in the process of raising adolescent children (which might color attitudes toward sexual license).

Mother's education and *father's education* are measured with a count of the number of years of the relevant parent's education. As with religion, a much richer variety of information is available about the respondents' education than about their parents' and probably to some extent reflects parental education even if it is also bound up with consequences of firstborn status. Using these various measures does not change the relevant portion of model results.

Table A.4.1.1. FIGURE 4.1 TOP PANEL[a]

	Reported, OLS Models			Ordered Logistic Models		
	Premarital	Cohabitation	Pill	Premarital	Cohabitation	Pill
Firstborn child	**−0.247**	**0.265**	0.099	**−0.365**	**0.369**	0.158
	(0.059)	(0.077)	(0.057)	(0.087)	(0.109)	(0.094)
Total siblings	**−0.058**	**0.055**	**0.033**	**−0.082**	**0.077**	**0.054**
	(0.013)	(0.016)	(0.012)	(0.019)	(0.024)	(0.020)
Constant	**3.074**	**2.801**	**2.226**			
	(0.055)	(0.072)	(0.054)			

OLS = ordinary least squares.
[a] Robust standard errors in parentheses.

Table A.4.1.2. FIGURE 4.1 BOTTOM PANEL[a]

	Reported, OLS Models			Ordered Logistic Models		
	Premarital	Cohabitation	Pill	Premarital	Cohabitation	Pill
Firstborn child	**−0.191**	**0.263**	0.098	**−0.289**	**0.399**	0.172
	(0.068)	(0.088)	(0.066)	(0.109)	(0.136)	(0.115)
Total siblings	**−0.033**	**0.047**	0.020	**−0.054**	**0.068**	0.035
	(0.015)	(0.019)	(0.015)	(0.025)	(0.030)	(0.027)
Fundamen-talism, age 16	**−0.236**	**0.179**	0.051	**−0.367**	**0.249**	0.083
	(0.043)	(0.054)	(0.042)	(0.072)	(0.084)	(0.072)
Age	0.005	0.012	−0.001	0.011	0.024	−0.004
	(0.010)	(0.013)	(0.010)	(0.017)	(0.022)	(0.018)
Age squared/1,000	**−0.306**	0.175	0.168	**−0.502**	0.205	0.305
	(0.100)	(0.130)	(0.098)	(0.174)	(0.213)	(0.181)
Mother's education	−0.013	−0.013	−0.007	−0.013	−0.026	−0.008
	(0.013)	(0.015)	(0.011)	(0.021)	(0.024)	(0.020)
Father's education	0.006	−0.009	−0.017	0.001	−0.019	**−0.035**
	(0.010)	(0.013)	(0.010)	(0.017)	(0.020)	(0.018)
Constant	**3.808**	**1.914**	**2.198**			
	(0.285)	(0.367)	(0.287)			

OLS = ordinary least squares.
[a] Robust standard errors in parentheses.

Table A.4.2.1. FIGURE 4.2 TOP PANEL[a]

	Reported, OLS Models			(Ordered) Logistic Models		
	2-Point Abortion	5-Point Abortion	7-Point Abortion	2-Point Abortion	5-Point Abortion	7-Point Abortion
Firstborn child	0.047	0.179	**0.264**	0.189	0.219	**0.232**
	(0.026)	(0.092)	(0.108)	(0.105)	(0.112)	(0.098)
Total siblings	**0.012**	**0.056**	**0.084**	**0.050**	**0.070**	**0.074**
	(0.005)	(0.019)	(0.023)	(0.022)	(0.023)	(0.021)
Constant	**1.483**	**2.804**	**1.546**	−0.068		
	(0.025)	(0.088)	(0.101)	(0.099)		

OLS = ordinary least squares.
[a] Robust standard errors in parentheses.

Table A.4.2.2. FIGURE 4.2 BOTTOM PANEL[a]

	Reported, OLS Models			Ordered Logistic Models		
	2-Point Abortion	5-Point Abortion	7-Point Abortion	2-Point Abortion	5-Point Abortion	7-Point Abortion
Firstborn child	0.031	0.191	0.167	0.130	0.226	0.171
	(0.031)	(0.113)	(0.129)	(0.131)	(0.137)	(0.121)
Total siblings	0.002	0.040	**0.061**	0.007	0.049	0.053
	(0.007)	(0.025)	(0.030)	(0.030)	(0.030)	(0.027)
Fundamentalism, age 16	**0.058**	**0.205**	**0.227**	**0.242**	**0.220**	**0.233**
	(0.019)	(0.068)	(0.079)	(0.081)	(0.082)	(0.074)
Age	**−0.012**	−0.016	−0.039	**−0.054**	−0.018	**−0.043**
	(0.005)	(0.018)	(0.020)	(0.021)	(0.021)	(0.018)
Age squared/1,000	**0.128**	0.234	0.359	**0.561**	0.255	**0.389**
	(0.048)	(0.172)	(0.203)	(0.213)	(0.207)	(0.177)
Mother's education	−0.007	−0.004	−0.007	−0.031	−0.005	−0.010
	(0.005)	(0.020)	(0.025)	(0.024)	(0.024)	(0.023)
Father's education	**−0.016**	**−0.037**	**−0.060**	**−0.066**	**−0.044**	**−0.062**
	(0.004)	(0.016)	(0.019)	(0.018)	(0.019)	(0.018)
Constant	**1.966**	**3.278**	**3.076**			
	(0.137)	(0.500)	(0.568)			

OLS = ordinary least squares.
[a] Robust standard errors in parentheses.

Table A.4.3.1. FIGURE 4.3 TOP PANEL[a]

	Reported, OLS Models		Ordered Logistic Models	
	Homosexual Sex	Gay Rights	Homosexual Sex	Gay Rights
Firstborn child	−0.109 (0.060)	**0.111** (0.056)	−0.165 (0.100)	**0.211** (0.102)
Total siblings	**−0.069** (0.011)	**0.037** (0.012)	**−0.120** (0.022)	**0.067** (0.021)
Constant	**2.080** (0.057)	**3.593** (0.052)		

OLS = ordinary least squares.
[a] Robust standard errors in parentheses.

Table A.4.3.2. FIGURE 4.3 BOTTOM PANEL[a]

	Reported, OLS Models		Ordered Logistic Models	
	Homosexual Sex	Gay Rights	Homosexual Sex	Gay Rights
Firstborn child	−0.091 (0.072)	0.073 (0.065)	−0.125 (0.123)	0.133 (0.133)
Total siblings	**−0.063** (0.014)	0.009 (0.015)	**−0.114** (0.028)	0.007 (0.028)
Fundamentalism, age 16	**−0.250** (0.043)	**0.144** (0.044)	**−0.425** (0.075)	**0.293** (0.091)
Age	0.007 (0.011)	**−0.029** (0.011)	0.027 (0.021)	−0.042 (0.022)
Age squared/1,000	−0.164 (0.105)	**0.363** (0.112)	**−0.470** (0.213)	**0.556** (0.212)
Mother's education	**0.029** (0.014)	**−0.034** (0.013)	**0.060** (0.027)	**−0.057** (0.025)
Father's education	**0.026** (0.010)	**−0.030** (0.009)	**0.044** (0.018)	**−0.078** (0.018)
Constant	**1.806** (0.320)	**4.699** (0.301)		

OLS = ordinary least squares.
[a] Robust standard errors in parentheses.

CHAPTER 5 CONTROL VARIABLES (IN ORDER OF APPEARANCE)

Age is, as usual, measured as self-reported age in years; also as in prior chapters, age squared is also included to allow for nonlinear effects.

Education measures number of years of formal education.

Female is the usual binary indicator variable, coded 1 for women and zero for men.

Party ID is the same 7-point scale from strong Democrat (lowest) to strong Republican (highest) that was used in chapter 3. It is self-reported by the survey respondent.

Church attendance, the proxy for religiosity, is on a 5-point scale of frequency of attendance of religious services (which may be at a synagogue, mosque, temple, or other facility rather than a "church" as such).

South indicates whether the respondent was from the Census-defined region of the South. This includes the states of the Confederacy plus Delaware, Kentucky, Maryland, Oklahoma, West Virginia, and the District of Columbia.

Urban is a binary indicator variable coded as 1 for those who reside in places the US Census Bureau deems to be urban and zero for those who live elsewhere.

Veteran is an indicator coded as 1 for those who claim to be veterans of the armed forces, including those who are currently active-duty military personnel, and zero for everyone else.

Household income is self-reported on a 23-point scale. This is much more precise than is the 5-point scale used in the National Election Study-based analyses in chapter 2 (and chapter 6), which include years of data for which the more detailed measure is unavailable. As a result, being "one income category higher" as reported on the figures involves a much smaller change in income than do analogous shifts in those chapters. Smaller effect sizes associated with that one-category change consequently are to be expected.

Table A.5.1.1. FIGURE 5.1 TOP PANEL[a]

	Reported, OLS Models		Ordered Logistic Models	
	Proliferation	Terrorism	Proliferation	Terrorism
Boys in household	**0.037** (0.013)	0.021 (0.020)	0.439 (0.228)	0.114 (0.132)
Girls in household	**0.044** (0.012)	−0.030 (0.029)	**0.469** (0.225)	−0.129 (0.142)
Constant	**2.840** (0.014)	**2.806** (0.015)		

OLS = ordinary least squares.
[a] Robust standard errors in parentheses.

Table A.5.1.2. FIGURE 5.1 BOTTOM PANEL[a]

	Reported, OLS Models		Ordered Logistic Models	
	Proliferation	Terrorism	Proliferation	Terrorism
Boys in household	**0.050** (0.015)	**0.049** (0.021)	**0.598** (0.271)	0.299 (0.168)
Girls in household	**0.044** (0.014)	−0.022 (0.031)	**0.540** (0.260)	−0.129 (0.194)
Age	0.005 (0.005)	**0.015** (0.005)	0.040 (0.035)	**0.095** (0.029)
Age squared/1,000	−0.037 (0.049)	**−0.125** (0.053)	−0.280 (0.359)	**−0.800** (0.307)
Education	0.003 (0.009)	−0.003 (0.007)	−0.003 (0.063)	−0.031 (0.046)
Female	−0.026 (0.027)	−0.058 (0.031)	−0.204 (0.218)	−0.355 (0.206)
Party ID	0.008 (0.006)	**0.041** (0.006)	0.063 (0.049)	**0.278** (0.044)
Church attendance	0.008 (0.009)	−0.002 (0.010)	0.088 (0.072)	0.015 (0.067)
South	0.032 (0.026)	0.017 (0.029)	0.206 (0.232)	0.116 (0.201)

(Continued)

Table A.5.1.2. (CONTINUED)

	Reported, OLS Models		Ordered Logistic Models	
	Proliferation	Terrorism	Proliferation	Terrorism
Urban	−0.028 (0.029)	−0.003 (0.033)	−0.329 (0.297)	−0.099 (0.257)
Veteran	−0.005 (0.035)	−0.028 (0.041)	−0.117 (0.319)	−0.201 (0.307)
Household income	0.002 (0.003)	−0.001 (0.003)	0.010 (0.021)	−0.006 (0.017)
Constant	**2.599** (0.147)	**2.382** (0.144)		

OLS = ordinary least squares.
[a] Robust standard errors in parentheses.

Table A.5.2.1. FIGURE 5.2 TOP PANEL[a]

	Reported, OLS Models		(Ordered) Logistic Models	
	Isolationism	Intervention	Isolationism	Intervention
Boys in household	**0.060** (0.023)	**−0.269** (0.093)	**0.327** (0.115)	**−0.254** (0.091)
Girls in household	0.005 (0.022)	**0.265** (0.093)	0.036 (0.134)	**0.255** (0.095)
Constant	**0.175** (0.012)	**3.767** (0.061)	**−1.544** (0.083)	

OLS = ordinary least squares.
[a] Robust standard errors in parentheses.

Table A.5.2.2. FIGURE 5.2 BOTTOM PANEL[a]

	Reported, OLS Models		(Ordered) Logistic Models	
	Isolationism	Intervention	Isolationism	Intervention
Boys in household	**0.084** (0.024)	−0.179 (0.102)	**0.474** (0.128)	−0.191 (0.120)
Girls in household	0.002 (0.024)	**0.225** (0.094)	0.001 (0.165)	**0.256** (0.116)
Age	−0.004 (0.004)	−0.005 (0.018)	−0.021 (0.026)	−0.015 (0.022)
Age squared/1,000	0.044 (0.043)	0.074 (0.191)	0.246 (0.265)	0.196 (0.228)
Education	**−0.020** (0.006)	**−0.129** (0.024)	**−0.133** (0.037)	**−0.149** (0.028)
Female	0.042 (0.025)	−0.202 (0.112)	0.319 (0.182)	−0.215 (0.124)
Party ID	**−0.019** (0.005)	**0.348** (0.025)	**−0.145** (0.041)	**0.415** (0.032)
Church attendance	**−0.016** (0.008)	−0.033 (0.035)	**−0.122** (0.060)	−0.052 (0.040)
South	0.010 (0.025)	**0.357** (0.116)	0.058 (0.177)	**0.383** (0.133)
Urban	0.026 (0.030)	−0.221 (0.148)	0.175 (0.224)	−0.246 (0.164)
Veteran	0.002 (0.038)	0.311 (0.164)	0.005 (0.290)	0.415 (0.186)
Household income	**−0.007** (0.003)	0.008 (0.011)	**−0.041** (0.016)	0.015 (0.013)
Constant	**0.662** (0.114)	**4.680** (0.508)	**1.539** (0.739)	

OLS = ordinary least squares.
[a] Robust standard errors in parentheses.

Table A.5.3.1. FIGURE 5.3 TOP PANEL[a]

	Reported, OLS Models		Logistic Models	
	Iraq	Afghanistan	Iraq	Afghanistan
Boys in household	**−0.057** (0.022)	−0.029 (0.023)	**−0.256** (0.110)	−0.138 (0.105)
Girls in household	**0.059** (0.026)	0.037 (0.021)	**0.246** (0.107)	0.188 (0.118)
Constant	**0.395** (0.016)	**0.702** (0.015)	**−0.426** (0.066)	**0.858** (0.070)

OLS = ordinary least squares.
[a] Robust standard errors in parentheses.

Table A.5.3.2. FIGURE 5.3 BOTTOM PANEL[a]

	Reported, OLS Models		Logistic Models	
	Iraq	Afghanistan	Iraq	Afghanistan
Boys in household	**−0.056** (0.019)	−0.025 (0.024)	**−0.404** (0.151)	−0.131 (0.135)
Girls in household	0.037 (0.024)	0.046 (0.021)	0.208 (0.175)	**0.341** (0.162)
Age	0.005 (0.004)	0.008 (0.005)	0.038 (0.029)	0.038 (0.026)
Age squared/1,000	−0.058 (0.041)	−0.066 (0.047)	−0.460 (0.294)	−0.298 (0.262)
Education	**−0.012** (0.006)	**0.018** (0.006)	**−0.086** (0.039)	**0.115** (0.035)
Female	0.009 (0.026)	**−0.164** (0.028)	0.014 (0.181)	**−0.944** (0.169)
Party ID	**0.135** (0.005)	**0.071** (0.006)	**0.754** (0.047)	**0.426** (0.040)
Church attendance	**0.017** (0.008)	−0.004 (0.009)	**0.110** (0.053)	−0.011 (0.052)
South	**0.053** (0.026)	0.018 (0.027)	**0.366** (0.178)	0.126 (0.171)
Urban	−0.045 (0.034)	−0.039 (0.033)	−0.251 (0.225)	−0.288 (0.224)
Veteran	0.001 (0.039)	0.043 (0.037)	−0.023 (0.272)	0.372 (0.292)
Household income	0.003 (0.002)	**0.006** (0.003)	0.019 (0.016)	**0.037** (0.015)
Constant	−0.016 (0.117)	0.073 (0.126)	**−2.773** (0.795)	**−2.640** (0.715)

OLS = ordinary least squares.
[a] Robust standard errors in parentheses.

Table A.5.4.1. FIGURE 5.4 TOP PANEL[a]

	Reported, OLS Models				(Ordered) Logistic Models			
	Isolationism	Intervention	Iraq	Afghanistan	Isolationism	Intervention	Iraq	Afghanistan
Boys in household	**0.067** (0.032)	−0.179 (0.121)	−0.035 (0.025)	−0.036 (0.033)	**0.374** (0.172)	−0.189 (0.144)	−0.236 (0.199)	−0.175 (0.165)
Girls in household	−0.024 (0.030)	0.165 (0.124)	0.036 (0.032)	0.013 (0.033)	−0.172 (0.208)	0.163 (0.139)	0.233 (0.287)	0.101 (0.198)
Age	−0.002 (0.006)	0.009 (0.026)	0.009 (0.006)	0.007 (0.007)	−0.009 (0.035)	−0.002 (0.031)	0.072 (0.045)	0.034 (0.033)
Age squared/1,000	0.016 (0.060)	−0.039 (0.262)	−0.093 (0.054)	−0.072 (0.067)	0.083 (0.344)	0.082 (0.325)	−0.823 (0.447)	−0.351 (0.333)
Education	**−0.022** (0.008)	**−0.117** (0.033)	−0.005 (0.007)	0.021 (0.009)	**−0.129** (0.049)	**−0.125** (0.037)	−0.050 (0.053)	**0.106** (0.044)
Party ID	**−0.024** (0.008)	**0.355** (0.033)	**0.141** (0.007)	0.086 (0.008)	**−0.163** (0.054)	**0.420** (0.043)	**0.829** (0.069)	**0.430** (0.050)
Church attendance	−0.011 (0.012)	−0.027 (0.049)	0.012 (0.010)	−0.003 (0.013)	−0.076 (0.075)	−0.040 (0.056)	0.086 (0.077)	−0.004 (0.066)
South	−0.005 (0.037)	**0.399** (0.168)	0.061 (0.034)	0.033 (0.041)	−0.057 (0.233)	**0.439** (0.189)	0.483 (0.266)	0.195 (0.219)
Urban	0.038 (0.043)	−0.051 (0.204)	0.008 (0.044)	−0.079 (0.050)	0.221 (0.283)	−0.092 (0.237)	0.195 (0.346)	−0.430 (0.278)
Veteran	0.008 (0.106)	−0.054 (0.362)	0.023 (0.079)	0.143 (0.112)	0.045 (0.662)	0.003 (0.404)	−0.075 (1.019)	0.841 (0.655)
Household income	−0.007 (0.004)	−0.002 (0.016)	0.004 (0.003)	0.005 (0.004)	−0.041 (0.022)	0.003 (0.018)	0.025 (0.025)	0.025 (0.019)
Constant	**0.711** (0.173)	**3.925** (0.746)	−0.235 (0.162)	−0.062 (0.187)	−1.602 (0.984)		**4.687** (1.245)	**2.865** (0.928)

OLS = ordinary least squares.
[a] Robust standard errors in parentheses.

Table A.5.4.2. FIGURE 5.4 BOTTOM PANEL[a]

	Reported, OLS Models				(Ordered) Logistic Models			
	Isolationism	Intervention	Iraq	Afghanistan	Isolationism	Intervention	Iraq	Afghanistan
Boys in household	**0.114** (0.035)	-0.118 (0.175)	**-0.085** (0.030)	-0.027 (0.036)	**0.374** (0.172)	-0.189 (0.144)	-0.236 (0.199)	-0.175 (0.165)
Girls in household	0.029 (0.037)	**0.291** (0.142)	0.032 (0.037)	**0.079** (0.024)	-0.172 (0.208)	0.163 (0.139)	0.233 (0.287)	0.101 (0.198)
Age	-0.008 (0.006)	-0.019 (0.028)	-0.001 (0.006)	0.007 (0.006)	-0.009 (0.035)	-0.002 (0.031)	0.072 (0.045)	0.034 (0.033)
Age squared/1,000	0.095 (0.065)	0.174 (0.295)	0.018 (0.065)	-0.040 (0.062)	0.083 (0.344)	0.082 (0.325)	-0.823 (0.447)	-0.351 (0.333)
Education	**-0.017** (0.008)	**-0.128** (0.036)	-0.018 (0.009)	0.014 (0.008)	**-0.129** (0.049)	**-0.125** (0.037)	-0.050 (0.053)	**0.106** (0.044)
Party ID	-0.011 (0.008)	**0.338** (0.039)	**0.127** (0.009)	**0.051** (0.008)	**-0.163** (0.054)	**0.420** (0.043)	**0.829** (0.069)	**0.430** (0.050)
Church attendance	**-0.023** (0.011)	-0.049 (0.051)	0.021 (0.013)	-0.003 (0.011)	-0.076 (0.075)	-0.040 (0.056)	0.086 (0.077)	-0.004 (0.066)
South	0.028 (0.035)	**0.328** (0.161)	0.045 (0.040)	-0.014 (0.036)	-0.057 (0.233)	**0.439** (0.189)	0.483 (0.266)	0.195 (0.219)
Urban	0.003 (0.043)	-0.397 (0.216)	**-0.107** (0.054)	0.004 (0.043)	0.221 (0.283)	-0.092 (0.237)	0.195 (0.346)	-0.430 (0.278)
Veteran	-0.006 (0.042)	**0.498** (0.196)	-0.035 (0.048)	-0.007 (0.041)	0.045 (0.662)	0.003 (0.404)	-0.075 (1.019)	0.841 (0.655)
Household income	**-0.007** (0.003)	0.020 (0.015)	0.002 (0.004)	**0.008** (0.004)	-0.041 (0.022)	0.003 (0.018)	0.025 (0.025)	0.025 (0.019)
Constant	**0.686** (0.158)	**5.071** (0.721)	0.294 (0.177)	0.110 (0.175)	-1.602 (0.984)		**4.687** (1.245)	**2.865** (0.928)

OLS = ordinary least squares.

[a] Robust standard errors in parentheses.

CHAPTER 6 CONTROL VARIABLES (IN ORDER OF APPEARANCE)

Age (and age squared) are again the respondent's self-reported age in years.

Female is the usual indicator variable: Female respondents are assigned a value of 1 and males zero.

Education, as in chapter 5, is the respondent's number of years of formal education.

Ruralness is measured using the same 3-point scale as in chapter 2 (see for fuller discussion).

South indicates whether the respondent is from the Census-designated South (see discussion of chapter 5 for a list of states included in that definition).

Church attendance, the measure used for religiosity, is the same as that used in previous chapters. Alternative measures, or excluding of a religion measure altogether to avoid reverse-causation problems, produces similar results.

Income is measured here with the same five-category scale grouped by percentile rankings as used in most previous chapters (though not chapter 5).

Minority is once more a simple indicator noting whether the respondent identifies with any nonwhite racial group or as a Hispanic.

Table A.6.1.1. FIGURE 6.1 TOP PANEL[a]

	Reported, OLS Models		(Ordered) Logistic Models	
	Job Insecurity	Delay Treatment	Job Insecurity	Delay Treatment
Children in household	**−0.065** (0.006)	**0.040** (0.006)	**−0.208** (0.018)	**0.189** (0.029)

OLS = ordinary least squares.
[a] Robust standard errors in parentheses. All regressions also control for year of survey.

Table A.6.1.2. FIGURE 6.1 BOTTOM PANEL[a]

	Reported, OLS Models		(Ordered) Logistic Models	
	Job Insecurity	Delay Treatment	Job Insecurity	Delay Treatment
Children in household	**−0.030** (0.007)	**0.022** (0.008)	**−0.052** (0.024)	**0.109** (0.043)
Age	**−0.017** (0.002)	**0.011** (0.003)	**−0.145** (0.013)	**0.074** (0.017)
Age squared/1,000	**0.238** (0.022)	**−0.154** (0.025)	**1.951** (0.149)	**−0.985** (0.176)

(Continued)

Table A.6.1.2. (CONTINUED)

	Reported, OLS Models		(Ordered) Logistic Models	
	Job Insecurity	Delay Treatment	Job Insecurity	Delay Treatment
Female	**0.045** (0.013)	0.022 (0.016)	**0.220** (0.055)	0.123 (0.092)
Education	**0.035** (0.004)	−0.002 (0.005)	**0.157** (0.019)	−0.025 (0.032)
Ruralness	**0.022** (0.009)	0.001 (0.011)	**0.097** (0.037)	0.005 (0.062)
South	**0.042** (0.015)	0.014 (0.018)	**0.170** (0.062)	0.064 (0.101)
Church attendance	**−0.014** (0.004)	**0.015** (0.005)	**−0.044** (0.019)	**0.082** (0.031)
Income	**0.073** (0.008)	**−0.135** (0.008)	**0.272** (0.029)	**−0.737** (0.049)
Minority	**−0.121** (0.018)	**0.051** (0.022)	**−0.407** (0.064)	**0.252** (0.115)

OLS = ordinary least squares.
[a] Robust standard errors in parentheses. All regressions also control for year of survey.

Table A.6.2.1. FIGURE 6.2 TOP PANEL[a]

	Reported, OLS Models			Ordered Logistic Models		
	Welfare Recipients	Poor People	Government Trust	Welfare Recipients	Poor People	Government Trust
Children in household	**0.483** (0.172)	**0.392** (0.136)	**0.799** (0.125)	**0.032** (0.014)	**0.038** (0.013)	**0.055** (0.010)

OLS = ordinary least squares.
[a] Robust standard errors in parentheses. All regressions also control for year of survey.

Table A.6.2.2. FIGURE 6.2 BOTTOM PANEL[a]

	Reported, OLS Models			Ordered Logistic Models		
	Welfare Recipients	Poor People	Government Trust	Welfare Recipients	Poor People	Government Trust
Children in household	**1.094** (0.218)	0.203 (0.168)	0.278 (0.191)	**0.088** (0.018)	0.019 (0.017)	0.017 (0.015)
Age	0.092 (0.083)	**0.533** (0.062)	**−0.529** (0.069)	0.012 (0.007)	**0.060** (0.006)	**−0.044** (0.006)
Age squared/1,000	0.350 (0.855)	**−4.841** (0.635)	**5.036** (0.709)	0.005 (0.071)	**−0.544** (0.064)	**0.420** (0.056)
Female	0.434 (0.459)	**1.939** (0.360)	−0.241 (0.397)	0.039 (0.038)	**0.194** (0.036)	−0.014 (0.032)
Education	0.201 (0.156)	**−0.938** (0.119)	0.153 (0.131)	0.010 (0.013)	**−0.110** (0.012)	0.020 (0.010)

(Continued)

Table A.6.2.2. (CONTINUED)

	Reported, OLS Models			Ordered Logistic Models		
	Welfare Recipients	Poor People	Government Trust	Welfare Recipients	Poor People	Government Trust
Ruralness	**−1.994**	−0.120	**−0.825**	**−0.151**	−0.015	**−0.068**
	(0.316)	(0.246)	(0.267)	(0.026)	(0.025)	(0.021)
South	**1.665**	**2.836**	0.297	**0.147**	**0.323**	0.012
	(0.518)	(0.401)	(0.443)	(0.043)	(0.040)	(0.035)
Church	**−0.547**	**−0.680**	**−0.706**	**−0.047**	**−0.071**	**−0.058**
attendance	(0.152)	(0.118)	(0.130)	(0.012)	(0.012)	(0.010)
Income	**−3.118**	**−1.589**	**0.415**	**−0.273**	**−0.180**	**0.055**
	(0.240)	(0.181)	(0.200)	(0.020)	(0.018)	(0.016)
Minority	**7.097**	**6.121**	**1.565**	**0.659**	**0.692**	**0.112**
	(0.617)	(0.456)	(0.534)	(0.052)	(0.047)	(0.043)

OLS = ordinary least squares.
[a] Robust standard errors in parentheses. All regressions also control for year of survey.

Table A.6.3.1. FIGURE 6.3 TOP PANEL[a]

	Reported, OLS Models			Ordered Logistic Models		
	Welfare Spending	Spending on Poor	Food Stamps	Welfare Spending	Spending on Poor	Food Stamps
Children in	**−0.033**	**−0.017**	**0.032**	**−0.080**	**−0.072**	**0.084**
household	(0.009)	(0.008)	(0.007)	(0.024)	(0.028)	(0.018)

OLS = ordinary least squares.
[a] Robust standard errors in parentheses. All regressions also control for year of survey.

Table A.6.3.2. FIGURE 6.3 BOTTOM PANEL[a]

	Reported, OLS Models			Ordered Logistic Models		
	Welfare Spending	Spending on Poor	Food Stamps	Welfare Spending	Spending on Poor	Food Stamps
Children in	−0.038	**−0.039**	**0.027**	−0.103	**−0.137**	**0.074**
household	(0.020)	(0.016)	(0.007)	(0.057)	(0.055)	(0.021)
Age	−0.003	−0.008	**0.011**	−0.008	−0.025	**0.031**
	(0.007)	(0.006)	(0.003)	(0.018)	(0.021)	(0.007)
Age squared/	0.036	0.075	**−0.112**	0.088	0.242	**−0.305**
1,000	(0.068)	(0.062)	(0.026)	(0.180)	(0.214)	(0.076)
Female	**−0.128**	**−0.130**	**0.070**	**−0.337**	**−0.401**	**0.201**
	(0.040)	(0.035)	(0.015)	(0.111)	(0.115)	(0.044)

(Continued)

	Reported, OLS Models			Ordered Logistic Models		
	Welfare Spending	Spending on Poor	Food Stamps	Welfare Spending	Spending on Poor	Food Stamps
Education	−0.002	**0.049**	**−0.013**	−0.008	**0.172**	**−0.038**
	(0.014)	(0.011)	(0.005)	(0.037)	(0.038)	(0.015)
Ruralness	0.027	0.025	**−0.100**	0.070	0.079	**−0.285**
	(0.027)	(0.023)	(0.010)	(0.075)	(0.078)	(0.030)
South	0.038	0.029	**−0.103**	0.120	0.074	**−0.314**
	(0.043)	(0.038)	(0.017)	(0.119)	(0.127)	(0.050)
Church	**−0.033**	**−0.027**	**0.027**	**−0.083**	**−0.089**	**0.074**
attendance	(0.013)	(0.011)	(0.005)	(0.035)	(0.037)	(0.014)
Income	**0.109**	**0.056**	**−0.130**	**0.298**	**0.180**	**−0.370**
	(0.021)	(0.017)	(0.008)	(0.058)	(0.057)	(0.023)
Minority	**−0.196**	**−0.288**	**0.267**	**−0.517**	**−1.062**	**0.763**
	(0.050)	(0.037)	(0.019)	(0.131)	(0.148)	(0.057)

OLS = ordinary least squares.
[a] Robust standard errors in parentheses. All regressions also control for year of survey.

CHAPTER 7 CONTROL VARIABLES (IN ORDER OF APPEARANCE)

Age is measured in years. This is another analysis where the age-squared term is particularly important, because of the typical peak in childbearing in early middle adulthood and hence highly nonlinear relationships between age of respondent and likelihood of new children.

Income measures the percentile rank of the respondent's annual household rank among all survey respondents, so that those at the median of the income distribution (with half of respondents richer and half of respondents poorer) get a score of 50. The very richest respondents, likewise, get a score of 100.

Education is measured with a 7-point scale of educational qualification, ranging from no qualification to higher degree. Those listed as having "other qualification" are excluded from the reported results; inferring from the name of the separate "other higher qualification" category that these are lowerlevel qualifications and putting them with the pre-O–level qualifications produces substantially similar results. Those listed as having no qualification and still being in school are also uncoded for educational attainment.

Partnered is an indicator variable noting whether the respondent claims to be partnered, either in a formal marriage or in a more informal liaison that the respondent regards as permanent.

Table A.7.1. FIGURE 7.1 MODELS[a]

	Reported, OLS Models		Logistic Models	
	New Parent (One-year lags)	New Parent (Two-year lags)	New Parent (One-year lags)	New Parent (Two-year lags)
Partisan intensity	**0.003** (0.001)	**0.002** (0.001)	**0.166** (0.046)	**0.117** (0.051)
Age	−0.000 (0.000)	−0.000 (0.000)	**0.482** (0.043)	**0.581** (0.052)
Age squared/ 1,000	**−0.020** (0.003)	**−0.018** (0.003)	**−8.737** (0.623)	**−10.184** (0.765)
Income	**0.000** (0.000)	**0.000** (0.000)	**0.024** (0.001)	**0.026** (0.002)
Education	**−0.001** (0.000)	**−0.001** (0.000)	**−0.079** (0.019)	**−0.052** (0.021)
Partnered	**0.024** (0.001)	**0.019** (0.001)	**1.200** (0.074)	**0.894** (0.075)
Constant	**0.022** (0.005)	**0.026** (0.006)	**−11.84** (0.695)	**−13.371** (0.855)

OLS = ordinary least squares.
[a] Robust standard errors in parentheses. All regressions include only respondents under the age of 60. The logistic models do not employ the King and Zeng (2001) rare-events correction; doing so produces substantively identical results.

NOTES

CHAPTER 1

1. Luhmann et al. 2012.
2. Healy et al. 2010.
3. Rahn et al. 1996, 46–49.
4. Srivastava et al. 2003, 1043.
5. Carney et al. 2008.
6. See, for one exposition, Nagle 2006. More recently, *The Simpsons'* Marge pointed to the inextricable bonds among identity, politics, and kinfolk, expressing support for her preferred gubernatorial candidate by asserting that "We're a Mary Bailey family, Homer."
7. McCarthy 2007. See also the common trope comparing government deficits to family budgets.
8. Whittington and Alm 1997.
9. Hill 2006.
10. Drewianka 2008.
11. Landsburg 2007.
12. Emeka 2006.
13. Fishback et al. 2007.
14. Crump et al. 2011.
15. Wilson 1993.
16. Cahn and Carbone 2010.
17. Chapter 7 returns to the idea of political attitudes, particularly partisanship, as an influence on family formation.
18. Jennings and Niemi 1968.
19. Achen 2002.
20. Hatemi, Funk et al. 2009.
21. Hand 2002.
22. Jennings et al. 2009.
23. Jennings and Niemi 1971; Zuckerman et al. 2007.
24. Wolak 2009.
25. Kroh and Selb 2009.
26. Zuckerman et al. 2007, particularly chapter 5.
27. Alford et al. 2005; Kandler et al. 2012.
28. Socialization may mediate the genetic factors. Suppose that people react distinctively to darker-skinned people, treating them less generously than they treat the lighter-skinned. If this unfair treatment causes those with darker complexions to

be more concerned about injustice and inequality, then the socialization by others was a necessary part of the development of political attitudes. Nevertheless, the ultimate cause that kicked off the process was skin color; since identical twins are likely to be more similar in skin color than are fraternal twins, they will end up more politically similar because their genetic heritage causes others to socialize them more similarly.

29. Smith et al. 2012.
30. Harris 2006.
31. Fowler et al. 2008.
32. Charney and English 2012.
33. Especially in matters of political participation, such as voter turnout; see Stoker and Jennings 1995.
34. Beck and Jennings 1975.
35. Watson et al. 2004; Alford et al. 2011—but see Klofstad et al. 2012 for a cautionary note.
36. Coffé and Need 2010.
37. Feng and Baker 1994 (who find no evidence of spousal convergence in attitudes).
38. Kenny 1994.
39. Stoker and Jennings 2005, 57.
40. van Berkel 1998; Martin 2006.
41. Zipp et al. 2004.
42. Zuckerman et al. 2007, chapter 4.
43. Osborn and Mendez 2011.
44. Hayes 1993; Wilson and Lusztig 2004.
45. Plutzer and McBurnett 1991.
46. Divorce, too, may have predictable political consequences, although this is usually argued in terms of behavior (i.e., likelihood of turning out to vote) rather than preferences (Kern 2010; Voorpostel and Coffé 2012).
47. van Deth et al. 2011.
48. Sears and Funk 1999.
49. For example, Stoddard 2009.
50. Elder and Greene 2012b.
51. Vavrus 2000; Elder and Greene 2007.
52. The following recapitulates the case made by Arnold and Weisberg 1996, 196.
53. Welch 2011.
54. Ross and van Willigen 1996.
55. Elder and Greene 2012b.
56. Solomon 2012.
57. Gender has also historically been more independent of conscious parental influence than has been most other child characteristics, which reduces the problem of determining whether the seeming influence of a child actually reflected whatever factors caused the parents to decide to have a baby.
58. Prokos et al. 2010, but see Conley and Rauscher 2013 for the opposite claim.
59. Oswald and Powdthavee 2010.
60. Shafer and Malhotra 2011.
61. Washington 2008.
62. In recent decades, sex-selective abortion appears to have emerged in at least some ethnic subpopulations in the rich world, though probably not in ways that would affect national figures (Abrevaya 2009).
63. Zuckerman et al. 2007.

64. See also Kroh 2009.
65. Burnet 2011.
66. For example, Newman and Taylor 1994; Steinberg 2001; Andeweg and van den Berg 2003.
67. For example, Mutz and Mondak 2006; Hibbing et al. 2011.
68. Schreckhise and Shields 2003.
69. Fitzgerald and Curtis 2012.
70. Parker et al. 2008.
71. Healy and Malhotra 2013.
72. Malmendier and Nagel 2011.
73. Scholars can successfully plumb the studies that do cover both family ties and political views to examine single political questions in depth, as demonstrated by, among others, Zuckerman et al. 2007. But, as that study also demonstrates, many of the most promising questions for more sustained analysis have already been explored.
74. Regrettably, this rules out the possibility for any systematic attention to the effects of grandparents, grandchildren, or other extended relations, about whom systematic data is very hard to come by in political surveys. Focusing on closer relationships is in any case more liable to produce substantively appreciable effects, because of the greater degree of interaction. In the terms of the previous section, the potential effects looked at with this nearer family will be more plausible even if they are less surprising.
75. The discussion of those sorts of specification checks typically appears in the endnotes, rather than in the main text.
76. An analogy could be made to a pointillist canvas, where no individual dot of paint is notable even if the whole picture can be revelatory. We need not pursue this analogy too far, since a fleck of paint for each study/chapter here would produce a canvas with only a half-dozen colored points, which would probably be pretty underwhelming.
77. Of course, parents', particularly mothers', decisions to work outside the home have become highly politicized (Morgan 2003; Zimmerman et al. 2008). Also, it is worth noting that parents' political behaviors such as involvement in elections have been looked at as a source for children's political attitudes; see, for instance, Gidengil et al. 2010.
78. Gelman et al. 2002; Kastellec and Leoni 2007.

CHAPTER 2

1. Ronald Reagan identified as a Democrat for many decades of his life (albeit mostly before his children with Nancy were likely to be absorbing explicit political lessons), and his other children, most vocally (adopted) son Michael, retained more conservative beliefs. Nevertheless, the point that some of Reagan's children diverged from his ideological persona stands.
2. For an early exception, see Jennings and Niemi 1971, 80–81.
3. Carney et al. 2008.
4. Kulik 2002; Sinno and Killen 2009.
5. Burns and Gallagher 2010.
6. Youngblade 2003.
7. Indeed, not all scholars accept the idea that parents' choices are important to children's outcomes. Most prominently, Judith Rich Harris (2009) has marshaled a great deal of evidence showing that parents who meet basic thresholds of

providing for their children and not being abusive have relatively little influence on their offspring's personalities. Instead, she argues that family resemblances largely stem from genetic factors. Yet her story need not be inconsistent with that told here: Harris concedes that parents do have influence in how their children act *within the home*. If the children cognitively relate political questions to the in-home context, which may be especially likely with issues such as gender equality, then these differences in home environment are compatible with different political viewpoints even absent any personality effects of parenting. It is worth emphasizing that Harris focuses mostly on personality rather than on political beliefs or behaviors when finding null effects (although some of the potential mechanisms linking mothers' workforce participation to child political development do rely on personality effects).

8. Yi et al. 2004.

9. Nomaguchi 2004.

10. Jost et al. 2008.

11. Fraley et al. 2012.

12. Waldfogel et al. 2002; Bianchi and Milkie 2010.

13. Kanazawa 2010.

14. One alternative question that is available is respondents' difference in opinion about "liberals" and "conservatives." This produces quite similar results to those above simply considering self-reported conservatism.

15. The larger sample insures against the potential for selection bias if, for some reason, liberals with stay-at-home mothers or conservatives with working mothers were particularly reticent about their own ideologies and thus less apt to answer the question asking directly about conservatism.

16. As mentioned earlier, the 1970 survey is already excluded for lacking ideology data when self-declared liberalism or conservatism is the variable being predicted.

17. The appendix includes a full description of how the control variables were coded in the models, along with discussion of some of the alternative codings used.

18. Raley and Bianchi 2006, 407.

19. Dancygier and Saunders 2006.

20. For technical reasons, regression models are in any event likely to underestimate actual effect sizes; see Taagepera 2008 for a thorough discussion.

21. Parental partisanship is likely to influence party identification more than ideology, since partisan categories serve as identity groups—one may feel a cultural affinity for one's parents' political party, even if the actual content of that party's ideology is less appealing (Zuckerman et al. 2007).

22. Jennings and Langton 1969; Zuckerman et al. 2007.

23. This is contrary to the findings of, among others, Dancygier and Saunders (2006), though the difference in results may merely reflect differences in measurement: The available measures are not comparable to those authors' in their inclusion of second-generation migrants.

24. The meaning of "conservatism" varies substantially according to country and context. Since the data used here are from a political survey in the United States, the interpretation follows the American political sense of what it means to be conservative.

25. Luker 1984.

26. The wording of this question changed after the 1980 survey, but looking only at the years using either question wording produces similar results.

27. Ruckstuhl et al. 2010.

CHAPTER 3

1. Rosenzweig 1986; Whitworth and Stephenson 2002.
2. Melby et al. 2008.
3. The most storied pattern of differential parental investment in their children, known as the Trivers-Willard hypothesis, suggests that parents concentrate effort on children likely to produce the most grandchildren (typically, daughters among the poor and sons among the rich). See Trivers and Willard 1973; Mulder 1998.
4. For example, Perner et al. 1994; Thapar et al. 1995; McGue et al. 1996.
5. Riggio 1999, for example, disputes the idea that siblings alter personality traits.
6. For a particularly nice example, see Vogl 2013.
7. Srivastava et al. 2003.
8. Examples include Holmgren et al. 2007; Mazan and Gagnon 2007.
9. Szobiová 2008.
10. Regnier-Loilier 2006.
11. For reviews of the sex-of-sibling literature, see Conley 2000 and Steelman et al. 2002.
12. Butcher and Case 1994.
13. Cicirelli 1980; Stocker et al. 1989.
14. Cicirelli 1994; Ruffman et al. 1998. One exception is Crouter et al. (1995), who find younger siblings' sexes to be more influential than older siblings'. But their findings focus on parental socializing behavior: When the children in one family are of opposite sexes, daughters receive more feminized treatment and sons receive more masculinized treatment. That they observe this fact only among older siblings is suggestive: It may be that for younger siblings, the cross-sex influence of the older sibling neutralizes the gender-typed socialization from the parent. Healy and Malhotra (2013) take a similar look at younger siblings' influence via the parents in a more political context.
15. Henderson and Berenbaum 1997.
16. Some societies in East Asia have seen fertility rates plunge (e.g., where the average woman has 0.8 children) to the point where elder siblings are rare. But even in a country like China, with stringent, widely enforced population policies, the average woman has 1.5 children; see Morgan et al. 2009. If half of all Chinese women have one child and half have two children, this translates into one child in three having an elder sibling; any more skewed distribution of family sizes increases the proportion of children with elder siblings.
17. Whiteman et al. 2007.
18. Stoneman et al. 1986; Iervolino et al. 2005.
19. Hatemi, Medland, et al. 2009.
20. Desposato and Norrander 2009.
21. Mason and Lu 1988; Hicks and Lee 2006.
22. For example, Konisky et al. 2008; Cochran and Sanders 2009.
23. Box-Steffensmeier et al. 2004.
24. Ary et al. 1993; McHale et al. 2009; Wang et al. 2009. As the next chapter discusses further, these socialization behaviors are most frequently studied and observed in proscribed activities—sexual relations, alcohol and drug abuse, and the like—but they do encompass many other actions as well.
25. Kam and Simas 2010.
26. Morrongiello and Rennie 1998.
27. Sallis et al. 1996; Linville and Huebner 2005.

28. In the data used in this chapter, for example, respondents whose next-older siblings are male are more likely to report membership in sporting clubs and veterans' groups.

29. Although this is theoretically possible, most studies of opinion formation find a relatively small role for self-interest (or for the personal interest of friends and relations); see Sears and Funk 1991.

30. For example, Mulick and Butter 2002; Washington 2008, 311.

31. Mondschein et al. 2000.

32. Fagot et al. 1992; Owen Blakemore 1998.

33. Gneezy et al. 2009.

34. Conover 1988; McCue and Gopoian 2000.

35. Schlesinger and Heldman 2001.

36. Alvarez and McCaffery 2003.

37. Bolzendahl and Olafsdottir 2008.

38. Other effects, for example of birth order, might produce other sibling differences, but the purely sex-based consideration here abstracts away from these.

39. Brody and Steelman 1985; Crouter et al. 1995.

40. Weichselbaumer and Winter-Ebmer 2005; King and Leigh 2010.

41. When sex selection occurs in Western cultures, it tends to aim for a child to have the opposite sex of its siblings. This sort of selection would not affect the central hypothesis here: If all previous children were girls, aborting a female fetus before having a male baby would not alter the fact that his next-older sibling was female. Thus even an intent-to-treat study would have the male baby in the same treatment group. By contrast, if people are selecting for children to have the same gender, for example because they have a strong bias in favor of sons, the study design becomes more complex. Healy and Malhotra (2013) argue that this invalidates the quasi-experimental design used here, although their alternative proposal is equally subject to sex-selection problems. The problem is likely minor in both their design and this one, however, as explicit sex selection appears rare in most populations in the United States.

42. This concept is undefined for eldest siblings and only children. Regressions including older-sibling sex as an independent variable accordingly drop 1,081 respondents (from the survey's 2,992) from the data set. An alternative coding that does not drop these people might consider "feminizing effect of older sibling," thus being valued at +1 for those with a next-older sister, –1 for those with a next-older brother, and zero for those with no older siblings. This alternative produces substantially similar results to those reported.

43. Henderson and Berenbaum 1997.

44. Twinship is assumed when the sibling born in the same year is a full sibling and the respondent's month of birth is between March and October. For those months in the middle of the year, allowing a nine-month gestation period—and nine months would be an extremely quick turnaround for having a second baby—would push any birth from the same mother into a different year. It is, though, just possible that a mother could give birth in both January and December of the same year, so that months toward either end of the year might represent an actual older or younger sibling.

45. In seventeen cases, the sex of the next-older full sibling differs from that of the next-older non-full sibling; a further 154 respondents have no older full siblings but do have older non-full siblings.

46. Raley and Bianchi 2006.

47. Chahnazarian 1988.
48. Almond and Edlund 2008.
49. The focus on circumstances at age sixteen rather than, say, age eight or thirteen is entirely data-driven: Sixteen happens to be the one age about which the GSS asked.
50. The original question assigns higher values to more conservative answers. The scale is reversed here for consistency with chapter 2.
51. Miller 1992.
52. In fact, excluding respondents who grew up in the South from the analysis consistently increases the predicted Republican ward pull of an older brother by over 50%. The uncertainty of the estimate also increases because of the smaller sample size but not by proportionately as much.
53. Kaufmann and Petrocik 1999.
54. Indeed, support for Perot shows suggestive patterns. Respondents whose next-older sibling was female were more likely to support Perot: 22.3% of such respondents did, compared to only 18.1% of respondents whose next-older sibling was male. (The 95% confidence interval on this difference ranged from +0.0% to 7.9%.) This effect is especially strong among male respondents, as might be expected because Perot's support was generally concentrated among men. 28.8% of men with next-older sisters supported Perot, compared to only 20.4% with a next-older brother. (The 95% confidence interval on that difference ranged from 2.2% to 14.6%.) Older-sister-induced support for Perot seems to have come at the expense of George H.W. Bush; 38.4% of men with next-older brothers supported Bush, but only 27.4% of men with next-older sisters did. (The 95% confidence interval on the difference ranged from 4.2% to 17.7%.)
55. For example, Jacobs and Shapiro 1994.
56. Eriksen and Jensen 2006.
57. Stocker et al. 1997.
58. Powell and Steelman 1993; Lindstrom and Berhanu 2000.
59. An alternative, somewhat more sophisticated approach might transform the age gap with a logarithm or some other mathematical function. Even a logarithm leaves the variable skewed, though, and the fact that age gaps are rounded to the nearest year (months of birth are unavailable for respondents' siblings) makes the left end of the logged distribution lumpy.
60. The table omits control variable coefficients for brevity; they are very similar to those given in earlier tables in both size and direction.
61. Bogaert 2006. For biological sibling effects on behaviors other than sexual orientation, see also Bressan et al. 2009.

CHAPTER 4
1. This was the conclusion of the classic, gargantuan review of the literature in Ernst and Angst (1983).
2. Sulloway 1997.
3. Bjerkedal et al. 2007.
4. Blanchard 2004. In particular, the usual finding in this literature is that boys are more likely to be gay if they have a greater number of elder brothers.
5. See, for typical examples, Freese et al. 1999 or Førland et al. 2012.
6. Somit et al. 1996, 105–106.
7. For example, Eaves and Hatemi 2008.
8. Argys et al. 2006.

9. Harris 2006, 104.
10. For example, Buonanno and Vanin 2013.
11. Zweigenhaft 2002.
12. For example, Rodgers et al. 1992.
13. Widmer 1997.
14. Averett et al. 2011.
15. Whiteman et al. 2003.
16. Granberg 1982.
17. Zucker 1999.
18. Hooghe and Wilkenfeld 2008.
19. Michalski and Shackelford 2002.
20. For example, Stone and Ingham 2011.
21. Also as in chapter 3, variations on these coding choices (dropping from the sample any potential twin births, for example) produce similar results to those reported in this chapter.
22. Factors that are determined simultaneously with birth order may also be worth controlling for, especially as they reflect, and can act as proxies for, other potential causally important factors. The most prominent of these is likely to be gender. However, finding a statistically significant relationship between birth order and sex—laterborns are more likely to be female—requires enormous sample sizes to overcome an effect size that is substantively vanishingly small (James 1987, 729).
23. Lewis 2003.
24. Because the data used here (unlike chapter 2's National Election Survey data) comes from a single year, respondents' ages provide the same information as would their years of birth.
25. Age may relate to firstborn status in the sample in interesting ways as well. For parents born in the 1890s, say, older children are more likely to have died by the time of the survey than are the younger children. For parents born in the post-WWII baby boom, the situation is reversed: Their firstborn children are more likely to be adults who are eligible for the survey than would any laterborn children they had.
26. The discussion also touched on the age of parents, which one might accordingly expect as another control variable. The 1994 GSS asks about parents' years of birth, which theoretically allows calculation of the extent to which effects here come not from older siblings but from older parents. Unfortunately, the parent-cohort questions were answered only by a small minority of the sample. Losing three-quarters of the observations naturally produces less confident estimates, but statistical significance sometimes increases because the coefficients increase. This largely seems to be because older fathers are associated with less permissive attitudes; older mothers usually associate with more permissive attitudes. Where these parental-age effects are smaller, the coefficients on being firstborn tend not to increase much in magnitude, so that the statistical significance of firstborn status decreases.
27. Holmlund et al. 2011.
28. Tanfer and Schoorl 1992.
29. Finer 2007.
30. Santorum 2005.
31. Santelli et al. 2006.
32. Firstborns in the sample are also slightly less likely to have lived with their spouses before marriage: 27.0% of firstborns admit to having done so, as compared with

30.4% of laterborns. The average difference between the two rises to five percentage points when controlling for family size.

33. The reduction in effect size between the top and bottom panels of the figure can be reversed by replacing the measure of education with measures of the respondent's parents' education.
34. Jelen and Wilcox 2003.
35. Freese et al. 1999 considered birth-order effects on abortion attitudes in passing using the same data set looked at here. Their results, using a variety of different configurations of control variables, matched that here, dancing on the fringes of statistical significance.
36. The three not given in the sentence in the text are whether the woman is unmarried and does not want to marry the baby's father, whether she is married but does not want more children, and whether there is a strong chance that the baby has a serious birth defect.
37. In the extreme cases, three respondents who said abortion should be legal under any circumstances proceeded to say abortion should be illegal in five of the six specific circumstances.
38. This may be because parts of the population (perhaps disproportionately including firstborns) think that rape victims brought the crime upon themselves; see Lambert and Raichle 2000 for discussion of the prevalence and predictors of this attitude.
39. Meier and Geis 1997.
40. That 8% of respondents who rejected abortion's availability in every circumstance the survey asked about includes some who were (possibly erroneously) coded as being relatively acceptant of abortion in the 5-point scale variable.

CHAPTER 5

1. For example, Hetherington and Globetti 2002.
2. This point is discussed more fully in chapter 1. For more extended discussions, see especially Arnold and Weisberg 1996; Elder and Greene 2006; Elder and Greene 2007; and Elder and Greene 2012b.
3. Toft 2006, 56.
4. Kopczuk and Lupton 2007.
5. For example, Dupont 2004.
6. Considering the policy preferences of individuals who ended up with responsibility for children without planning to (or those who unexpectedly ended up childless, as through miscarriages) would speak to this point, though the data set used here does not include the relevant information.
7. Garfinkle and Skaperdas 2000.
8. Pickering and Kisangani 2006.
9. Organski and Kugler 1977. This tendency for societies to bounce back economically after wars is somewhat countered by the potential that defense policy has long-run effects on other aspects of society, most notably in the connection between military spending and economic growth. If more active military policies retard growth, children and their guardians have stronger reason to oppose such activities, just as any future costs or benefits of a particular military action may weigh more heavily in the opinions of those with children. This effect is at best indirect, however, and since analysts still debate even the direction of the relationship—let alone its size—between military spending and macroeconomic

outcomes, its theoretical claims are weak and ambiguous. See Heo 2010 for further discussion.

10. Going to war can present the ethical problem of trading off the costs of causing immediate deaths through military action but preventing a (possibly larger) number of subsequent deaths, a variant of the philosophical problem sometimes known as the "Survival Lottery" (Harris 1975). In this framing, even the costs incurred by death and mourning might be compensated for by avoiding the deaths of others. The question is not an idle one in national security debates (Tobey 2012).

11. Growing up during times of war might inflict psychological costs on children (Pesonen et al. 2007), though the evidence gives most cause for concern with direct exposure to intense war. Children seem to be more resilient to indirect cases or less severe war (Jensen and Shaw 1993). It may in fact be adults, more cognizant of the conflict and less psychologically flexible, who are more likely to be traumatized by these less acute exposures to war. It is not clear, then, that incorporating a child's welfare would naturally lead to less opposition to conflict, especially in the case considered here, that of the United States, whose conflicts have since the nineteenth century mostly been fought overseas.

12. Lebel 2007.

13. Gifford 2006. A variant of this crowding-out argument could run via cognitive costs rather than limited government budgets: Parents' cognitive attention to personally relevant domestic policy, such as education, reduces their interest in and attention to foreign policy. The theoretical implications of such apathy are ambiguous. It is plausible that less interest in foreign affairs motivates demands for reduced outlays on related expenditure. However, being less attentive to international events may also make the costs of military sorties less salient.

14. Caverley 2010.

15. Elder et al. 2010.

16. Segal et al. 1999.

17. Wolfe et al. 2005.

18. Lane 2001.

19. Of course, a variety of mechanisms do allow for child sex selection, some of which were not as directly available to the siblings considered in chapter 3: Adoptive and stepparents can select children of a preferred gender, for example. These sorts of behaviors could potentially produce reverse causation, where people with one particular foreign-policy preference tend to have children of a particular gender or be more likely to keep having children until they have one of each sex. For this to contaminate this chapter's quasi-experimental design, though, military hawkishness would have to be the *cause* of having more female children. Few causal stories seem to follow that trajectory. Still, speaking more conclusively to the point would require a study that tracked adults' foreign-policy preferences before and after the birth of their children.

20. See also Kelty et al. 2010's figures on the age distribution of those in the military.

21. More technically, the increased random error should also increase standard errors, so that a causal effect of any given size is less likely to attain statistical significance.

22. Thomson et al. 1992.

23. Hofferth and Anderson 2003.

24. Another alternative, particularly relevant to the hypotheses involving gender, would look at the proportion of children that are girls and separately control for

the total number of children. This is especially useful in case family size has an independent effect on policy preferences, as the chapter 4 models suggested it sometimes might. In the event, though, this also produces comparable results to those reported.

25. A special motivation for selecting two security-related variables is that both inherently implicate risk. As chapter 6 explores, parents may have reason to react differently from nonparents where risks are concerned, so this parallelism is important.

26. Jacobs 2006.

27. While the range of this variable theoretically covers three points, in practice few respondents called either priority "not at all important." (Only 1.6% of respondents—17 out of 1,062—gave that answer for nuclear proliferation; 2.0%—21 out of 1,062—did for terrorism.) This might raise questions about how meaningful the results of modeling of those few outlying observations could be. Combining the "not at all" and "somewhat important" categories into a single group on a 2-point scale produces similar results to the 3-point coding, though, so the results here stick with the original, more precise rendition of the variable.

28. The original question wording: "Some people believe the United States should solve international problems by using diplomacy and other forms of international pressure and use military force only if absolutely necessary. Suppose we put such people at '1' on this scale. Others believe diplomacy and pressure often fail and the US must be ready to use military force. Suppose we put them at number 7. And of course others fall in positions in-between, at points 2, 3, 4, 5, and 6. Where would you place yourself on this scale, or haven't you thought much about this?"

29. Lavine et al. 1996.

30. Controlling for other concepts (minority status, having a parent born abroad, etc.) do not appreciably affect the results. The reported results are also robust to most alternative specifications of the listed control variables: age and/or education squared, a measure of professed strength of religious belief rather than a measure of attendance, decadal dummy variables for age, whether or not there is a veteran or active-duty military member in the respondent's family, and so on. The largest exception is noted below.

31. The (two-tailed) statistical confidence that girls' and boys' effects differ is just under 88%. Boys' effect can be distinguished from zero but not from the putatively negative effect of girls because of the uncertainty around the size of the latter effect. Allowing for the possibility, clearly visible in Figure 5.1, that girls could, like boys, associate with increased prioritization of fighting terrorism, reduces the confidence that the two estimated effects differ.

32. As with nuclear war, most respondent placed the highest possible prioritization on antiterrorism: The average value was just over 2.80 out of 3. This narrow variation again raises the proportion of variation explained by relatively small shifts.

33. As discussed above, partisan identification raises endogeneity issues that might be expected to bias downward the coefficients on the variables of interest. Partisan identification in fact mostly diminishes the child-in-household coefficients. Rerunning the lower-right model of Figure 5.2 without partisan identification, for example, produces coefficients on the numbers of boys and girls in the house that closely match those in the models without control variables in Figure 5.2's top panel.

34. As of November 2004, near the end of the sampling period for the survey, there had been 1,263 U. S. military deaths (combat and noncombat) in Iraq since combat

operations began in 2003 compared with 159 US military deaths in Afghanistan since 2001.
35. Goldstone et al. 2012.
36. For example, Mesquida and Wiener 1999; Hesketh and Xing 2006.
37. Using an interaction—multiplying respondent gender by child gender—rather than subdividing sample produces similar results.
38. Control variables, omitted for brevity, are the same as in Figure 5.3, except that there is no control for the respondent's gender—that control is superfluous since each sample contains respondents of only one gender.
39. They might also not apply in societies such as Israel's where both sexes are subject to military conscription.
40. The data set used here has data on how many children in the household are in each of several age groups (zero to four years, five to nine years, ten to thirteen years, fourteen to seventeen years) but does not distinguish those age groups by gender.

CHAPTER 6
1. Wisman and Capehart 2010.
2. Schlesinger 2011.
3. Mastekaasa 2000; Bianchi and Milkie 2010.
4. Scott et al. 2006.
5. Correll et al. 2007.
6. Budig and England 2001. As chapter 2 noted, these consequences can feed into children's ultimate political attitudes.
7. Elder and Greene 2006. There and in subsequent work (see particularly chapter 5 of Elder and Greene 2012a), these authors emphasize causal mechanisms involving mothers becoming more compassionate through the experience of nurturing, a slightly different story from that explored here. They also argue that fathers will typically be *less* interested in social welfare programs than will men who are not parents.
8. Nomaguchi and Milkie 2003.
9. Jost et al. 2003; De Vries and Edwards 2009.
10. Mughan 2007.
11. Huddy et al. 2005.
12. Rehm 2009.
13. Pailhe and Solaz 2012.
14. The measure may actually have additional relevance to the psychological aspect of the argument here, since, as Ross and van Willigen (1996, 573) put it, "Living with children is the stressful aspect of parenthood." In other words, some of the child-induced stress and sensitivity to risk may affect individuals who live with the child, even if those individuals are not biological parents.
15. In years where both variables (children in household and all children) are available, the correlation coefficient—Pearson's r—between the two is slightly over 0.3, where 1 indicates that the two variables always move in the same direction, −1 indicates that they move in opposite directions, and zero indicates that movements of one variable give no information about movements in the other.
16. Valletta 1999.
17. Johnson and Neumark 1997.
18. Shams and Jackson 1993.
19. Scheve and Stasavage 2006.
20. Regnerus and Smith 2005.

21. Norris and Inglehart 2004, 18.
22. Tversky and Kahneman 1991.
23. The wording varied slightly depending on the employment status of the respondent: those unemployed but seeking work at the time of the survey had the "losing your job" text replaced by "finding a job." Excluding the respondents who faced the alternative wording (and who accordingly were out of work) does not change the results, so the models include all respondents for generality. Note also that varying categories of respondents were not asked this question across the survey years. For example, in the 1996 and 1998 administrations of the survey, those who reported being retired yet having a job were given the question, even though other years did not. These differences from one year to the next are relatively minor; the survey treated the largest classes of respondent more consistently over time. The currently employed always received the question, for instance, while nonworking homemakers never did. Any remaining differences caused by the few whose inclusion depended on the administration of the survey should be accounted for by the models' controls for each particular year of survey.
24. For respondents not interviewed in person in their homes, the question text substitutes "there" for "here." In either case, then, the question aims to encompass health problems of any family member who lives with the respondent.
25. The correlation coefficient is 0.2.
26. The estimated effect is somewhat more substantial than it might appear because, like chapter 5's nonproliferation question, the job-insecurity results are highly skewed, with three-quarters of respondents giving the minimum possible answer (i.e., they were unworried about losing their jobs). Merging the much smaller categories where people expressed at least some concern about losing their job shows that each additional child increases co-householders' probability of expressing some insecurity about their job by four percentage points.
27. Scheve and Slaughter 2004.
28. Nelson 1999.
29. When the survey was administered in its usual face-to-face fashion, the survey-taker would show the respondent a card showing a thermometer specifying degrees of fondness at particular values. For example, an answer of 60 was marked as "60°: A bit more warm or favorable than cold feeling" while 15 was marked "15°: Quite cold or unfavorable feeling." The distribution of answers on feeling thermometers consequently tends to be extremely lumpy, with many more respondents choosing the values (such as 15) that had associated descriptions than choosing other values (such as 10, 20, or 14) that had no explicit description. Nonetheless, respondents were free to answer any whole-number value in the zero to 100 range, and these measures are treated as continuous over the whole range of possibilities.
30. Hogan et al. 2005 find a link between economic insecurity and attitudes to the poor before linking these attitudes toward preferences over criminal justice policy.
31. Gilens 1999.
32. Empirically, they do: They have a moderate correlation of only 0.4 with one another.
33. Keele 2005.
34. It could be that faith in social institutions leads to more optimism about and confidence in future outcomes, which in turn makes having children more appealing. This case, further examined in chapter 7, would reverse the causation discussed here.

35. This difference is well known, so much so that some (notably Gilens 1999) have argued that racial attitudes drive feelings toward welfare, especially among whites.

36. This is similar to, though less extreme than, the rescaling used in chapter 3.

37. Rehm 2009.

38. The bottom of the confidence interval is at –0.002; for technically inclined readers, the statistical significance (two-tailed p statistic) is .06.

39. The low observation counts for spending on welfare and the poor largely result from the NES's suppression of respondent data for privacy reasons after 2000. This eliminates information about urban or rural residence. Excluding this variable more than triples the number of respondents available. With this larger sample, each additional child increases one's desire for welfare spending by 0.026 (instead of 0.038 as seen in Figure 6.3), but the more precise estimation provided by the larger sample means that the smaller coefficient attains higher standards of statistical significance (the 95% confidence interval is entirely to the right of zero). Conversely, the effect of additional children on spending on the poor falls to almost exactly zero, far lower than its smaller-sample estimate and with no hope of statistical significance.

40. Greenlee 2010; Elder and Greene 2012b.

41. Nail et al. 2009.

42. Huddy et al. 2007.

CHAPTER 7

1. An anecdotal sense that this might be true comes from news reports on the 2012 death of Ben-Zion Netanyahu, father of the then-prime minister of Israel, which speculated that the younger Netanyahu would feel freer to moderate his positions once he would not face rebukes from his hardline father.

2. Crandall 1995.

3. Ellison and Bradshaw 2009.

4. Wildsmith et al. 2010.

5. Leventhal and Brooks-Gunn 2000.

6. Billy and Moore 1992.

7. Morgan and King 2001. Most consistently, belief in the permanence of the romantic partnership associates with increased willingness to bear children (even unintended children; see Sassler et al. 2009).

8. Hakim 2003.

9. Rossier and Bernardi 2009.

10. Mansyur et al. 2008.

11. Sheldon and Bettencourt 2002.

12. Billy and Moore 1992, 982.

13. Mosher et al. 1992.

14. Dupont 2004.

15. For example, Schoen et al. 1997; Astone et al. 1999.

16. Singerman 2006.

17. Studies can ask whether respondents are trying to have children, but they rarely do if they are concerned with political factors. This approach also focuses on the slightly different question of whether potential parents have *intended* children; if those with strong political beliefs are more likely to have intended children (e.g., are less likely to abort unintended fetuses or to use birth control more effectively) than are less politically committed individuals, this question would provide an

inaccurate impression of actual family formation. Intentions, in any case, can be a poor guide to behavior (ask most dieters).

18. There is a striking pattern in the likelihood of mothers being outside of the household. Only one newborn is listed as having an out-of-household mother (whether dead or living elsewhere) in 1991–1998. From 1999 on, by contrast, there are infants living with their fathers but not their mothers almost every year, with seventeen such observations over the 1999–2007 period. Whether this reflects random chance, an upsurge in women living separately from their infants, or changed reporting practices in the survey is unclear.

19. The data set includes not only month of birth but also information on whether the child was born on the expected date and, if not, how many weeks early or late it was. This would allow reasonably precise timing of conception and therefore a closer match with waxing or waning partisan identification—or it would if self-reported due dates can be trusted; there is reason to doubt. Birth certificate based data all too often includes such peculiarities as seemingly healthy, seven-pound babies said to be born in the fifteenth week of gestation.

20. When used in conjunction with those who did not identify with any party at all, this could produce a 4-point scale. Indeed, we can get even more precise. Those who had no party association were asked to identify what party they would be most likely to support in a hypothetical general election the following day. Distinguishing between those who named a party and those who responded that they did not know or would not support any party would allow for a 5-point scale of partisan feeling: those who show no signs of any partisan stirrings, those who do not identify with a party but who can express a leaning, and the three levels of explicit identification with a party. Using any of these finer scales typically produces similar results to those reported, although sometimes the expected effect of partisan intensity increases slightly in magnitude.

21. Sears and Funk 1999.

22. van Balen et al. 1997.

23. Caldwell 1980.

24. Note that none of these variables measure religion. This is in part because the BHPS does not ask questions about religion with much regularity. Including measures of frequency of church attendance or membership in religious groups accordingly drops half the sample. One might still argue that the theoretical case for inclusion is strong—that there is cause to believe religiosity increases likelihood of having children as well as partisan intensity—but it also turns out that religion has, with the available measures, an incredibly paltry effect on childbirth in this sample. Thus adding religion controls tend not to add any information even as they systematically slash the sample size. If they are included, partisanship becomes a more important determinant of fertility in the model with one-year lags but less important in the model with two-year lags.

25. Special statistical methods exist for rare events; see King and Zeng (2001). Using these more sophisticated techniques does not change the tenor of the results here.

26. The results are similar when including other control variables, such as indicators for year of survey, region of residence, and the party with which the voter associates (both in terms of its ideology—Conservative instead of Labour—and in terms of its incumbency status).

27. Storey et al. 2000.

28. Some work along these behavioral lines has begun. Šerek et al. (2012) find that having parents who fight seems to lead to less of a sense that one's political actions will make a difference (a sense that social scientists call "efficacy"). In contrast, Sances (2013) finds that children of divorce do not systematically have lower turnout rates, though there may be exceptions for some subpopulations.

29. That is to say: even if family is not relevant as the causal variable in a model, a wider range of family variables ought to be taken into account far more often when testing hypotheses relating to public attitudes.

APPENDIX

1. Any *straight* line. Models can involve curved lines—in fact, some in this book are parabolas, lines shaped like the letter U either rightside up or upside down, by predicting outcomes based not just on a variable (such as age) but also the square of that variable (age times age). In this case, predicted values could hit zero and 1 without ever getting to 2, if the vertex (peak) of the parabola is between 1 and 2. Even then, though, the basic point here holds, since the parabola that never gets as high as 2 will make predictions that are below zero as well as those between zero and 1. While some functions (anything sinusoidal, for example) would avoid this problem, they are generally implausible to the point of absurdity.

2. The difference between 40% and 42% can be substantively and statistically significant. If something affects 42% of Americans instead of 40%, for example, it affects around 6 million more people. Even the smallish-seeming two percentage points may then hold a great deal of interest.

3. King et al. 2000.

4. Angrist and Pischke 2009, 197–198 (see also pp. 105–107).

5. Taagepera 2008.

6. Ai and Norton 2003.

7. Allison 1999.

8. Angrist and Pischke 2009, 197–198.

9. For example, Sinclair et al. 2012.

REFERENCES

Abrevaya, Jason. 2009. "Are There Missing Girls in the United States? Evidence from Birth Data." *American Economic Journal: Applied Economics* 1 (2): 1–34.

Achen, Christopher H. 2002. "Parental Socialization and Rational Party Identification." *Political Behavior* 24 (2): 151–170.

Ai, Chunrong, and Edward C. Norton. 2003. "Interaction Terms in Logit and Probit Models." *Economics Letters* 80 (1): 123–129.

Alford, John R., Carolyn L. Funk, and John R. Hibbing. 2005. "Are Political Orientations Genetically Transmitted?" *American Political Science Review* 99 (2): 153–167.

Alford, John R., Peter K. Hatemi, John R. Hibbing, Nicholas G. Martin, and Lindon J. Eaves. 2011. "The Politics of Mate Choice." *Journal of Politics* 73 (2): 362–379.

Allison, Paul D. 1999. "Comparing Logit and Probit Coefficients across Groups." *Sociological Methods and Research* 28 (2): 186–208.

Almond, Douglas, and Lena Edlund. 2008. "Son-Biased Sex Ratios in the 2000 United States Census." *Proceedings of the National Academy of Sciences* 105 (15): 5681–5682.

Alvarez, R. Michael, and Edward J. McCaffery. 2003. "Are There Sex Differences in Fiscal Political Preferences?" *Political Research Quarterly* 56 (1): 5–17.

Andeweg, Rudy B., and Steef B. Van Den Berg. 2003. "Linking Birth Order to Political Leadership: The Impact of Parents or Sibling Interaction?" *Political Psychology* 24 (3): 605–623.

Angrist, Joshua, and Jörn-Steffen Pischke. 2009. *Mostly Harmless Econometrics: An Empiricist's Companion*. Princeton, NJ: Princeton University Press.

Argys, Laura M., Daniel I. Rees, Susan L. Averett, and Benjama Witoonchart. 2006. "Birth Order and Risky Adolescent Behavior." *Economic Inquiry* 44 (2): 215–233.

Arnold, Laura W., and Herbert F. Weisberg. 1996. "Parenthood, Family Values, and the 1992 Presidential Election." *American Politics Quarterly* 24 (2): 194–220.

Ary, Dennis V., Elizabeth Tildesley, Hyman Hops, and Judy Andrews. 1993. "The Influence of Parent, Sibling, and Peer Modeling and Attitudes on Adolescent Use of Alcohol." *International Journal of the Addictions* 28 (9): 853–880.

Astone, Nan Marie, Constance A. Nathanson, Robert Schoen, and Young J. Kim. 1999. "Family Demography, Social Theory, and Investment in Social Capital." *Population and Development Review* 25 (1): 1–31.

Averett, Susan L., Laura M. Argys, and Daniel I. Rees. 2011. "Older Siblings and Adolescent Risky Behavior: Does Parenting Play a Role?" *Journal of Population Economics* 24 (3): 957–978.

Beck, Paul, and M. Kent Jennings. 1975. "Parents as Middle-Persons in Political Socialization." *Journal of Politics* 37 (1): 87–93.

Bianchi, Suzanne M., and Melissa A. Milkie. 2010. "Work and Family Research in the First Decade of the 21st Century." *Journal of Marriage and the Family* 72 (3): 705–725.

Billy, John O.G., and David E. Moore. 1992. "A Multilevel Analysis of Marital and Nonmarital Fertility in the United States." *Social Forces* 70 (4): 977–1011.

Bjerkedal, Tor, Petter Kristensen, Geir A. Skjeret, and John I. Brevik. 2007. "Intelligence Test Scores and Birth Order Among Young Norwegian Men (Conscripts) Analyzed Within and Between Families." *Intelligence* 35 (5): 503–514.

Blanchard, Ray. 2004. "Quantitative and Theoretical Analyses of the Relation Between Older Brothers and Homosexuality in Men." *Journal of Theoretical Biology* 230 (2): 173–187.

Bogaert, Anthony F. 2006. "Biological Versus Nonbiological Older Brothers and Men's Sexual Orientation." *Proceedings of the National Academy of Sciences* 103 (28): 10771–10774.

Bolzendahl, Catherine, and Sigrun Olafsdottir. 2008. "Gender Group Interest or Gender Ideology? Understanding US Support for Family Policy within the Liberal Welfare Regime." *Sociological Perspectives* 51 (2): 281–304.

Box-Steffensmeier, Janet M., Suzanna De Boef, and Tse-min Lin. 2004. "The Dynamics of the Partisan Gender Gap." *American Political Science Review* 98 (3): 515–528.

Bressan, Paola, Stephen M. Colarelli, and Mary Beth Cavalieri. 2009. "Biologically Costly Altruism Depends on Emotional Closeness Among Step-But Not Half or Full Siblings." *Evolutionary Psychology* 7 (1): 118–132.

Brody, Charles J., and Lala Carr Steelman. 1985. "Sibling Structure and Parental Sex-Typing of Children's Household Tasks." *Journal of Marriage and Family* 47 (2): 265–273.

Budig, Michelle J., and Paula England. 2001. "The Wage Penalty for Motherhood." *American Sociological Review* 66 (2): 204–225.

Buonanno, Paolo, and Paolo Vanin. 2013. "Bowling Alone, Drinking Together." *Empirical Economics* 44 (3): 1635–1672.

Burnet, Jennie E. 2011. "Women Have Found Respect: Gender Quotas, Symbolic Representation, and Female Empowerment in Rwanda." *Politics and Gender* 7 (3): 303–334.

Burns, Nancy, and Katherine Gallagher. 2010. "Public Opinion on Gender Issues: The Politics of Equity and Roles." *Annual Review of Political Science* 13: 425–443.

Butcher, Kristin F., and Anne Case. 1994. "The Effect of Sibling Sex Composition on Women's Education and Earnings." *Quarterly Journal of Economics* 109 (3): 531–563.

Cahn, Naomi, and June Carbone. 2010. *Red Families v. Blue Families: Legal Polarization and the Creation of Culture*. New York: Oxford University Press.

Caldwell, John C. 1980. "Mass Education as a Determinant of the Timing of Fertility Decline." *Population and Development Review* 6 (2): 225–255.

Carney, Dana R., John T. Jost, Samuel D. Gosling, and Jeff Potter. 2008. "The Secret Lives of Liberals and Conservatives: Personality Profiles, Interaction Styles, and the Things They Leave Behind." *Political Psychology* 29 (6): 807–840.

Caverley, Jonathan D. 2010. "The Myth of Military Myopia: Democracy, Small Wars, and Vietnam." *International Security* 34 (3): 119–157.

Chahnazarian, Anouch. 1988. "Determinants of the Sex Ratio at Birth: Review of Recent Literature." *Social Biology* 35 (3): 214–235.

Charney, Evan, and William English. 2012. "Candidate Genes and Political Behavior." *American Political Science Review* 106 (1): 1–34.

Cicirelli, Victor G. 1980. "Comparison of College Women's Feelings Toward Their Siblings and Parents." *Journal of Marriage and the Family* 42 (1): 111–118.

Cicirelli, Victor G. 1994. "Sibling Relationships in Cross-Cultural Perspective." *Journal of Marriage and Family* 56 (1): 7–20.

Cochran, John K., and Beth A. Sanders. 2009. "The Gender Gap in Death Penalty Support: An Exploratory Study." *Journal of Criminal Justice* 37 (6): 525–533.

Coffé, Hilde, and Ariana Need. 2010. "Similarity in Husbands and Wives Party Family Preference in the Netherlands." *Electoral Studies* 29 (2): 259–268.

Conley, Dalton. 2000. "Sibship Sex Composition: Effects on Educational Attainment." *Social Science Research* 29 (3): 441–457.

Conley, Dalton, and Emily Rauscher. 2013. "The Effect of Daughters on Partisanship and Social Attitudes Toward Women." *Sociological Forum* 28 (4): 700–718.

Conover, Pamela Johnston. 1988. "Feminists and the Gender Gap." *Journal of Politics* 50 (4): 985–1010.

Correll, Shelley J., Stephen Benard, and In Paik. 2007. "Getting a Job: Is There a Motherhood Penalty?" *American Journal of Sociology* 112 (5): 1297–1338.

Crandall, Christian S. 1995. "Do Parents Discriminate Against Their Heavyweight Daughters?" *Personality and Social Psychology Bulletin* 21 (7): 724–735.

Crouter, Ann C., Beth A. Manke, and Susan M. McHale. 1995. "The Family Context of Gender Intensification in Early Adolescence." *Child Development* 66 (2): 317–329.

Crump, Richard, Gopi Shah Goda, and Kevin J. Mumford. 2011. "Fertility and the Personal Exemption: Comment." *American Economic Review* 101 (4): 1616–1628.

Dancygier, Rafaela, and Elizabeth N. Saunders. 2006. "A New Electorate? Comparing Preferences and Partisanship Between Immigrants and Natives." *American Journal of Political Science* 50 (4): 962–981.

De Vries, Catherine E., and Erica E. Edwards. 2009. "Taking Europe to Its Extremes: Extremist Parties and Public Euroscepticism." *Party Politics* 15 (1): 5–28.

Desposato, Scott, and Barbara Norrander. 2009. "The Gender Gap in Latin America: Contextual and Individual Influences on Gender and Political Participation." *British Journal of Political Science* 39 (1): 141–162.

Drewianka, Scott. 2008. "Divorce Law and Family Formation." *Journal of Population Economics* 21 (2): 485–503.

Dupont, Diane P. 2004. "Do Children Matter? An Examination of Gender Differences in Environmental Valuation." *Ecological Economics* 49 (3): 273–286.

Eaves, Lindon J., and Peter K. Hatemi. 2008. "Transmission of Attitudes Toward Abortion and Gay Rights: Effects of Genes, Social Learning and Mate Selection." *Behavior Genetics* 38 (3): 247–256.

Elder, Glen H., Jr., Lin Wang, Naomi J. Spence, Daniel E. Adkins, and Tyson H. Brown. 2010. "Pathways to the All-Volunteer Military." *Social Science Quarterly* 91 (2): 455–475.

Elder, Laurel, and Steven Greene. 2006. "The Children Gap on Social Welfare and the Politicization of American Parents, 1984–2000." *Politics and Gender* 2 (4): 451–472.

Elder, Laurel, and Steven Greene. 2007. "The Myth of 'Security Moms' and 'NASCAR Dads': Parenthood, Political Stereotypes, and the 2004 Election." *Social Science Quarterly* 88 (1): 1–19.

Elder, Laurel, and Steven Greene. 2012a. *The Politics of Parenthood: Causes and Consequences of the Politicization and Polarization of the American Family.* Albany: SUNY Press.

Elder, Laurel, and Steven Greene. 2012b. "The Politics of Parenthood: Parenthood Effects on Issue Attitudes and Candidate Evaluations in 2008." *American Politics Research* 40 (3): 419–449.

Ellison, Christopher G., and Matt Bradshaw. 2009. "Religious Beliefs, Sociopolitical Ideology, and Attitudes Toward Corporal Punishment." *Journal of Family Issues* 30 (3): 320–340.

Emeka, Amon. 2006. "Birth, Fortune, and Discrepant Fertility in Twentieth-Century America." *Social Science History* 30 (3): 327–357.

Eriksen, Shelley, and Vickie Jensen. 2006. "All in the Family? Family Environment Factors in Sibling Violence." *Journal of Family Violence* 21 (8): 497–507.

Ernst, Cécile, and Jules Angst. 1983. *Birth Order: Its Influence on Personality.* New York: Springer.

Fagot, Beverly I., Mary D. Leinbach, and Cherie O'Boyle. 1992. "Gender Labeling, Gender Stereotyping, and Parenting Behaviors." *Developmental Psychology* 28 (2): 225–230.

Feng, Du, and Laura Baker. 1994. "Spouse Similarity in Attitudes, Personality, and Psychological Well-Being." *Behavior Genetics* 24 (4): 357–364.

Finer, Lawrence B. 2007. "Trends in Premarital Sex in the United States, 1954–2003." *Public Health Reports* 122 (1): 73–78.

Fishback, Price V., Michael R. Haines, and Shawn Kantor. 2007. "Births, Deaths, and New Deal Relief During the Great Depression." *Review of Economics and Statistics* 89 (1): 1–14.

Fitzgerald, Jennifer, and K. Amber Curtis. 2012. "Partisan Discord in the Family and Political Engagement: A Comparative Behavioral Analysis." *Journal of Politics* 74 (1): 129–141.

Førland, Tor Egil, Trine Rogg Korsvik, and Knut-Andreas Christophersen. 2012. "Brought Up to Rebel in the Sixties: Birth Order Irrelevant, Parental Worldview Decisive." *Political Psychology* 33 (6): 825–838.

Fowler, James H., Laura A. Baker, Christopher T. Dawes. 2008. "Genetic Variation in Political Participation." *American Political Science Review* 102 (2): 233–248.

Fraley, R. Chris, Brian N. Griffin, Jay Belsky, and Glenn I. Roisman. 2012. "Developmental Antecedents of Political Ideology: A Longitudinal Investigation from Birth to Age 18 Years." *Psychological Science* 23 (11): 1425–1431.

Freese, Jeremy, Brian Powell, and Lala Carr Steelman. 1999. "Rebel Without a Cause or Effect: Birth Order and Social Attitudes." *American Sociological Review* 64 (2): 207–231.

Garfinkel, Michelle R., and Stergios Skaperdas. 2000. "Conflict Without Misperceptions or Incomplete Information: How the Future Matters." *Journal of Conflict Resolution* 44 (6): 793–807.

Gelman, Andrew, Cristian Pasarica, and Rahul Dodhia. 2002. "Let's Practice What We Preach: Turning Tables into Graphs." *American Statistician* 56 (2): 121–130.

Gidengil, Elisabeth, Brenda O'Neill, and Lisa Young. 2010. "Her Mother's Daughter? The Influence of Childhood Socialization on Women's Political Engagement." *Journal of Women, Politics and Policy* 31 (4): 334–355.

Gifford, Brian. 2006. "Why No Trade-Off Between 'Guns and Butter'? Armed Forces and Social Spending in the Advanced Industrial Democracies, 1960–1993." *American Journal of Sociology* 112 (2): 473–509.

Gilens, Martin. 1999. *Why Americans Hate Welfare.* Chicago: University of Chicago Press.

Gneezy, Uri, Kenneth L. Leonard, and John A. List. 2009. "Gender Differences in Competition: Evidence from a Matrilineal and a Patriarchal Society." *Econometrica* 77 (5): 1637–1664.

Goldstone, Jack A., Eric P. Kaufmann, and Monica Duffy Toft, eds. 2012. *Political Demography: How Population Changes Are Reshaping International Security and National Politics.* New York: Oxford University Press.

Granberg, Donald. 1982. "Family Size Preferences and Sexual Permissiveness as Factors Differentiating Abortion Activists." *Social Psychology Quarterly* 45 (1): 15–23.

Greenlee, Jill S. 2010. "Soccer Moms, Hockey Moms and the Question of 'Transformative' Motherhood." *Politics and Gender* 6 (3): 405–431.

Hakim, Catherine. 2003. "A New Approach to Explaining Fertility Patterns: Preference Theory." *Population and Development Review* 29 (3): 349–374.

Hand, Michael. 2002. "Religious Upbringing Reconsidered." *Journal of Philosophy of Education* 36 (4): 545–557.

Harris, John. 1975. "The Survival Lottery." *Philosophy* 50 (191): 81–87.

Harris, Judith Rich. 2006. *No Two Alike: Human Nature and Human Individuality.* New York: W.W. Norton.

Harris, Judith Rich. 2009. *The Nurture Assumption.* New York: Free Press.

Hatemi, Peter K., Carolyn L. Funk, Sarah E. Medland, Hermine M. Maes, Judy L. Silberg, Nicholas G. Martin, and Lindon J. Eaves. 2009. "Genetic and Environmental Transmission of Political Attitudes over a Life Time." *Journal of Politics* 71 (3): 1141–1156.

Hatemi, Peter K., Sarah E. Medland, and Lindon J. Eaves. 2009. "Do Genes Contribute to the 'Gender Gap?'" *Journal of Politics* 71 (1): 262–276.

Hayes, Bernadette C. 1993. "Partisanship and Political Attitudes: Is There a Marriage Gap?" *Australian Journal of Political Science* 28 (2): 242–257.

Healy, Andrew, and Neil Malhotra. 2013. "Childhood Socialization and Political Attitudes: Evidence from a Natural Experiment." *Journal of Politics* 75 (4): 1023–1037.

Healy, Andrew J., Neil Malhotra, and Cecilia Hyunjung Mo. 2010. "Irrelevant Events Affect Voters' Evaluations of Government Performance." *Proceedings of the National Academy of Sciences* 107 (29): 12804–12809.

Henderson, Brenda A., and Sheri A. Berenbaum. 1997. "Sex-Typed Play in Opposite-Sex Twins." *Developmental Psychobiology* 31 (2): 115–123.

Heo, Uk. 2010. "The Relationship Between Defense Spending and Economic Growth in the United States." *Political Research Quarterly* 63 (4): 760–770.

Hesketh, Therese, and Zhu Wei Xing. 2006. "Abnormal Sex Ratios in Human Populations: Causes and Consequences." *Proceedings of the National Academy of Sciences* 103 (36): 13271–13275.

Hetherington, Mark J., and Suzanne Globetti. 2002. "Political Trust and Racial Policy Preferences." *American Journal of Political Science* 46 (2): 253–275.

Hibbing, Matthew V., Melinda Ritchie, and Mary R. Anderson. 2011. "Personality and Political Discussion." *Political Behavior* 33 (4): 601–624.

Hicks, Gary R., and Tien-tsung Lee. 2006. "Public Attitudes Toward Gays and Lesbians: Trends and Predictors." *Journal of Homosexuality* 51 (1): 57–77.

Hill, Twyla J. 2006. "Grandchild, Grandparent, and Parent Coresidence from 1970 to 1990: Structural Factors Affecting State Patterns." *International Journal of Aging and Human Development* 62 (2): 117–142.

Hofferth, Sandra L., and Kermyt G. Anderson. 2003. "Are All Dads Equal? Biology Versus Marriage as a Basis for Paternal Investment." *Journal of Marriage and Family* 65 (1): 213–232.

Hogan, Michael J., Ted Chiricos, and Marc Gertz. 2005. "Economic Insecurity, Blame, and Punitive Attitudes." *Justice Quarterly* 22 (3): 392–412.

Holmgren, Sara, Bo Molander, and Lars-Göran Nilsson. 2007. "Episodic Memory in Adult Age and Effects of Sibship Size and Birth Order: Longitudinal Data." *Journal of Adult Development* 14 (1): 37–46.

Holmlund, Helena, Mikael Lindahl, and Erik Plug. 2011. "The Causal Effect of Parents' Schooling on Children's Schooling: A Comparison of Estimation Methods." *Journal of Economic Literature* 49 (3): 615–651.

Hooghe, Marc, and Britt Wilkenfeld. 2008. "The Stability of Political Attitudes and Behaviors Across Adolescence and Early Adulthood: A Comparison of Survey Data on Adolescents and Young Adults in Eight Countries." *Journal of Youth and Adolescence* 37 (2): 155–167.

Huddy, Leonie, Stanley Feldman, Charles Taber, and Gallya Lahav. 2005. "Threat, Anxiety, and Support of Antiterrorism Policies." *American Journal of Political Science* 49 (3): 593–608.

Huddy, Leonie, Stanley Feldman, and Christopher Weber. 2007. "The Political Consequences of Perceived Threat and Felt Insecurity." *Annals of the American Academy of Political and Social Science* 614: 131–153.

Iervolino, Alessandra C., Melissa Hines, Susan E. Golombok, John Rust, and Robert Plomin. 2005. "Genetic and Environmental Influences on Sex-Typed Behavior During the Preschool Years." *Child Development* 76 (4): 826–840.

Jacobs, Lawrence R., and Robert Y. Shapiro. 1994. "Public Opinion's Tilt Against Private Enterprise." *Health Affairs* 13 (1): 285–298.

Jacobs, Scott. 2006. "Nonfallacious Rhetorical Strategies: Lyndon Johnson's Daisy Ad." *Argumentation* 20 (4): 421–442.

James, William H. 1987. "The Human Sex Ratio. Part 1: A Review of the Literature." *Human Biology* 59 (5): 721–752.

Jelen, Ted G., and Clyde Wilcox. 2003. "Causes and Consequences of Public Attitudes Toward Abortion: A Review and Research Agenda." *Political Research Quarterly* 56 (4): 489–500.

Jennings, M. Kent, and Kenneth P. Langton. 1969. "Mothers Versus Fathers: The Formation of Political Orientations Among Young Americans." *Journal of Politics* 31 (2): 329–358.

Jennings, M. Kent, and Richard G. Niemi. 1968. "The Transmission of Political Values from Parent to Child." *American Political Science Review* 62 (1): 169–184.

Jennings, M. Kent, and Richard G. Niemi. 1971. "The Division of Political Labor Between Mothers and Fathers." *American Political Science Review* 65 (1): 69–82.

Jennings, M. Kent, Laura Stoker, and Jake Bowers. 2009. "Politics Across Generations: Family Transmission Reexamined." *Journal of Politics* 71 (3): 782–799.

Jensen, Peter S., and John Shaw. 1993. "Children as Victims of War: Current Knowledge and Future Research Needs." *Journal of the American Academy of Child and Adolescent Psychiatry* 32 (4): 697–708.

Johnson, Richard W., and David Neumark. 1997. "Age Discrimination, Job Separations, and Employment Status of Older Workers: Evidence from Self-Reports." *Journal of Human Resources* 32 (4): 779–811.

Jost, John T., Jack Glaser, Arie W. Kruglanski, and Frank J. Sulloway. 2003. "Political Conservatism as Motivated Social Cognition." *Psychological Bulletin* 129 (3): 339–375.

Jost, John T., Brian A. Nosek, and Samuel D. Gosling. 2008. "Ideology: Its Resurgence in Social, Personality, and Political Psychology." *Perspectives on Psychological Science* 3 (2): 126–136.

Kam, Cindy D., and Elizabeth N. Simas. 2010. "Risk Orientations and Policy Frames." *Journal of Politics* 72 (2): 381–396.

Kanazawa, Satoshi. 2010. "Why Liberals and Atheists Are More Intelligent." *Social Psychology Quarterly* 73 (1): 33–57.

Kandler, Christian, Wiebke Bleidorn, and Rainer Riemann. 2012. "Left or Right? Sources of Political Orientation: The Roles of Genetic Factors, Cultural Transmission, Assortative Mating, and Personality." *Journal of Personality and Social Psychology* 102 (3): 633–645.

Kastellec, Jonathan P., and Eduardo L. Leoni. 2007. "Using Graphs Instead of Tables in Political Science." *Perspectives on Politics* 5 (4): 755–771.

Kaufmann, Karen M., and John R. Petrocik. 1999. "The Changing Politics of American Men: Understanding the Sources of the Gender Gap." *American Journal of Political Science* 43 (3): 864–887.

Keele, Luke. 2005. "The Authorities Really Do Matter: Party Control and Trust in Government." *Journal of Politics* 67 (3): 873–886.

Kelty, Ryan, Meredith Kleykamp, and David R. Segal. 2010. "The Military and the Transition to Adulthood." *Future of Children* 20 (1): 181–207.

Kenny, Christopher B. 1994. "The Microenvironment of Attitude Change." *Journal of Politics* 56 (3): 715–728.

Kern, Holger Lutz. 2010. "The Political Consequences of Transitions out of Marriage in Great Britain." *Electoral Studies* 29 (2): 249–258.

King, Amy, and Andrew Leigh. 2010. "Bias at the Ballot Box? Testing Whether Candidates' Gender Affects Their Vote." *Social Science Quarterly* 91 (2): 324–343.

King, Gary, Michael Tomz, and Jason Wittenberg. 2000. "Making the Most of Statistical Analyses: Improving Interpretation and Presentation." *American Journal of Political Science* 44 (2): 341–355.

King, Gary, and Langche Zeng. 2001. "Logistic Regression in Rare Events Data." *Political Analysis* 9 (2): 137–163.

Klofstad, Casey A., Rose McDermott, and Peter K. Hatemi. 2012. "Do Bedroom Eyes Wear Political Glasses? The Role of Politics in Human Mate Attraction." *Evolution and Human Behavior* 33 (2): 100–108.

Konisky, David, Jeffrey Milyo, and Lilliard E. Richardson, Jr. 2008. "Environmental Policy Attitudes: Issues, Geographical Scale, and Political Trust." *Social Science Quarterly* 89 (5): 1066–1085.

Kopczuk, Wojciech, and Joseph P. Lupton. 2007. "To Leave or Not to Leave: The Distribution of Bequest Motives." *Review of Economic Studies* 74 (1): 207–235.

Kroh, Martin. 2009. "The Preadult Origins of Postmaterialism: A Longitudinal Sibling Study." *European Journal of Political Research* 48 (5): 598–621.

Kroh, Martin, and Peter Selb. 2009. "Inheritance and the Dynamics of Party Identification." *Political Behavior* 31 (4): 559–574.

Kulik, Liat. 2002. "The Impact of Social Background on Gender-Role Ideology: Parents' Versus Children's Attitudes." *Journal of Family Issues* 23 (1): 53–73.

Lambert, Alan J., and Katherine Raichle. 2000. "The Role of Political Ideology in Mediating Judgments of Blame in Rape Victims and Their Assailants: A Test of the Just World, Personal Responsibility, and Legitimization Hypotheses." *Personality and Social Psychology Bulletin* 26 (7): 853–863.

Landsburg, Steven. 2007. *More Sex Is Safer Sex: The Unconventional Wisdom of Economics.* New York: Free Press.

Lane, Robert E. 2001. "Self-Reliance and Empathy: The Enemies of Poverty and of the Poor." *Political Psychology* 22 (3): 473–492.

Lavine, Howard, John L. Sullivan, Eugene Borgida, and Cynthia J. Thomsen. 1996. "The Relationship of National and Personal Issue Salience to Attitude Accessibility on Foreign and Domestic Policy Issues." *Political Psychology* 17 (2): 293–316.

Lebel, Uri. 2007. "Civil Society Versus Military Sovereignty: Cultural, Political, and Operational Aspects." *Armed Forces and Society* 34 (1): 67–89.

Leventhal, Tama, and Jeanne Brooks-Gunn. 2000. "The Neighborhoods They Live In: The Effects of Neighborhood Residence on Child and Adolescent Outcomes." *Psychological Bulletin* 126 (2): 309–337.

Lewis, Gregory B. 2003. "Black–White Differences in Attitudes Toward Homosexuality and Gay Rights." *Public Opinion Quarterly* 67 (1): 59–78.

Lindstrom, David P., and Betemariam Berhanu. 2000. "The Effects of Breastfeeding and Birth Spacing on Infant and Early Childhood Mortality in Ethiopia." *Social Biology* 47 (1): 1–17.

Linville, Deanna C., and Angela J. Huebner. 2005. "The Analysis of Extracurricular Activities and Their Relationship to Youth Violence." *Journal of Youth and Adolescence* 34 (5): 483–492.

Luhmann, Maike, Wilhelm Hofmann, Michael Eid, and Richard E. Lucas. 2012. "Subjective Well-Being and Adaptation to Life Events: A Meta-Analysis." *Journal of Personality and Social Psychology* 102 (3): 592–615.

Luker, Kristin. 1984. *Abortion and the Politics of Motherhood.* Berkeley: University of California Press.

Malmendier, Ulrike, and Stefan Nagel. 2011. Depression Babies: Do Macroeconomic Experiences Affect Risk Taking? *Quarterly Journal of Economics* 126 (1): 373–416.

Mansyur, Carol, Benjamin C. Amick, Ronald B. Harrist, and Lulsa Franzini. 2008. "Social Capital, Income Inequality, and Self-Rated Health in 45 Countries." *Social Science and Medicine* 66 (1): 43–56.

Martin, Sherry L. 2006. "Keeping Women in Their Place? Spousal Influence, Vote Choice and Changing Marital Dynamics in Japan." *Journal of Women, Politics and Policy* 28 (2): 29–55.

Mason, Karen Oppenheim, and Yu-Hsia Lu. 1988. "Attitudes Toward Women's Familial Roles: Changes in the United States, 1977–1985." *Gender and Society* 2 (1): 39–57.

Mastekaasa, Arne. 2000. "Parenthood, Gender, and Sickness Absence." *Social Science and Medicine* 50 (12): 1827–1842.

Mazan, Ryan, and Alain Gagnon. 2007. "Familial and Environmental Influences on Longevity in Historical Quebec." *Population* 62 (2): 315–338.

McCarthy, Kate. 2007. "Pluralist Family Values: Domestic Strategies for Living with Religious Difference." *Annals of the American Academy of Political and Social Science* 612: 188–208.

McCue, Clifford P., and J. David Gopoian. 2000. "Dispositional Empathy and the Political Gender Gap." *Women and Politics* 21 (2): 1–20.

McGue, Matt Anu Sharma, and Peter Benson. 1996. "Parent and Sibling Influences on Adolescent Alcohol Use and Misuse: Evidence from a US Adoption Cohort." *Journal of Studies on Alcohol* 57 (1): 8–18.

McHale, Susan M., Joanna Bissell, and Ji-Yeon Kim. 2009. "Sibling Relationship, Family, and Genetic Factors in Sibling Similarity in Sexual Risk." *Journal of Family Psychology* 23 (4): 562–572.

Meier, Robert F., and Gilbert Geis. 1997. *Victimless Crime? Prostitution, Drugs, Homosexuality, Abortion*. Los Angeles: Roxbury.

Melby, Janet N., Rand D. Conger, Shu-Ann Fang, K.A.S. Wickrama, and Katherine J. Conger. 2008. "Adolescent Family Experiences and Educational Attainment During Early Adulthood." *Developmental Psychology* 44 (6): 1519–1636.

Mesquida, Christian G., and Neil I. Wiener. 1999. "Male Age Composition and Severity of Conflicts." *Politics and the Life Sciences* 18 (2): 181–189.

Michalski, Richard L., and Todd K. Shackelford. 2002. "Birth Order and Sexual Strategy." *Personality and Individual Differences* 33 (4): 661–667.

Miller, Alan S. 1992. "Are Self-Proclaimed Conservatives Really Conservative? Trends in Attitudes and Self-Identification Among the Young." *Social Forces* 71 (1): 195–210.

Mondschein, Emily R., Karen E. Adolph, and Catherine S. Tamis-LeMonda. 2000. "Gender Bias in Mothers' Expectations About Infant Crawling." *Journal of Experimental Child Psychology* 77 (4): 304–316.

Morgan, Kimberly J. 2003. "The Politics of Mothers' Employment: France in Comparative Perspective." *World Politics* 55 (2): 259–289.

Morgan, S. Philip, and Rosalind Berkowitz King. 2001. "Why Have Children in the 21st Century? Biological Predisposition, Social Coercion, Rational Choice." *European Journal of Population* 17 (1): 3–20.

Morgan, S. Philip, Guo Zhigang, and Sarah R. Hayford. 2009. "China's Below-Replacement Fertility: Recent Trends and Future Prospects." *Population and Development Review* 35 (3): 605–629.

Morrongiello, Barbara A., and Heather Rennie. 1998. "Why Do Boys Engage in More Risk Taking than Girls? The Role of Attributions, Beliefs, and Risk Appraisals." *Journal of Pediatric Psychology* 23 (1): 33–43.

Mosher, William D., Linda B. Williams, and David P. Johnson. 1992. "Religion and Fertility in the United States: New Patterns." *Demography* 29 (2): 199–214.

Mughan, Anthony. 2007. "Economic Insecurity and Welfare Preferences: A Micro-Level Analysis." *Comparative Politics* 39 (3): 293–310.

Mulder, Monique Borgerhoff. 1998. "Brothers and Sisters: How Sibling Interactions Affect Optimal Parental Allocations." *Human Nature* 9 (2): 119–161.

Mulick, James A., and Eric M. Butter. 2002. "Educational Advocacy for Children with Autism." *Behavioral Interventions* 17 (2): 57–74.

Mutz, Diana C., and Jeffery J. Mondak. 2006. "The Workplace as a Context for Cross-Cutting Political Discourse." *Journal of Politics* 68 (1): 140–155.

Nagle, D. Brendan. 2006. *The Household as the Foundation of Aristotle's Polis*. New York: Cambridge University Press.

Nail, Paul R., Ian McGregor, April E. Drinkwater, Garrett M. Steele, and Anthony W. Thompson. 2009. "Threat Causes Liberals to Think Like Conservatives." *Journal of Experimental Social Psychology* 45 (4): 901–907.

Nelson, Thomas E. 1999. "Group Affect and Attribution in Social Policy Opinion." *Journal of Politics* 61 (2): 331–362.

Newman, Joan, and Alan Taylor. 1994. "Family Training for Political Leadership: Birth Order of United States State Governors and Australian Prime Ministers." *Political Psychology* 15 (3): 435–442.

Nomaguchi, Kei M. 2004. "Maternal Employment, Nonparental Care, Mother–Child Interactions, and Child Outcomes During Preschool Years." *Journal of Marriage and Family* 68 (5): 1341–1369.

Nomaguchi, Kei M., and Melissa A. Milkie. 2003. "Costs and Rewards of Children: The Effects of Becoming a Parent on Adults' Lives." *Journal of Marriage and Family* 65 (2): 356–374.

Norris, Pippa, and Ronald Inglehart. 2004. *Sacred and Secular: Religion and Politics Worldwide*. New York: Cambridge University Press.

Organski, A.F.K., and Jacek Kugler. 1977. "The Costs of Major Wars: The Phoenix Factor." *American Political Science Review* 71 (4): 1347–1366.

Osborn, Tracy, and Jeanette Morehouse Mendez. 2011. "Two Become One? Spouses and Agreement in Political Opinions." *American Politics Research* 39 (5): 783–803.

Oswald, Andrew J., and Nattavudh Powdthavee. 2010. "Daughters and Left-Wing Voting." *Review of Economics and Statistics* 92 (2): 213–227.

Owen Blakemore, Judith E. 1998. "The Influence of Gender and Parental Attitudes on Preschool Children's Interest in Babies: Observations in Natural Settings." *Sex Roles* 38 (1): 73–94.

Pailhe, Ariane, and Anne Solaz. 2012. "The Influence of Employment Uncertainty on Childbearing in France: A Tempo or Quantum Effect?" *Demographic Research* 26 (1): 1–40.

Parker, Suzanne L., Glenn R. Parker, and James A. McCann. 2008. "Opinion Taking Within Friendship Networks." *American Journal of Political Science* 52 (2): 412–420.

Perner, Josef, Ted Ruffman, and Susan R. Leekam. 1994. "Theory of Mind Is Contagious: You Catch It from Your Sibs." *Child Development* 65 (4): 1228–1238.

Pesonen, Anu-Katriina, Katri Räikkönen, Kati Heinonen, Eero Kajantie, Tom Forsén, and Johan G. Eriksson. 2007. "Depressive Symptoms in Adults Separated from Their Parents as Children: A Natural Experiment During World War II." *American Journal of Epidemiology* 166 (10): 1126–1133.

Pickering, Jeffrey, and Emizet E. Kisangani. 2006. "Political, Economic, and Social Consequences of Foreign Military Intervention." *Political Research Quarterly* 59 (3): 363–376.

Plutzer, Eric, and Michael McBurnett. 1991. "Family Life and American Politics: The 'Marriage Gap' Reconsidered." *Public Opinion Quarterly* 55 (1): 113–127.

Powell, Brian, and Lala Carr Steelman. 1993. "The Educational Benefits of Being Spaced Out: Sibship Density and Educational Progress." *American Sociological Review* 58 (3): 367–381.

Prokos, Anastasia H., Chardie L. Baird, and Jennifer Reid Keene. 2010. "Attitudes About Affirmative Action for Women: The Role of Children in Shaping Parents' Interests." *Sex Roles* 62 (5): 347–360.

Rahn, Wendy M., Brian Kroeger, and Cynthia M. Kite. 1996. "A Framework for the Study of Public Mood." *Political Psychology* 17 (1): 29–58.

Raley, Sara, and Suzanne Bianchi. 2006. "Sons, Daughters, and Family Processes: Does Gender of Children Matter?" *Annual Review of Sociology* 32: 401–421.

Regnerus, Mark D., and Christian Smith. 2005. "Selection Effects in Studies of Religious Influence." *Review of Religious Research* 47 (1): 23–50.

Regnier-Loilier, Arnaud. 2006. "Influence of Own Sibship Size on Number of Children Desired at Various Times of Life: The Case of France." *Population* 61 (3): 193–223.

Rehm, Philipp. 2009. "Risks and Redistribution: An Individual-Level Analysis." *Comparative Political Studies* 42 (7): 855–881.

Riggio, Heidi R. 1999. "Personality and Social Skill Differences Between Adults With and Without Siblings." *Journal of Psychology* 133 (5): 514–522.

Rodgers, Joseph Lee, David C. Rowe, and David F. Harris. 1992. "Sibling Differences in Adolescent Sexual Behavior: Inferring Process Models from Family Composition Patterns." *Journal of Marriage and Family* 54 (1): 142–152.

Rosenzweig, Mark R. 1986. "Birth Spacing and Sibling Inequality: Asymmetric Information Within the Family." *International Economic Review* 27 (1): 55–76.

Ross, Catherine E., and Marieke van Willigen. 1996. "Gender, Parenthood, and Anger." *Journal of Marriage and Family* 58 (3): 572–584.

Rossier, Clementine, and Laura Bernardi. 2009. "Social Interaction Effects on Fertility: Intentions and Behaviors." *European Journal of Population* 25 (4): 467–485.

Ruckstuhl, Kathreen E., Grant P. Colijn, Volodymyr Amiot, and Erin Vinish. 2010. "Mother's Occupation and Sex Ratio at Birth." *BMC Public Health* 10: 269.

Ruffman, Ted, Josef Perner, Mika Naito, Lindsay Parkin, and Wendy A. Clements. 1998. "Older (But Not Younger) Siblings Facilitate False Belief Understanding." *Developmental Psychology* 34 (1): 161–174.

Sallis, James F., Joy M. Zakarian, Melbourne F. Hovell, and C. Richard Hofstetter. 1996. "Ethnic, Socioeconomic, and Sex Differences in Physical Activity Among Adolescents." *Journal of Clinical Epidemiology* 49 (2): 125–134.

Sances, Michael W. 2013. "Disenfranchisement Through Divorce? Estimating the Effect of Parental Absence on Voter Turnout." *Political Behavior* 35 (1): 199–213.

Santelli, John, Mary A. Ott, Maureen Lyon, Jennifer Rogers, Daniel Summers, and Rebecca Schleifer. 2006. "Abstinence and Abstinence-Only Education: A Review of U.S. Policies and Programs." *Journal of Adolescent Health* 38 (1): 72–81.

Santorum, Rick. 2005. *It Takes a Family: Conservatism and the Common Good.* Wilmington, DE: Intercollegiate Studies Institute.

Sassler, Sharon, Amanda Miller, and Sarah M. Favinger. 2009. "Planned Parenthood? Fertility Intentions and Experiences Among Cohabiting Couples." *Journal of Family Issues* 30 (2): 206–232.

Scheve, Kenneth, and Matthew J. Slaughter. 2004. "Economic Insecurity and the Globalization of Production." *American Journal of Political Science* 48 (4): 662–674.

Scheve, Kenneth, and David Stasavage. 2006. "Religion and Preferences for Social Insurance." *Quarterly Journal of Political Science* 1 (3): 255–286.

Schlesinger, Mark. 2011. "Making the Best of Hard Times: How the Nation's Economic Circumstances Shaped the Public's Embrace of Health Care Reform." *Journal of Health Politics, Policy, and Law* 36 (6): 989–1020.

Schlesinger, Mark, and Caroline Heldman. 2001. "Gender Gap or Gender Gaps? New Perspectives on Support for Government Action and Policies." *Journal of Politics* 63 (1): 59–92.

Schoen, Robert, Young J. Kim, Constance A. Nathanson, Jason Fields, and Nan Marie Astone. 1997. "Why Do Americans Want Children?" *Population and Development Review* 23 (2): 333–358.

Schreckhise, William D., and Todd G. Shields. 2003. "Ideological Realignment in the Contemporary U.S. Electorate Revisited." *Social Science Quarterly* 84 (3): 596–612.

Scott, Linda D., Wei-Ting Hwang, and Ann E. Rogers. 2006. "The Impact of Multiple Care-Giving Roles on Fatigue, Stress, and Work Performance Among Hospital Staff Nurses." *Journal of Nursing Administration* 36 (2): 86–95.

Sears, David O., and Carolyn L. Funk. 1991. "The Role of Self-Interest in Social and Political Attitudes." *Advances in Experimental Social Psychology* 24: 1–91.

Sears, David O., and Carolyn L. Funk. 1999. "Evidence of the Long-Term Persistence of Adults' Political Predispositions." *Journal of Politics* 61 (1): 1–28.

Segal, David R., Jerald G. Bachman, Peter Freedman-Doan, and Patrick O'Malley. 1999. "Propensity to Serve in the U.S. Military: Secular Trends and Sub-Group Differences." *Armed Forces and Society* 25 (3): 407–427.

Šerek, Jan, Lenka Lacinová, and Petr Macek. 2012. "Does Family Experience Influence Political Beliefs? Relation Between Interparental Conflict Perceptions and Political Efficacy in Late Adolescence." *Journal of Adolescence* 35 (3): 577–586.

Shafer, Emily Fitzgibbons, and Neil Malhotra. 2011. "The Effect of a Child's Sex on Support for Traditional Gender Roles." *Social Forces* 90 (1): 209–222.

Shams, Manfusa, and Paul R. Jackson. 1993. "Religiosity as a Predictor of Well-Being and Moderator of the Psychological Impact of Unemployment." *British Journal of Medical Psychology* 66 (4): 341–352.

Sheldon, Kennon M., and Ann B. Bettencourt. 2002. "Psychological Need-Satisfaction and Subjective Well-Being Within Social Groups." *British Journal of Social Psychology* 41 (1): 25–38.

Sinclair, Betsy, Margaret McConnell, Margaret, and Donald P. Green. 2012. "Detecting Spillover Effects: Design and Analysis of Multilevel Experiments." *American Journal of Political Science* 56 (4): 1055–1069.

Singerman, Diane. 2006. "Restoring the Family to Civil Society: Lessons from Egypt." *Journal of Middle East Women's Studies* 2 (1): 1–32.

Sinno, Stefanie M., and Melanie Killen. 2009. "Moms at Work and Dads at Home: Children's Evaluations of Parental Roles." *Applied Developmental Science* 13 (1): 16–29.

Smith, Kevin, John R. Alford, Peter K. Hatemi, Lindon J. Eaves, Carolyn Funk, and John R. Hibbing. 2012. "Biology, Ideology, and Epistemology: How Do We Know Political Attitudes Are Inherited and Why Should We Care?" *American Journal of Political Science* 56 (1): 17–33.

Solomon, Andrew. 2012. *Far from the Tree: Parents, Children and the Search for Identity*. New York: Scribner.

Somit, Albert, Alan Arwine, and Steven A. Peterson. 1996. *Birth Order and Political Behavior*. Lanham, MD: University Press of America.

Srivastava, Sanjay, Oliver P. John, Samuel D. Gosling, and Jeff Potter. 2003. "Development of Personality in Early and Middle Adulthood: Set Like Plaster or Persistent Change?" *Journal of Personality and Social Psychology* 84 (5): 1041–1053.

Steelman, Lala Carr, Brian Powell, Regina Werum, and Scott Carter. 2002. "Reconsidering the Effects of Sibling Configuration: Recent Advances and Challenges." *Annual Review of Sociology* 28: 243–269.

Steinberg, Blema S. 2001. "The Making of Female Presidents and Prime Ministers: The Impact of Birth Order, Sex, of Siblings, and Father–Daughter Dynamics." *Political Psychology* 22 (1): 89–110.

Stocker, Clare, Judy Dunn, and Robert Plomin. 1989. "Sibling Relationships: Links with Child Temperament, Maternal Behavior, and Family Structure." *Child Development* 60 (3): 715–727.

Stocker, Clare M., Richard P. Lanthier, and Wyndol Furman. 1997. "Sibling Relationships in Early Adulthood." *Journal of Family Psychology* 11 (2): 210–221.

Stoddard, Christiana. 2009. "Why Did Education Become Publicly Funded? Evidence from the Nineteenth-Century Growth of Public Primary Schooling in the United States." *Journal of Economic History* 69 (1): 172–201.

Stoker, Laura, and M. Kent Jennings. 1995. "Life-Cycle Transitions and Political-Participation: The Case of Marriage." *American Political Science Review* 89 (2): 421–433.

Stoker, Laura, and M. Kent Jennings. 2005. "Political Similarity and Influence Between Husbands and Wives." In Alan S. Zuckerman, ed., *The Social Logic of Politics: Personal Networks as Contexts for Political Behavior*, 51–74. Philadelphia: Temple University Press.

Stone, Nicole, and Roger Ingham. 2011. "Who Presents More Than Once? Repeat Abortion Among Women in Britain." *Journal of Family Planning and Reproductive Health Care* 37 (4): 209–215.

Stoneman, Zolinda, Gene H. Brody, and Carol E. MacKinnon. 1986. "Same-Sex and Cross-Sex Siblings: Activity Choices, Roles, Behavior, and Gender Stereotypes." *Sex Roles* 15 (9): 495–511.

Storey, Anne E., Carolyn J. Walsh, Roma L. Quinton, and Katherine E. Wynne-Edwards. 2000. "Hormonal Correlates of Paternal Responsiveness in New and Expectant Fathers." *Evolution and Human Behavior* 21 (2): 79–95.

Sulloway, Frank J. 1997. *Born to Rebel: Birth Order, Family Dynamics, and Creative Lives.* New York: Vintage.

Szobiová, Eva. 2008. "Birth Order, Sibling Constellation, Creativity and Personality Dimensions of Adolescents." *Studia Psychologica* 50 (4): 371–381.

Taagepera, Rein. 2008. *Making Social Sciences More Scientific: The Need for Predictive Models.* New York: Oxford University Press.

Tanfer, Koray, and Jeannette J. Schoorl. 1992. "Premarital Sexual Careers and Partner Change." *Archives of Sexual Behavior* 21 (1): 45–68.

Thapar, Anita, Amaia Hervas, and Peter McGuffin. 1995. "Childhood Hyperactivity Scores Are Highly Heritable and Show Sibling Competition Effects: Twin Study Evidence." *Behavior Genetics* 25 (6): 537–544.

Thomson, Elizabeth, Sara S. McLanahan, and Roberta Braun Curtin. 1992. "Family Structure, Gender, and Parental Socialization." *Journal of Marriage and Family* 54 (2): 368–378.

Tobey, William. 2012. "Nuclear Scientists as Assassination Targets." *Bulletin of the Atomic Scientists* 68 (1): 61–69.

Toft, Monica Duffy. 2006. "Issue Indivisibility and Time Horizons as Rationalist Explanations for War." *Security Studies* 15 (1): 34–69.

Trivers, Robert L., and Dan E. Willard. 1973. "Natural Selection of Parental Ability to Vary the Sex Ratio of Offspring." *Science* 179 (4068): 90–92.

Tversky, Amos, and Daniel Kahneman. 1991. "Loss Aversion in Riskless Choice: A Reference-Dependent Model." *Quarterly Journal of Economics* 106 (4): 1039–1061.

Valletta, Robert G. 1999. "Declining Job Security." *Journal of Labor Economics* 17 (S4): S170–S197.

van Balen, F., J.E. Verdurmen, and E. Ketting. 1997. "Age, the Desire to Have a Child and Cumulative Pregnancy Rate." *Human Reproduction* 12 (3): 623–627.

van Berkel, Michel. 1998. "Political Preferences and Class Identity Among Spouses. Who Dominates When?" *Netherlands Journal of Social Sciences* 34 (1): 23–43.

van Deth, Jan W., Simone Abendschön, and Meike Vollmar. 2011. "Children and Politics: An Empirical Reassessment of Early Political Socialization." *Political Psychology* 32 (1): 147–173.

Vavrus, Mary Douglas. 2000. "From Women of the Year to 'Soccer Moms': The Case of the Incredible Shrinking Women." *Political Communication* 17 (2): 193–213.

Vogl, Tom S. 2013. "Marriage Institutions and Sibling Competition: Evidence from South Asia." *Quarterly Journal of Economics* 128 (3): 1017–1072.

Voorpostel, Marieke, and Hilde Coffé. 2012. "Transitions in Partnership and Parental Status, Gender, and Political and Civic Participation." *European Sociological Review* 28 (1): 28–42.

Waldfogel, Jane, Wen-Jui Han, and Jeanne Brooks-Gunn. 2002. "The Effects of Early Maternal Employment on Child Cognitive Development." *Demography* 39 (2): 369–392.

Wang, X. T., Daniel J. Kruger, and Andreas Wilke. 2009. "Life History Variables and Risk-Taking Propensity." *Evolution and Human Behavior* 30 (2): 77–84.

Washington, Ebonya L. 2008. "Female Socialization: How Daughters Affect Their Legislator Fathers' Voting on Women's Issues." *American Economic Review* 98 (1): 311–332.

Watson, David, Eva C. Klohnen, Alex Casillas, Ericka Nus Simms, Jeffrey Haig, and Diane S. Berry. 2004. "Match Makers and Deal Breakers: Analyses of Assortative Mating in Newlywed Couples." *Journal of Personality* 72 (5): 1029–1068.

Weichselbaumer, Doris, and Rudolf Winter-Ebmer. 2005. "A Meta-Analysis of the International Gender Wage Gap." *Journal of Economic Surveys* 19 (3): 479–511.

Welch, Kelly. 2011. "Parental Status and Punitiveness: Moderating Effects of Gender and Concern About Crime." *Crime and Delinquency* 57 (6): 878–906.

Whiteman, Shawn D., Susan M. McHale, and Ann C. Crouter. 2003. "What Parents Learn from Experience: The First Child as a First Draft?" *Journal of Marriage and Family* 65 (3): 608–621.

Whiteman, Shawn D., Susan M. McHale, and Ann C. Crouter. 2007. "Explaining Sibling Similarities: Perceptions of Sibling Influences." *Journal of Youth and Adolescence* 36 (7): 963–972.

Whittington, Leslie A., and James Alm. 1997. "'Til Death or Taxes Do Us Part: The Effect of Income Taxation on Divorce." *Journal of Human Resources* 32 (2): 388–412.

Whitworth, Alison, and Rob Stephenson. 2002. "Birth Spacing, Sibling Rivalry and Child Mortality in India." *Social Science and Medicine* 55 (12): 2107–2119.

Widmer, Eric D. 1997. "Influence of Older Siblings on Initiation of Sexual Intercourse." *Journal of Marriage and Family* 59 (4): 928–938.

Wildsmith, Elizabeth, Karen Benjamin Guzzo, and Sarah R. Hayford. 2010. "Repeat Unintended, Unwanted and Seriously Mistimed Childbearing in the United States." *Perspectives on Sexual and Reproductive Health* 42 (1): 14–22.

Wilson, James Q. 1993. "The Family-Values Debate." *Commentary* 95 (4): 24–31.

Wilson, J. Matthew, and Michael Lusztig. 2004. "The Spouse in the House: What Explains the Marriage Gap in Canada?" *Canadian Journal of Political Science* 37 (4): 979–995.

Wisman, Jon D., and Kevin W. Capehart. 2010. "Creative Destruction, Economic Insecurity, Stress, and Epidemic Obesity." *American Journal of Economics and Sociology* 69 (3): 936–982.

Wolak, Jennifer. 2009. "Explaining Change in Party Identification in Adolescence." *Electoral Studies* 28 (4): 573–583.

Wolfe, Jessica, Kiban Turner, Marie Caulfield, Tamara L. Newton, Katherine Melia, James Martin, and Jill Goldstein. 2005. "Gender and Trauma as Predictors of Military Attrition: A Study of Marine Corps Recruits." *Military Medicine* 170 (12): 1037–1043.

Yi, Chin-Chun, Chin-Fen Chang, and Ying-Hwa Chang. 2004. "The Intergenerational Transmission of Family Values: A Comparison Between Teenagers and Parents in Taiwan." *Journal of Comparative Family Studies* 35 (4): 523–545.

Youngblade, Lise M. 2003. "Peer and Teacher Ratings of Third- and Fourth-Grade Children's Social Behavior as a Function of Early Maternal Employment." *Journal of Child Psychology and Psychiatry* 44 (4): 477–488.

Zimmerman, Toni Schindler, Jennifer T. Aberle, Jennifer L. Krafchick, and Ashley M. Harvey. 2008. "Deconstructing the 'Mommy Wars': The Battle over the Best Mom." *Journal of Feminist Family Therapy* 20 (3): 203–219.

Zipp, John F., Ariane Prohaska, and Michelle Bemiller. 2004. "Wives, Husbands, and Hidden Power in Marriage." *Journal of Family Issues* 25 (7): 933–958.

Zucker, Gail Sahar. 1999. "Attributional and Symbolic Predictors of Abortion Attitudes." *Journal of Applied Social Psychology* 29 (6): 1218–1245.

Zuckerman, Alan S., Josip Dasović, and Jennifer Fitzgerald. 2007. *Partisan Families*. New York: Cambridge University Press.

Zweigenhaft, Richard L. 2002. "Birth Order Effects and Rebelliousness: Political Activism and Involvement with Marijuana." *Political Psychology* 23 (2): 219–233.

INDEX

Page numbers followed by *f* or *t* indicate figures or tables, respectively. Numbers followed by n indicate endnotes.

government intervention
attitudes toward, 55–58, 96–97, 96*f*, 147–148, 149*t*, 151*t*
international, 96–97, 96*f*, 99–100, 101, 101*f*
US intervention in Afghanistan, 93, 99–100, 101, 101*f*, 147–148, 150*t*, 151*t*
US intervention in Iraq, 147–148, 150*t*
government spending, 116, 117, 117*f*, 118, 139*t*, 140*t*, 142*t*, 143*t*, 155*t*, 156*t*
grandparents, 21, 161n74
Great Society programs, 119
Green Party, 28
GSS (General Social Survey), 50–51, 52, 55, 59, 68–69, 71, 75, 79, 165n49, 166n26
guardian figures. *See* parents

Harris, Judith Rich, 161n7
health-care reform, 57
home
stay-at-home fathers, 24–25
stay-at-home mothers, 21–42
staying at, 23–27
homosexuality, 79–81, 80*f*, 144, 147*t*
horizontal identity, 10–11
household income, 148, 149*t*, 150*t*, 151*t*

identity
horizontal, 10–11
partisan identification, 33–35, 34*f*, 35–36
ideology
control variables, 140–144, 141*t*, 142*t*
right-leaning, 28
self-rated, 33–35, 34*f*, 35–36
sex and left-right positions, 53–55
sibling closeness and, 60–61, 61*f*
sibling effects, 43–63, 120–121
income variables, 136–137, 138*t*, 148, 149*t*, 150*t*, 151*t*, 152, 154*t*, 155*t*, 156, 156*t*, 157*t*
independents, 28
insecurity
economic, 103–119, 110*f*, 121–122
economic insecurity-influenced policy preferences, 117, 117*f*, 118
economic insecurity-influenced political attitudes, 113–115, 114*f*

job insecurity, 110–111, 110*f*, 152, 152*t*, 153*t*
international intervention, 96–97, 96*f*, 99–100, 101, 101*f*
international wars, 98–99, 98*f*, 99–100
interventionism. *See* government intervention; international intervention
Iraq, 93, 99, 101, 101*f*, 147–148, 150*t*, 151*t*
isolationism, 101, 101*f*, 147–148, 149*t*, 151*t*
issue-area preferences, 39–41, 41*f*

job insecurity
control variables, 152, 152*t*, 153*t*
indicators of, 110–111, 110*f*
Johnson, Lyndon, 119

left-right positions, 53–55
liberalism, 26, 53–55, 162n14
Libertarian Party, 28
linear ("ordinary least squares") models, 19–20

marital status, 156, 157*t*
maternal work, 26–27
effects of, 31–33, 33–35, 34*f*, 35–36, 39–41, 41*f*
survey responses, 27–31
mating, assortative, 8
medical treatment: delaying, 110, 110*f*, 111, 132–133, 153*t*, 154*t*
methodology, 19–20
control variables, 135–140
data and predictor variables, 50–52
statistical methods, 19–20
statistical models, 19–20, 131–157
militarism, 83–102, 121, 147–148, 148*t*
military intervention
international, 96–97, 96*f*, 101, 101*f*
international wars, 98–99, 98*f*, 99–100
US intervention in Afghanistan, 93, 99–100, 101, 101*f*, 147–148, 150*t*, 151*t*
US intervention in Iraq, 147–148, 150*t*
minority status, 135, 137*t*, 138*t*, 139*t*, 140, 140*t*, 142*t*, 143*t*, 152, 154*t*, 155*t*, 156*t*

morality, 64–82, 121
mothers
    attitudes of, 23
    influence of, 27
    out-of-household, 173n18
    stay-at-home, 21–42
    working, 26–27, 27–31, 31–33, 33–
        35, 34f, 35–36, 39–41, 41f

National Election Study (NES), 28, 31,
    33, 89, 92–93, 106–107, 109, 112,
    113, 116, 172n39
Netanyahu, Ben-Zion, 172n1
new parents, 156, 157t
nonlinear models, 131, 132, 133, 134–135
nuclear proliferation, 91, 94–95, 94f, 97,
    121, 147–148, 148t, 149t

older siblings, 49–50, 62, 65, 66,
    163n16, 165n42
only children, 69
"ordinary least squares" (linear) models,
    19–20
out-of-household mothers, 173n18

parental figures. *See* parents
parental partisanship, 162n21
parenting differences, 163n3
parents
    control variables, 135, 136
    definition of, 17, 21
    economic insecurity, 103–119, 110f,
        121–122, 152, 152t, 153t
    foreign-policy concerns, 88–94, 94–
        100, 101, 101f, 121
    influence of, 5–7, 120–121
    new, 156, 157t
    out-of-household mothers, 173n18
    stay-at-home fathers, 24–25
    stay-at-home mothers, 21–42
    stress effects, 170n14
    support for big government, 103–119
    world outlook, 84–88
partisanship, 28
    bounded, 6
    control variables, 136, 137t, 138t,
        139t, 140t
    demographic factors, 125–126, 127
    fertility and, 127–128
    having children and, 125–126
    parental, 162n21

sibling closeness and, 60–61, 61f
socioeconomic factors, 125–126
variables affecting, 33–35, 34f, 35–36,
    126
partnerships, 156, 157t
Perot, Ross, 53, 165n54
personal experience, 14, 27
policy preferences, 116–118
    domestic policy concerns, 84–88
    economic-policy concerns, 104, 105
    foreign-policy concerns, 85–86, 88–
        94, 90–91, 94–100, 101, 101f, 121
    insecurity-influenced, 117, 117f, 118
political affiliation, 147, 148t, 150t, 151t
political attitudes, 112–115
    control variables, 136, 137t, 138t,
        139t, 140t
    family and, 3–5, 5–7, 7–9, 9–11
    having children and, 125
    indicators of, 113–115, 114f
    insecurity-influenced, 113–115, 114f
    and making of family, 122–128
    measures of, 54–55, 54f
    sex and left-right positions, 53–55
    sibling effects, 43–63
    support for welfare state, 57, 57f, 60–
        61, 61f, 112–113, 116, 117, 117f,
        118, 121–122, 142t, 155t, 156t
poor people
    deserving poor, 112–113
    support for spending on, 112–113,
        113–115, 114f, 117, 117f, 118,
        142t, 153, 154t, 155t, 156t
    undeserving poor, 112–113
predictor variables, 50–52
premarital sex, 71–74, 72f, 129, 144,
    145t
private enterprise, 56, 60–61, 61f, 142t,
    143t
proliferation of nuclear weapons, 91,
    94–95, 94f, 97, 121, 147–148, 148t,
    149t

rape, 167n38
Reagan, Michael, 161n1
Reagan, Nancy, 21, 41, 161n1
Reagan, Patti Davis, 21
Reagan, Ron, 21
Reagan, Ronald, 21, 41, 161n1
regression models, 162n20
religiosity, 70